BOUNDARIES UNDERMINED

DELWAR HUSSAIN

Boundaries Undermined

The Ruins of Progress on the Bangladesh-India Border

HURST & COMPANY, LONDON

First published in the United Kingdom in 2013 by
C. Hurst & Co. (Publishers) Ltd.,
41 Great Russell Street, London, WC1B 3PL
© Delwar Hussain, 2013
Printed in India

The right of Delwar Hussain to be identified as the author
of this publication is asserted by him in accordance with the
Copyright, Designs and Patents Act, 1988.

A Cataloguing-in-Publication data record for this book
is available from the British Library.

ISBN: 978-1-84904-232-1

www.hurstpublishers.com

To
Arful Nessa

CONTENTS

ACKNOWLEDGEMENTS

The first incarnation of this book was as a doctoral thesis, the production and completion of which simply would not have been possible without the help, guidance and support, both personal and professional, given to me by many people. I wish to thank James Laidlaw for his unfailing commitment throughout. His knowledge, friendship, kindness, time and discipline have been pivotal and will never be forgotten. Thank you also to Susan Bayly who had to wade through earlier drafts of the chapters. Others at the University of Cambridge include the staff at the Department for Social Anthropology, my PhD writing-up colleagues, David Sneath and the Centre for South Asian Studies.

In Bangladesh, I would like to thank all of my friends in Khonighat and Boropani. A number of people and their families made my life extremely comfortable in Dhaka and Sylhet by giving me shelter, food, companionship, laughter and much more besides. Sudipta Chowdhury and his family and Diane, James and Hannah Jennings and the rest of their family. Thanks also to Isaac Sairs for letting me live with him. I hope I will be in a position to reciprocate all of their generosity.

At the LSE, I would like to thank Laura Bear, Chris Fuller and the late Olivia Harris for kick-starting the project and thinking it worthwhile to pursue. I would like to show my appreciation to the many individuals, seminars and conferences that invited me to speak, including the Bangladesh Studies Workshop 2010, the South Asia Anthropology Group 2010, LSE Labour Seminar, Delhi University, the University of Wisconsin, Dhaka University, Jahangirnagar University and BRAC University. Other colleagues and friends whose help, comments, conversations and suggestions for ways to improve the material include David

ACKNOWLEDGEMENTS

Lewis, Willem van Schendel, John Hutnyk, Benji Zeitlyn, David Ludden, Malini Sur, Chloe Nahum Claudel and Ela Drazkiewicz. I am much obliged. Thank you to Daniel Ramos for the maps.

I made many new friends during the process of this work and also strengthened my relationships with many old ones. Support, love and, importantly, distractions, were provided by Simon Chambers, Nick Boston, Julie Begum, Abdul Shohid, Tony Stevens, Henrik Aspengren, Jeremy Seabrook and the Spalding set, including Jared Rossouw, Zak Hulstrom and Desha Osborne. Thank you especially to Aiyaz Ahmed for allowing me to drown him in PhD and then book manuscript gunk and for helping me to steer through it all. My family's encouragement, love and support have been continuous throughout. I shall always remain grateful for the detachment they provided: the two new babies, three weddings and a funeral.

I would finally like to express my gratitude to the Royal Anthropological Institute for the Emslie Horniman Scholarship Fund, the LSE Anthropology Departmental Funding, the Economic and Social Research Council and the Ferris Grant at Kings College for taking care of all my financial needs.

LIST OF MAPS

A NOTE ON CURRENCY

The exchange rate is correct at the time of going to press.

Bangladesh: 100 taka—80 pence
1 lakh—£900

India: 100 rupees—£1.30
1 lakh—£1,300

ABBREVIATIONS

BCIC	Bangladesh Chemical Industries Corporation
BDR	Bangladesh Rifles
BSF	(Indian) Border Security Force
EPIDC	East Pakistan Industrial Development Corporation
LC	Letter of Credit
NGO	Non-Governmental Organisation
PF	Pension Fund

GLOSSARY

adivasi	indigenous tribal
Ansar	auxiliary law enforcement force employed by the government
azaan	call to prayer
babuchis	cooks
basti	slum
bekkar	unemployed
bezal	trouble
bhai	brother
bhitore	inside
bikaler prarthona	evening prayer
boli	sacrifice during Durga Puja
bongsho	origins
cela	disciple
chunapathor	limestone
coila	coal
coila netha	coal labour leader
desher bari	village home
dui nombori kaj	illicit work
geeti	song
ghorib	the poor
goosh	bribe
guru	teacher
haor	wetland
iftar	the meal that breaks the Ramadan fast
Jamaat	Eid prayer

GLOSSARY

kalo shuna	black gold
kula	open
lakh	thousand
lathi	wooden staff
maidan	lawn
madrassa	religious school
mal	goods
malik	owner
mandir	temple
mazaar	shrine of a local saint
murrobi	respected elder
murti	idol
netha	leader
paan	betel leaf
panthi	(in Ultapalta: lovers)
pariks	(in Ultapalta: husbands)
prasad	food blessings
purohit	priest
rit	the formal marker of an allegiance to a hijra lineage
sanda	donation
shomithi	committee
tella gharis	pushcarts
Terrabi	special prayers following the breaking of fast
ultapalta	the hijra language
Union Parishad	local council
urus	worship ceremony of local saint

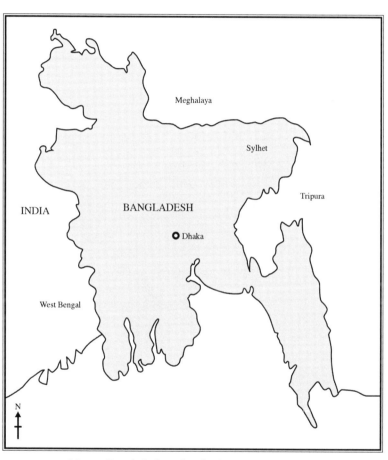

Map 1: Bangladesh and India (1971–Present day).

Map 2: East and West Pakistan (1947–1971).

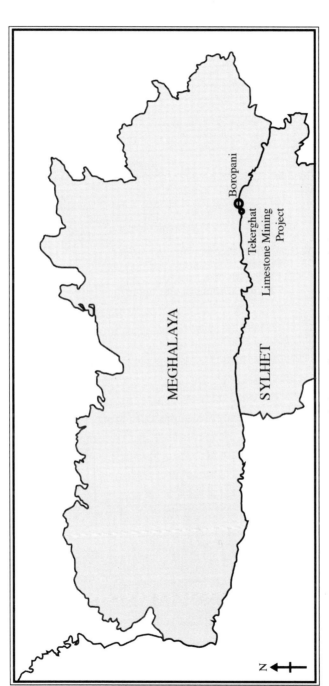

Map 3: Meghalaya-Sylhet Border (Present day).

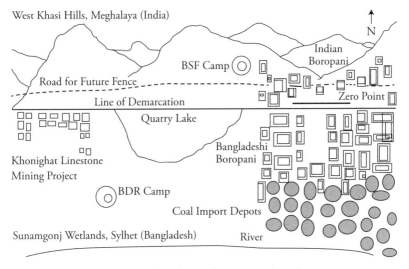

Map 4: Khonighat and Boropani (2010).

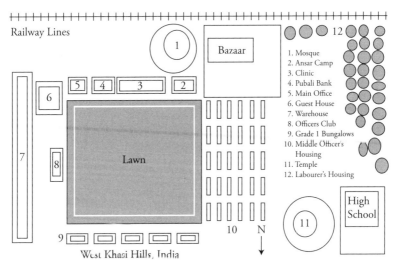

Map 5: Khonighat Limestone Mining Project (2010).

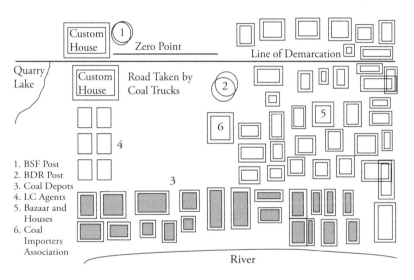

Map 6: Boropani (2010).

INTRODUCTION

THE RISE AND FALL OF GRAND MASTER PLANS

There is a small coal-mining village that lies in-between the vast stretches of the West Khasi Hills to one side and the seemingly never-ending wetlands of Sunamgonj on the other. Boropani shall be its name. It is this particular ecology, of the hills and the floodplains, that provides the village and its inhabitants with their livelihood and identities, and which is at the heart of the monumental transformations that have shaped the entire region. The distinction between the two terrains and the subsistence associated with them have meant that interdependency is the norm for the area's inhabitants. In pre-colonial times, rice, chicken and fish found in the plains were traded for fruit, betel nut and spices from the hills. During the colonial period, ivory and timber were sent down by river to be sold in the markets of Calcutta. Today there is an international border running through the centre of Boropani, dividing it in two. One half of the village is in the floodplains, in Sylhet district on the Bangladeshi side, the other half of Boropani is in the hills, in the state of Meghalaya, on the Indian side. Historically composed relationships persist in spite of all the ruptures that border demarcations have brought in their wake. Lives and livelihoods have simply adjusted, taking account of new and ever-changing realities. Both halves of Boropani have retained the same name.[1] Those on the hill now buy Chinese-made mobile phones and Bangladeshi sim cards alongside the fish and rice from the plains. There, people buy Chinese-made sandals, ginger, oranges and alcohol from the hills. At one time these transactions were out in the open. With the drawing of state boundaries, however, much

1

is now surreptitious. But these days, it is coal, or what is sometimes referred to with irony around these parts as '*kalo shuna*' (black gold), that everyone is chiefly interested in. The coal trade between the Indian side (who export it) and the Bangladeshi side (who import it) is the main industry here. Traditionally inhabited by the indigenous Garo and Khasi communities, the hills—where all the mines are located—remain relatively sparsely populated, which means a scarcity of labour. This draws in hundreds of thousands of migrants from all over Bangladesh who illegally cross the border to work the mines, joining other labourers from across the subcontinent. The trade itself is ostensibly legal, the market for the *kalo shuna* being the mushrooming numbers of brick kilns that feed the ongoing development of Bangladesh.

Indian and Bangladeshi Boropani are located in extremely remote and isolated parts of both countries. The journey from Dhaka city is slow and tiring: an overnight bus north-east to Sylhet, a three-hour rickety bus ride to Sunamgonj town, a slow and noisy boat ride across the Surma River and then a bumpy two-hour journey on the back of a motorbike over unpaved paths, through tangled bamboo groves and sleepy bazaars and hamlets. As I get closer to the hills and with it, the border, there are scenes of men in riverbeds collecting stones that have come down from the hills and women sieving sand: essential ingredients in the building of cities elsewhere in the country. The blue limestone West Khasi Hills are spectacular. They are not very tall, but it is their sheer breadth that makes them look magnificent. Initially I assume that the hills act as a natural boundary against the plains, which is why, over the centuries, borders have continuously been (re)drawn here. It doesn't take long to realise how futile this endeavour is. Rather than preventing connections between both sides, the hills actually enable, facilitate and even provide the motives for the interconnections in the first place. In the dry season, which is when I arrive, the *haors* (wetlands) on the Bangladeshi side are devoid of water. Rice had been planted and the sheaves were acid green. Occasionally a human head or two could be seen bobbing up and down amongst the fluttering tips. Migratory ducks from Siberia, pintails, pochards and widgeons, fly past in sequence. It will be a few months later that I experience the full force of the climatic orchestra that plays out here annually. During the monsoon, it rains for days and nights without abating. The sound is deafening. Rain water as well as the bloated rivers, streams and waterfalls that emanate from the hills come straight down into the plains. As they do so, the waters slowly colonise each and every stretch of land including the fields where the paddy grow. Soon there will be water as far as the eye can see. The occasional mud huts, built on raised land, look like floating islands. The floods, rather than being catastrophic, which they can be, are a moment of opportunity with possibilities for travel and transportation opening up, impossible in the dry season. The season is crucial for the coal trade too. The water is the colour of grey slate. Often the sky reflects on to the still waters making it difficult to see where one ends and the other begins.

Boropani bazaar is at the centre of the Bangladesh–India coal trade in this part of the border region. It has the impermanent feel of a frontier town, a scene out of a country and western film, though the usual noise, people and the frenetic hurriedness of other rural Bangladeshi bazaars is evident here. It is teeming with thousands of dark-skinned, gaunt labourers, a fretwork of bones protruding out of their sweaty, taut muscles, their backs and hamstrings tight in desperate effort. I jump out of their way as they push, lug, heave and pull carts laden with bulky sacks of coal towards the river. Soot has ground itself into their skin and it clouds the paths they walk on. The men speak a mixture of languages, some which I recognise and others I don't. Their homes, made out of corrugated sheets of tin, mud and bamboo, are scattered around the outskirts of the bazaar. Indian Boropani can easily be seen from the Bangladeshi side, only a few metres ahead. Though the no-man's-land that divides both parts is itself clear of buildings and structures, the other side looks as scruffy and raucous as here. Little huts covered in blue tarpaulin dot the hills. People walk around, going about their business, working, laughing and drinking tea in the same way they do here. But an invisible force field seems to stop anyone from crossing the boundary (this is not the case all the time as I am to find out later). Is this a result of history, nationalism or just the threat of violence? It only applies to people on foot, however, because every so often heavy trucks lumber into Bangladeshi Boropani with coal on their backs. The Khasi men who drive them have the crucifix dangling from their necks and painted on the side of their noisy juggernauts. What country do these men belong to, India or Bangladesh? Children and women wearing tattered clothes and thick soot run after the vehicles as they cross into Bangladesh. A troupe of Bangladesh Rifles guards in camouflage uniforms, berets and rifles bid goodbye to an Indian Border Security Force guard, a Sikh, on the other side. Having just finished their shift at the Zero Point, they head towards their barracks, looking tired and bored rather than full of purpose and nationalist zeal.

* * *

I have come to Boropani to study the fence India is building around Bangladesh. It does not appear to have arrived here yet, but the road that the double, barbed-wire barrier will be constructed upon can be seen from the village. It is a scar of earth carved out on the side of the limestone hills. No one knows when the work to erect the fencing will start let alone finish. More importantly, no one knows what it will mean for the coal trade which so many individuals, families and communities on both sides of the border and further afield are dependent upon. What locals do say is that they will just adjust their lives to it as they have done with all other changes that have occurred here. 'What else can we do?' they say. Once complete, the metal curtain will totally surround Bangladesh. It is intended to define hitherto opaque state margins and delineate once and for all the recalcitrant populations who live alongside it, sorting out 'India' from 'Bangladesh' and 'Indians' from 'Bangladeshis'. In many other parts of the two countries where the fence has already been erected, the barrier divides villages, agricultural lands and markets. In north-west Bangladesh its twists and turns separate families and communities, with some borderland residents finding their homes in one country and their fields in another. The Bangladesh–India border is one of the most violent in the world with more than 1,000 people killed alongside it between 2001 and 2011.[2] In India, the last BJP government argued that a staggering 20 million Bangladeshis have apparently illegally moved there (van Schendel 2009: 227). The current Congress government also alleges that there are terrorist camps on Bangladeshi territory which are used as bases to attack Indian civilians. The result of the eight feet high barricade would, they claim, see a decrease in illegal Bangladeshi immigration, smuggling and terrorism. Depending upon domestic political expediencies, consecutive governments in Dhaka have argued that the fence is part of a wider aggressive strategy adopted by India to maintain its position as the regional hegemon. They dismiss the evidence of insurgents within their territory, claiming these are secessionist groups from India's own north-eastern states, a long, protracted issue exacerbated by Delhi's domestic policies in that region. The Bangladeshis also declare that there are no illegal immigrants in India and that the Bangladesh Rifles (the paramilitary force charged with protecting the border) are thwarting smugglers in the frontier regions between the two states.[3]

In the face of the rhetoric between Delhi and Dhaka over the (mis) management of their borders, two things are certain. Firstly, despite attempts to prevent them, cultural, social, economic and political connections continue between borderlanders who live and work in the margins of Bangladesh and India. New links and bonds continue to be relentlessly made. This is not just in the Sylhet-Meghalaya section, but arguably across the entire length of the border. Over the years there have even been half-hearted attempts on the part of the states to facilitate some of these linkages, with cross-border markets for example being set up. Secondly, it is pertinent to keep in mind that the current Bangladesh-India fence is not just a specific ad hoc development occurring in a specific site. It is taking place at the same time as many other barriers across the world are being erected to divide nation states, populations, spaces and resources. More walls, barricades, cordons, enclosures and fences are going up than are coming down. All of these experiments with bordering have very different aims, legitimacies, histories, political and economic realities, narratives and operational policies. These include the much-discussed US–Mexico border and the Israel–Palestine wall, as well as the Saudi Arabia–Yemen border and Catholic and Protestant 'peace lines' in Northern Ireland, amongst others. What all of them have in common is that they seem to be relics from an earlier time, a time when politics was carried out in a different, more visceral way. Their physicality—the barbed wire; the huge amounts of manpower required to build and police them; the carving of roads through deserts and forests and into mountain sides; observation towers and landmines—appear to belong to a long forgotten past. They could not be any more further away from the frontier traversing, digitalised, virtual, retina-reading era that many of us think we belong and are accustomed to.

Commentators have recently argued that contemporary borders are not actually remnants of a medieval past, but very much products and formations of contemporary realities and future concerns. They are apparently part of the same forces of globalisation that attempt to create the vision of a borderless globe, of motions, connectedness, exchange, movements, openness and flows. This is, in effect, the Janus face of globalisation. The anthropologist Yael Navaro-Yashin argues that the very process of globalisation which promotes mobility and flexibility also engenders the opposite: immobility, entrapment, confinement and incarceration (2003: 108). The political theorist, Wendy Brown asserts that these new boundaries are reactions to pressures on the sovereignty of nation states exerted by the process of neoliberal globalisation (2010: 21). In line with this reasoning then, one could argue that as India rapaciously opens its markets to transnational capital and corporations, and grows in wealth, power and influence, that it is these circumstances that see it attempting to close, militarise and police its borders against its poorer neighbour. The two processes are integrally connected to one another. It is then an attempt to reconstitute power over territory that globalisation is supposedly eroding. However, the danger with this line of thought is that this overarching explanation ignores local specificities. Borders are not simply a contemporary phenomenon reacting to present-day issues and thus materialising out of thin air. Globalisation may be a worldwide experience, but the consequences of it are produced, made sense of and experienced locally. If the Bangladesh–India fence tells us anything, it is that in the current era borders are historically constituted entities that are (re)imagined and (re)fashioned in light of present conditions.

The Indian fence is the most recent permutation of a much longer history of border demarcations in the subcontinent. Sylhet and Meghalaya have experienced several attempts to (re)draw and (re)create their boundaries. This is possibly a reason why the inhabitants of Boropani I found are so relaxed in their opinions of the impending fence that aims to be one of the largest barriers in the world. The physical debris of past efforts to demarcate the margins are strewn around the borderlands, reminding everyone of the futility of such endeavours. They include rusting sections of fencing, remnants of previous Indian attempts at constructing barriers, which, alas, the annual flood waters have long destroyed. There are pieces of metal intermittently jutting out of the ground with 'EAST PAK' emblazoned on one side and 'IND' on the other and the more recent white conical concrete pillars with 'INDIA' written in English and 'BANGLA' written in Bangla. A historian of South Asia, David Ludden argues that the oldest part of the 2,500 mile Bangladesh–India border is the segment that separates northern Sylhet from Meghalaya (2003a). Boropani is located roughly in this area. In the

1700s, following a series of bloody wars between the British East India Company and the Khasi rajas (who lived on the hills), a line was drawn between the hills and the plains. This divided the northern borderlands of Sylhet from the hills of Assam (which Meghalaya was a part of then). It consequently produced the distinctions between the lands of the Bengal Nawabs and the East India Company against those of the mountain Khasis. It also created a distinction between the Bengali (Muslim and Hindu) and non-Bengali (Khasi and Garo) populations. This frontier did not last long, as later, with the British takeover of the region, Sylhet district was incorporated into Assam in 1874.

After the first partition of Bengal in 1905, which the British government had to repeal six years later due to the level of protest and opposition against it, the 1947 partition of Sylhet from Assam, and with it the entire subcontinent, is the most salient of boundary formations in recent times. The maelstrom that it was, its reach and magnitude continues to be felt in a myriad of personal, psychological, social and spiritual traumas. Before departing, the British divided the subcontinent into Muslim-majority East and West Pakistan and Hindu-majority India. As a result, countless numbers of people criss-crossed the newly delineated borders of independent India and Pakistan, leaving behind age-old connections for new and imagined homelands.[4] Muslims headed for the two newly created wings of Pakistan (the East later becomes Bangladesh) and Hindus evacuated these territories for India. This was accompanied by immense political expediency at national, regional and local levels, bloodbaths that killed hundreds of thousands of Muslims, Hindus and Sikhs and displaced millions. But while the particulars of Partition concerning Punjab and Bengal have been widely written about in novels and academia as well as filmed, much less is known of the severing of Sylhet from Assam.

Assam was predominantly non-Muslim, but Sylhet, which is adjacent to East Bengal, was largely Muslim. It constituted only a small piece of the overall province but was economically the most prosperous. At Partition a referendum was held to decide whether Sylhet should remain within Assam and India or be amalgamated into East Bengal and Pakistan. Sylhetis overwhelmingly voted for the latter. The Indian historian Bidyut Chakrabarty believes this was due to communalism, the supposed perennial antagonism between Hindus and Muslims (2002: 323). Over the years huge numbers of Muslim migrants from various parts of East Bengal had settled into Sylhet district and Assam. Sylhetis also held many of the high-ranking positions in the colonial bureaucracy there. According to Chakrabarty, the tactics used by the Muslim League in the run-up to the referendum ensured that Muslim voters feared losing their lands and livelihoods were they to remain in Hindu-majority India. Dasgupta's first-hand work with Sylheti 'Partition refugees' conversely states that 'traditional Hindu–Muslim' rivalries were not a reason for the referendum result and that there were in fact only a few incidents of violence against Sylheti Hindus in Sylhet during and after the referendum anyway. Rather, it was the tensions between Hindu and Muslim Sylhetis and the Assamese, the latter who felt usurped, that was at the root of the referendum result. Dasgupta's Sylheti informants recall that all Partition riots were organised by Assamese Hindus who did not want Hindu Sylheti refugees to relocate themselves in the province (2001: 334). In fact the Assamese 'wanted Sylhet and all the Sylhetis to go to Pakistan' (ibid.: 235). Following the referendum, in 1947 Sylhet was partitioned from the rest of Assam and its borders redrawn. It became an extension of East Bengal, a region of East Pakistan and part of the experiment that was to be the Pakistan project. The Eastern wing was separated from the Western wing by more than 1,600 kilometres of Indian territory, and other than religion the two sides were economically, linguistically and socially vastly different. (Assam was subsequently subdivided again in 1972 in order to create the state of Meghalaya.)

Partition turned neighbours into the citizens of different states. It also made Pakistan and India obsessed about their borders. Anxieties over 'infiltration' and 'attempts to undermine' the new countries were pervasive (van Schendel 2001). Border pillars, guards and camps were set up.[5] For many in the Sylheti borderlands, encounters with the newly formed Pakistani border guards (made up of Muslim refugees from India) were the first and only interaction with the newly formed state (ibid.). The centres of administrative power were physically and symbolically a long way away. Though the anxieties were felt acutely by those who lived in border areas, movements across them for work or to visit family were initially relatively easy. It may have involved having to bribe a guard or most commonly, walking to a desired destination using old paths and networks. New ways of operating were also created. For Sylhetis who worked on the now Indian side, one of the problems was bringing wages, paid in bags of paddy or grain, back home. Many were accused of smuggling by border guards and arrested (ibid.).[6]

INTRODUCTION

But events that take place in 'places that matter' are—where borders are produced and inspired from in the first place and which are rarely the products of people that live in border zones themselves—felt in particular ways in the margins of states. So whilst increasingly the tensions between India and Pakistan were most visible in the border areas, simultaneously other potent failures of Partition were also gaining ground. Throughout the 1950s and 1960s, the myth of religious unity and its inability to glue the two wings of East and West Pakistan was also becoming obvious. Economic exploitation of the East by the West began to establish a colonial relationship between the two wings and together with the West's political, linguistic, military and cultural hegemony, the break-up of the two Pakistans was inevitable. During the eventual war in 1971, 10 million Bengali refugees would spill across the border into India for safety. Then, the neighbours saw one another as allies, rather than antagonists as they do today. After Partition, this would be the second time in history when the border would act as a refuge for such large numbers of people (van Schendel 2001: 412). The break-up of Pakistan derides the two-nation theory posited at the time of Partition which assumed that the Hindus and Muslims of India were two separate entities. With the founding of Bangladesh, Sylhet again became a region of yet another conglomeration and its border with its neighbour was simply adjusted to suit new conditions.

* * *

Boropani was exciting from the offset. It had the same raffish quality about it that border towns tend to have. I immediately had many questions about the place and its people. Is the peculiarity of the place a result of the border? How does the cross-border coal trade shape the place today? How did Partition and the events of 1971 play out here? I have always thought anthropologists should put themselves in precarious places and live and work with those that are ignored or marginalised for historical, political and economic reasons. This invariably means going out of zones of safety. But in my case I had to let practicalities outweigh these other considerations. I ultimately did not want to be killed or 'disappeared' in theatre. I end up choosing this place as opposed to other potential border areas that I had visited along the margins of the two countries because of security. There have been no shootings here between the border guards/civilians of either country for many years. The intermittent violence and deaths in other parts of the borderlands mean that my choices are limited. In such places, the local economy is on the whole based on smuggling and in particular the illicit cattle trade, which is what creates the heightened tension as border guards attempt to facilitate the trade between both sides (Hussain 2009b). Boropani on the other hand has a legitimate, legal cross-border trade in coal alongside a myriad of other illicit transactions. This makes the area less of a threatening place to be and one which also makes my presence slightly less conspicuous.

But there are some problems that need resolving before I can think about setting up my proverbial tent here. Firstly, I have come to the border to study the fence and how historically constituted interconnections are being transformed in its wake. But other than the makeshift bamboo barrier at the Zero Point, there is nothing else here. This will not be a problem, I realise. The fence is clearly on its way. The road that has been dug on the hillside attests to this. Now, instead of my work being just about the fence, the border and the relationship locals have to it, it will be able to encapsulate what life is like before the fence turns up and also the process of it being constructed. The second problem is legalities. As a British citizen, it is illegal for me to be in the border region and getting official permission was going to be time-consuming. My time was limited and I didn't want to have to spend it all in traffic jams in Dhaka waiting for bureaucratic acceptance. 'Not a problem', the Bangladeshi friend who initially introduces me to the area says. 'As someone whose family is from Sylhet, you are not that much of a foreigner anyway'. I attempt a protest. 'But it was my grandfather who had left Sylhet when it was part of the British Empire. Since then, there have been three generations of my family who are from the UK'. Tariq laughs. 'This does not matter. Once a Sylheti, always a Sylheti'. Nonetheless, I am able to be here without raising too many suspicions on account of my physical features which are supposedly quintessentially Bengali. My Bangla is also adequate. Tariq tries to further alleviate my concerns. 'Look around you', he says. 'Everyone here is busy doing something that they probably shouldn't be. You are the least threatening out of the lot'. So, by joining a multitude of other activities and people in Boropani that may be strictly illegal, but somewhat locally permissible, my second problem is ameliorated, for the time being at least.

INTRODUCTION

Six months after arriving in the area, however, I was held and taken to camp by a Bangladesh border guard for allegedly being an Indian smuggler. I telephoned Tariq who managed to placate the commander of the camp by explaining that I am not Indian but from the UK and that my family originated from Sylhet. The commander, whose moustache took up nearly half of his face, diffusing any sense of fear that the incident may have had, accepts this. He allows me to stay on condition that I do not attempt to cross the border, stay out of trouble and do not drink the smuggled Indian alcohol so pervasive in the area. The final difficulty that needs resolving is finding somewhere to stay. Boropani is not a place one can live in easily. There is little spare housing, no electricity, no clean drinking water or sanitation. Locals also say that because of the alcohol smugglers, it isn't very safe for someone to live alone. Again Tariq provides a solution. He suggests I live in the fenced-off perimeters of the Khonighat Limestone Mining Project.

To begin with, I had not been able to differentiate between Boropani and Khonighat, the latter where I do indeed end up living. Also on the Bangladeshi side of the border, I assume the two are neighbouring villages. In many respects, that is certainly what they are. The inhabitants of the two places are Bengali and largely Muslim though there are significant Hindu populations in both. However, the people and place of Boropani could not be more different to Khonighat, which until relatively recently played a small role in a larger master plan that was to revolutionise the entire country. A quarry lake separates the two places now, acting as a buffer, both physical and symbolic, between the contrasting narratives Boropani and Khonighat have to tell about one another and their different relationships to the border. While the coal village is teeming with life and activity, Khonighat is its exact opposite. It is eerily quiet and looks like an abandoned ghost town that has been picked up from somewhere else and dropped here. There is little sign of any of the grime and bustle of the coal trade here. Instead, scattered around the insides of the perimeters of the fence are the skeletons and entrails of a decomposing industrial past. Large debris of rusting machinery, lines of railway tracks (that have neither beginning nor end) and disintegrating earth diggers lie strewn around. A massive, metal crane perches gracelessly at the main entrance. The remnants act as an allegory of the collapse of the ideology that once created and sustained Khonighat. The houses, all concrete buildings, built uniformly and painted the same colour, are largely derelict. Around the central lawn are official looking buildings, closed down long ago. Everything seems to have been organised and planned here once, but has since fallen apart. Like all deserted places of the imagination, it also has few inhabitants that actually live here—the young and old. People of working age have left. There is something very sad about Khonighat, a sense of decay hanging all over it. Though I came here to study the border and the fence, these two separate and interweaving spaces—Khonighat and Boropani—the distinct groups of people that occupy them and what they represent were to form the actual basis of my work. It is by exploring their own particular histories, the thoughts of people who live in either place, about themselves and each other that I was able to learn about the contemporary realities of the Bangladesh–India border and, indeed, something about the wider world and how it makes itself felt in this very remote part of it.

* * *

Set up during the latter years of British colonial rule, the Assam Bengal Cement Factory was a large-scale industrial plant situated in Chhatak, on the banks of the Surma River in Sylhet. It was privately owned by the Assam Bengal Cement Company Ltd which had its offices in Calcutta. Its business was in the main extracting and processing limestone—a key ingredient in the production of cement—from the East Khasi Hills. The excavated rock would be lowered into the plains of Sylhet via a mechanical conveyer belt which would then be transported by river to the colonial metropolis of Calcutta, the foremost destination for the cement.[7] At Partition, with the severing of Sylhet from Assam, all social, political and economic life in the subcontinent had to adjust accordingly. The factory now found itself in East Pakistan, separated from its head office in India. Crucially, the border also disconnected the factory in Chhatak from the raw materials it needed from the hills, in Assam. The Boropani collieries, one of its auxiliary sites that provided the coal to fire the furnaces, located some miles west of Chhatak, was also on the Indian side. The village of Boropani was now divided: one half was on the Indian side and the other half, with the labourers, on the same side as the factory in East Pakistan. Over time, supplies of limestone and coal from the East Khasi Hills became increasingly erratic and often insufficient, which meant the factory was unable to run at maximum output. By the 1950s, the market itself was also altering. Much more cement was needed for Dhaka, now the provincial capital of East Pakistan. With the rising demand in both large-scale public and private development projects, the inconsistent supply was troubling. Previously, the biggest challenge faced by the factory had been dealing with the transportation of the raw materials between the hills and the plains. The difficulty now was negotiating an international boundary and all its concomitant obstacles. Partition had brought with it a raft of bureaucratic and administrative measures which had repercussions for the business. The presence of customs posts had rapidly increased across the newly demarcated borderlands. The anthropologist Willem van Schendel writes that there was pressure from local authorities to increase the numbers in order to tax and thus (il)legalise trade which before the border was drawn had been possible. As this now required both the Pakistani and Indian states to negotiate and come to a compromise, trade became a 'pawn in complex diplomatic games between the two governments' (2001: 408).[8] The ensuing disorder, common in other large-scale industries during this unprecedented period, was felt in particular ways in the border areas for many years to come. Not surprisingly, the factory's productivity declined to half the capacity from pre-Partition days (ibid.: 409).

The Assam Bengal Cement Factory staggered along until 1961 when reserves of limestone were discovered on the East Pakistani side of the border in the West Khasi Hills. This was an important breakthrough. The Geological Survey of Pakistan had been exploring the possibilities of reserves of natural resources in Pakistan including coal, gas and oil since the 1950s. It was considered important for newly de-colonialised countries to be independent not only of British colonial rule, but also each other, or at the very least be seen to be so. It was both an attempt at producing new nationalisms and strengthening fledgling national economies. The fact that East Pakistan was still reliant on limestone from India was therefore disconcerting for its new leaders. As a result, both countries prioritised rapid industrialisation as a way to develop their new states. This particular vision of modernity was practised by many de-colonising states at the time. Government-backed organisations that invested in private sector enterprises which pushed forward industrial development and who provided concessions to further these aims were established: this included the East Pakistan Industrial Development ment Corporation (EPIDC). The aim was that top-down state intervention in all matters of the economy would not only lead to accelerated industrialisation with the reduction of foreign imports, thus helping to develop indigenous industries and self-reliance, but also create 'domesticated' consumers for products. Pakistan and India on the other hand used import substitution simply to reinforce parochial ideas of the myth of no-dependency between Muslims and Hindus which had seen the separation of the subcontinent in the first place.[9]

The discovery of limestone on the East Pakistani side of the border coincided with larger forces elsewhere, bringing the factory's uncertainties to a head. Again, it is forces such as this, actions in other places impinging locally, that are a theme in the workings of this border. In 1965, the second war between India and Pakistan broke out over the disputed territory of Kashmir. Though the conflict took place primarily along the West Pakistan–India border and lasted a matter of weeks, the hostilities effectively ended all trade and movement between India and Pakistan. This included the trade in limestone and coal between the East Khasi Hills and the plains of Sylhet that had been a feature of this landscape for centuries. Consequently, the factory in Chhatak was taken over by the EPIDC and renamed the Chhatak Cement Factory. In that very same year, the EPIDC proceeded to excavate the ground where the new limestone reserves were discovered. The West Khasi Hills were some hours away from Chhatak but also on the margins between the highlands and plains. The location, called Khonighat, had been known to factory management for some time. The coal from the Boropani collieries which it once depended upon was brought to this exact place from the hills. From here it would be loaded on to waiting boats, destined for Chhatak.[10] The infrastructure was already in place to operate and manage the quarries. Much of this was from the original coal industry. The transport links required to transfer the raw material to Chhatak were also available. The railway tracks once used to move the coal from the hills to the waiting boats were recommissioned and used to transfer the limestone. Management knowledge existed to supervise the quarries, and the labourers who once worked in the collieries were employed to dig the limestone. Above all, the geography of the wetlands and its particular topography was understood. This was significant because for at least five months of the year the *haor* is under water. An understanding of this topography and ways to make use of it were crucial for the factory to work here. The topsoil was removed and deep, cavernous openings were excavated. The new enterprise was named the Khonighat Limestone Mining Project.

New opportunities began opening up and soon the demography of Khonighat and the border began changing. Much of it was unprecedented in scale. At Partition, 6.5 per cent of the total Pakistani workforce was made up of industrial workers (Alam 1995: 25). Of that, East Pakistan had less than 1 per cent (van Schendel 2009: 133). Joining the existing labourers to work the quarries, new workers began arriving from overpopulated neighbouring districts of East Pakistan as well as the *haor* region. Some high-level Hindu officers, fearing violence and/or discrimination, left their posts at the Chhatak Cement Factory for employment in India. With them, they took the intricate knowledge of an industry that they had amassed over years. The gaps were filled by Muslim officers, some of whom were from West Pakistan. Others were Urdu-speaking Muslim émigrés from places such as Bihar and West Bengal. With their experience of working in large-scale industries across the subcontinent, some of these migrants came to Khonighat to take part in the revolution. Elderly residents of Khonighat who continue to live in the Project remember there were *lakh lakh* (thousands upon thousands) of people who worked there at any given time. One such person recalls:

When I looked over the top of the quarry into the bottom, the workers looked like ants. The quarry was that deep and the numbers of people that many. It was impossible to even locate your father or uncle in there.

In Johnny Parry's chronicling of the Bhilai Steel Plant which began functioning in the Indian state of Chhattisgarh in the 1950s, he says a 'bicycle was still a wonder' before the steel industry established itself (2001: 789). Khonighat, though in a remote part of both countries then as well as now, was hardly a rural backwater in 1965 when the Project began operations. It was well accustomed to the coal industry operating before the quarries even commenced work. However, the limestone extraction was on such a scale that an unprecedented amount of new technology and machinery was required. For many of the newcomers, the industrial landscape they encountered would have been bewildering. The technological infrastructure and machinery would have seemed like it had emerged from another world. According to Project records, this was imported from China and Germany (there are no accounts of anything—formally—coming from across the border in India). At the time, there were only three metal cranes in the whole of East Pakistan, a Project resident recalls. One was in the Chittagong Port (in the southeast of the country and which itself was undergoing modernisation) and the other two were in Khonighat. Project records show that during the monsoon, officers travelled by speedboat between Khonighat and Sunamgonj town, the district's main administrative centre. Homes belonging to high-ranking officers too were decked out in modern amenities, electricity, running water and even indoor toilets and baths. The poverty and hunger rural migrants had left behind would have outweighed this initial uneasiness. Some had moved to the *haor* region a generation earlier as it was sparsely populated and met with little resistance from the communities of Khasi and Garos already living there. A local Garo man told me that they would allow Bengali migrants to take over a piece of land in exchange of a *lao* (gourd) as there was so much free, abundant land everywhere at the time.[11] Some of the long-term residents in Khonighat today as well as the long-term residents settled in Boropani are the decendents of these migrants who moved here in the middle of the twentieth century.

The developmental trajectory that newly independent, post-colonial states followed in the mid-twentieth century is writ small on the Khonighat Limestone Mining Project. Its spread is integrally connected to European colonialism. Modernisation, the theory and practice, dictated that once peasants make the move from working in the field to the factory, these so-called 'backward' people would be propelled into 'civilisation' and the future. By following this process, they would overcome poverty, share in the prosperity of the 'developed' world and take their place as equals in a worldwide family of nations (Ferguson 2006: 177). The idea was that the state was at the centre of development programmes, preoccupied as it was with national progress, or in other words, the development of the whole. Therefore, along with import substitution and backing private entrepreneurship, state-led development concentrated upon spectacular public works. Entire cities, such as Brasilia (Brazil), Islamabad (Pakistan) and Chandigarh (India) were carved out where none existed previously. More commonly, it involved building infrastructure (roads, bridges), developing large-scale power projects (hydroelectricity dams, power stations), constructing industries (manufacturing, refineries, factories) and civic institutions (courts, hospitals, schools, universities, libraries, parliaments). Most of this was concentrated in urban centres, but 'unknown', so-called 'peripheral' places (such as the region where Khonighat and Boropani are located) were also targeted. This is important because these spaces were to be instantiations of modernity, exemplars of what was to come, 'colonising the whole into which it has been inserted' (Caldeira and Holston 2005: 396). Their function was to act as transformers, changing everything around them and thus accelerating the teleological process even in the most remote of locations and amongst the most diverse ranges of people. James Holston (1999: 160) refers to it as a 'viral notion of development'. The 'radical fragments' were to create new forms of social experience, perceptions and habits, thus destabilising, subverting and negating those forms—historical, social, physical and celestial—deemed undesirable and 'backward'.

Although cement was required in huge quantities for the construction projects taking place throughout East and West Pakistan, the aim of the Khonighat Limestone Mining Project was not simply to extract limestone, though this was of course one of its core functions.[12] It found itself at the centre of a much larger, protracted utopian goal that constituted a project of a different order. As an inciter of modernity, it was to rewrite history, to unassailably question old structures, banish 'backwardness' to a distant past and be at the forefront of the new world order for everyone and everything that came into contact with it. In his exposition of the rise and fall of modernity in the West, Marshall Berman argues that in this spirit, modernity and history are diametrically opposed to one another, in that, for one to exist, the other has to be eradicated (1989: 331). So Project workers who came to live and work in this remote part of the then India–East Pakistan border in the 1960s were to be part of the modern Pakistani industrial workforce but more importantly, contemporary and enlightened citizens of the new Pakistani state. They were to be conditioned in body and soul and made to feel the full centrifugal force of the newly modernising state. This was not simply top-down state and Project management gobbledegook. Workers and their families at all levels of the industry truly believed in the rhetoric and vision. It is not difficult to see why. All around them much had already begun changing. Across both wings of Pakistan, there were many modernisation projects being realised. Schools, roads and hospitals were being built in new towns and cities. Much larger projects included the construction of the hydroelectric dam at Kaptai Lake in 1961 and Dhaka's parliament building in 1957.

* * *

The technology, the reliable source of limestone and labour and the ideological incentives meant increased output and soon the Project began to play its role in Pakistan's larger industrial revolution. Talk of the 'Pakistani miracle' began to surface. For a while at least, the optimism seemed to herald transformations that had once occurred in the industrialisation of Western countries. But it was not to last. By the late 1960s, it became clear amongst practitioners of the doctrine as well as academics and policy-makers that modernisation theory was not working. In spite of all the effort leaders put into programmes and the considerable foreign investment,[13] societies were not being propelled into the future. People remained as poor, hungry and 'backward' as they always were. In some cases there were even signs that poverty and inequalities were increasing (Gardner and Lewis 1996: 14). It was no different in Khonighat. The benefits of social welfare which the Project offered were meant exclusively for those who lived and worked within the enclave of modernity. They were not, in practice, shared out amongst its 'non-modern' neighbours in Boropani. Even within the perimeters of the Project, there were anomalies that were not being ironed out.[14] Around the world, the success of economic growth, technological advancement and rationality not only failed to materialise for the majority of people, but where it did take some sort of root, its far-reaching transformations were also at the heart of massive geopolitical ruptures, environmental and ecological degradation and social and individual conflicts. Veena Das says:

The goals of national organisation of life, the scientific management of society, modernisation and development to which great energies has been devoted in the 1960s and early 1970s, now seems like signposts to cities that are abandoned and empty (1990: 1).

The Project closed its gates for the last time in 1993. The trend in recent years has been to explain the closure of large-scale, formal sector industries on neo-liberalism. This is part of a larger argument which declares that states are no longer responsible for their territories and the incumbent political, economic or even social domains (hence the need to build borders, as a way to counteract such forces). Many smaller, poorer states, which modernisation theory had mostly been concerned with, so the argument goes, have lost the ability to manage their national economies altogether. Marcus Taylor for example writes that neo-liberalism emerged during a period of continual global political and economic crisis, becoming a programme of institutional transformation that sought to embed market relations as the pre-eminent form of social organisation by which societies reproduce themselves (2009: 22). For architects and theorists of neo-liberalism, what was preventing 'development' (or rather capitalist penetration) of post-colonial societies was the state itself. It was being blocked by inflated public sectors, distorted economic controls and an overemphasis on capital formation. The solution then was to limit the reach of the state. Rolling it back would lead to actual modernisation, greater freedoms, new private capital investment and ultimately to 'democratisation' (Ferguson and Gupta 2005: 118). As a result, all state institutions were aimed for: many public sectors were privatised, the scale and depth of public spending was reduced and policies that altered prices that could otherwise be managed by the market were sidelined (Leys 2005: 114). Particular targets included institutions that formed around economic planning, labour relations and social policy (Taylor 2009: 30). Such thinking was precisely what the World Bank and the International Monetary Fund, indebted to post-colonial countries, set out to propagate in the subsequent decades by implementing structural adjustment programmes.

In keeping with this overarching assessment, abandoned and empty is certainly how the Project finds itself today. The project of modernisation lasted around thirty years in Khonighat. The totalising master narrative that sustained it is as much of a rumour as the top-down state that championed it. The rusting carcasses of the machinery that lie next to the two limestone quarries which were dug continue to shape people's lives as does the border and landscape. The majority of the Project's high-level staff were transferred out of the area. Some fifty or so middle-ranking clerks, administrators and teachers and their families remained, as there were no positions for them to fill elsewhere. Not so long ago, these men would wear a shirt and tie to work. They would go to the photography studio in the bazaar on their day off to have pictures taken with their wife and children against the backdrop of the

West Khasi Hills. They could expect to be looked after when they were ill and their families to be provided for when old. All this has vanished. The ideals of full employment, centralised bureaucracies, state benefits or even the centrality of the state now seem like mythical tales in comparison to what currently exists. The old aristocracy of labour sit in the Khonighat tea shop (which used to be the labourers' subsidised canteen), in shabby clothes, reading days-old newspapers. They gather around each other as one imagines war veterans who have experienced shell-shock doing: their reduced horizons of life chances leave them with little to do but reminisce about the past. Whether this past actually existed in the way they remember is not the point. They believe it and act upon it, passing the memory on to their children who all behave and remember accordingly. Those who were at the bottom of the Project hierarchy, the limestone labourers, who once formed the backbone of the modernisation myth, were left behind in the borderlands by the Chhatak Cement Factory. Their fate was no longer its concern. With nowhere else to go, having loosened links with their rural homes, many of them moved to neighbouring Boropani. With the advantages of experience (as well as financial opportunities) that the Project provided, in time they gained pivotal positions in the coal trade that was operating there. It is they who have now become extremely wealthy and influential coal barons, running most of the cross-border industry on the Bangladeshi side.

Whilst the previous limestone workforce have bifurcated into those who languish in nostalgia and those who flourish in the resurgent coal industry, for recently arrived seasonal and temporary labour migrants life is altogether very different. These people constitute the majority involved in the coal trade. They toil all the hours their bodies will allow. They hew, collect, wash, sieve, breathe, talk, fight and dream about coal. Some even clean their teeth with it. They work in order to eat, to live. They live, simply to survive; a habit in itself. As the seasons change, so do their methods for collecting coal. It never stops. The effect it has had on the people and the environment is catastrophic and often the area looks like a particularly gruesome biblical scene. This is an outcome of the increased penetration of neo-liberal policies which has undercut the state's responsibilities for social welfare. The legislations that once protected Project labourers does not apply to coal labourers. They work outside of the law. Coupled with their illegal crossings into India to work the mines, the question to ask is, whose citizens are they? The coal industry is now un-mechanised. Intimate and public lives have changed accordingly. There are no public health facilities, sanitation or even electricity; signs and symbols of a modernity that had once existed here and were in the grasp of many ordinary people have now disappeared. Local and national NGOs located here do not concern themselves with such long-term issues; short-term micro-financing is what they are essentially interested in. In the past, some people at least had running water and even baths in their quarters. Today the majority of the people in Boropani and even many of the remaining residents in Khonighat wash in the rain waters that have filled the limestone quarries. This is a testament to what had gone on before and what came after.

It is tempting to understand the area and its people by as rewinding and going backwards when the Project closed down. The old Project aristocracy have (on the whole) been marginalised, and the mining is disastrous for the environment as well as the physical, emotional and mental health of those who labour in it on both sides of the border. However, on the other hand, the changes that have been wrought to the heterogeneous populations that live and work here are far from uniform. There are alternative accounts that have emerged in Boropani and Khonighat. The resultant dual tensions that have manifested between real troubled realities and what one may describe as 'multiple modernities' is a running theme throughout the entire book.[15] Local spaces of creative potentialities and possibilities, hitherto unseen in these parts, have emerged. This is not just in the obvious realm of the local economy but also within the wider domains of society, the individual and intimate lives. Many of these alternative forms were previously seen as challenges, ignored, or at worst repressed, during the Project regime; considered to go against the doctrine of modernisation. It, after all, was aiming for its own particular, singular, version of the future. Thus social groups that were earlier marginalised, sidelined and ostracised from the benefits of modernisation have managed to appropriate the discourse on their own terms, something they would not have previously been able to do. Amongst them are the rejected limestone labourers who have come to control the coal trade today, including women, hijras (widely known as the third sex), as well as religious communities. Their roles and positions are far from identical. In fact, as in the case of poor women, their subordinate status is not one to be desired, but the point is that where once they would have been economically marginalised, today they are able to make a living for themselves and their families in Boropani.

* * *

Much of the work that follows was based on serendipity, chance encounters and coincidences. Despite my best intentions, there was little formality or organisation in the piecing together of the story of this area and indeed its people. It was on the whole done bit by bit, in the process of doing other things such as walking, eating and bathing. I collected a fragment of an anecdote here, an observation there, recalled a part of a conversation I had with a person and linked this with gossip and stories I heard elsewhere. I read in-between lines, in the silences and omissions. It was impossible to work any other way here because of the nature of the place, the transitoriness and overt suspicion of the area's inhabitants and my own insecure position in amongst all of this. What I did manage to do was to establish a daily routine, one which developed out of necessities, rather than a planned course of action. In this way, I was able to carve a path that sliced through the lives, relationships and implicit/explicit networks of the myriad people that are to be found in the borderlands. In the course of walking this path (both metaphoric and physical), I had all sorts of encounters which enabled me to understand, question, share with and observe better the area's inhabitants. Often I would find myself veering off the carved path; sometimes this paid dividends, but more often than not, it highlighted the countless things that were taking place in the area that I knew nothing about, but for fear of self-preservation I would find myself retreating back to the known path. I scribbled the following into my notebook upon arrival to Khonighat:

Moved into Project bungalow. Covered in cobwebs, dried dead cockroaches. Smells. Looks like the records room. Shredded bits of paper strewn around like flowers for an honoured guest. I definitely do not feel honoured to be here. Stacks of rotting paper on veranda that have to be climbed over to get to room. One piece attached itself to my muddy sandal—handwritten letter in English from the Secretary of the Officers Club dated 22.04.1978:

'I have purchased 1 (one) teaset for the KLM [Khonighat Limestone Mining] Officers Club in presence of the finance secretary of the club from Sunamgonj market at an amount of TK150 (one hundred and fifty) only—cash memo enclosed. The said amount may please be approved and given to me for adjustment of my other advance'.

There are five signatures that have approved the letter. The building is really scary. Not sure how I will live here for foreseeable future. No running water from taps. Dirty room. Termite mounds adorn the veranda like some contemporary art work. But views of the haor on one side and the undulating hills on the other are incredibly beautiful. Records contain details about Project. Info on wages paid to peons, security guards, drivers, letters of absence and employees waiting for leave etc. Stuff about people paying subscriptions to the clubs, mosque, a mandir etc. Earlier records kept in English, later ones in Bangla.

The bungalow, I am to find out over the course of time, was not the records room of the Project. It was an old officer's quarter that had been commandeered to store the records, now all unwanted and getting in the way. The building was in the last stages of dilapidation, not so dissimilar to all the others in the colony. It looked sad and ignored, although it must have once been quite a pleasant home for a middle-ranking family. The sun had scorched the distinct yellow colour that all Project buildings were painted in, the shutters on the metal windows had come off their hinges and graffiti dating back to 1990 had not been cleaned off. Inside there were facilities one does not find in homes in rural Bangladesh, though all in poor condition: an indoor washroom with a Western toilet, shower, porcelain sink, mirror and metal soap-holder fixed to the wall. In another bungalow where I stayed later, there was even a tin bath. In the main room there was an electrical light and a ceiling fan. The latter two would work intermittently when there was power but the shower and toilet did not work at all. The plumbing had obviously broken down long ago.

My neighbour, the records, continued to be not very neighbourly. Great numbers of the ledgers spilled out of the room and lay scattered on the veranda and in the garden. Inside, they lay piled up on the floor, many in jute sacks, some on shelves, most of them rotting and eaten away. Sometimes I heard the voices of brave school children rummaging around in the spooky, echoing, dark room, foraging for empty pages which they would tear out of the hardbound records and use for their schoolwork. Frequently I would see a family of mongoose slinking in and out of the room. I was told by residents that there were snakes in there too. Yet it wasn't them I was frightened of but the ghosts that I heard had moved in. Occasionally, the wind would carry a page or two to my door. Whether I liked it or not, I had to engage with them. If I were more superstitious, I would say the records were beckoning me to find out what was contained in them. But I didn't want to risk my precarious position in the Project and in the border area itself by asking the management if I could peruse them. I knew too well that there is no way they would have allowed me to go through the 'private records'. But like most things, once something is gone, it is only then that one misses it. I woke up one morning and discovered that all the records, except the three I had salvaged and hidden in my room to nose through, had been taken away. No one I knew could say where they had gone. Someone said they had been sold to a bits-and-bobs man who would recycle the paper. Nonetheless, I wish I had interacted with my neighbour more than I did while I had the chance. In particular because when, much later, I had become aware of the relationship between the dilapidated state of the bungalow, the records that were spilling out of the adjacent room and the subject of my study, it was too late. But for a long time I did ignore it all, or more accurately, did not connect up the dots. After all, I had come here to 'study' the Bangladesh–India border and this house and the colony in which it was located were simply a base from which to live and work. *It* was not the subject of my study. Or so I thought for a long time after my arrival.

1

THE FUTURE THAT DID NOT HAPPEN

The ancients who wished to illustrate illustrious virtue throughout the empire, first ordered well their own States. Wishing to order well their states, they first regulated their families. Wishing to regulate their families, they first cultivated their persons. Wishing to cultivate their persons, they first rectified their hearts. Wishing to rectify their hearts, they first sought to be sincere in their thoughts. Wishing to be sincere in their thoughts, they first extended to the utmost their knowledge. Such extension of knowledge lay in the investigation of things (Confucius).[1]

Most evenings, groups of young men would climb to the top of one of the hillocks that litter the borderlands to watch the sun set. It is illegal to do so, as they are officially entering no-man's-land and, if caught, this carries with it the threat of either a Bangladesh Rifles grilling or an Indian Border Security Force beating. Local Bangladeshis join Indians in this most high risk of pursuits. A plastic bottle of whiskey, Officer's Choice, may be passed around. It is one of the many ways people on both sides of the border connect and socialise with each other, something the impending barbed-wire fence India is building will attempt to disrupt. The spot doubles up as the most auspicious place to be a diviner of time too. As the golden glow swathes everyone and everything in its warm, eternal embrace, the magnificent sight allows even the novices amongst these plucky men the ability to recall the past and prophesise about the future. Immediately below, on the Bangladeshi side, are the remnants of the Khonighat Limestone Mining Project. Once aiming to be much more than just about quarrying limestone for the newly independent (Pakistani and then later Bangladeshi) state, the industrial site now looks forgotten and melancholic. From this height one can see rusting machinery, decaying houses and abandoned office buildings. They all surround the luminous green lawn where grand parties would once be held. There is no difference between the few that continue to be occupied and the majority of the houses that are now deserted and abandoned. From the state of the place, it seems like it has forever been this way: timeless, static and unchanging, seemingly in suspension and disconnected from developments taking place in the rest of the world. But this is not so. Its present condition belies the monumental transformations that have occurred here. Looking at this historic ruin, one would be forgiven for not realising that the site before us had promised to be at the forefront of a bright national future.

To the north of the border are the West Khasi Hills. To the south and beyond the Project's ramshackle perimeters are the endless *haor* (wetlands), extending deep into Bangladesh. The plains have always been connected to life on the hills. From the homesteads scattered out there, peasants, having heard the call for the future, came to work in the Project's limestone quarries. It is from these same homesteads that current generations of men, women and children come to work the coal mines. Eastwards, the quarry lake physically and symbolically separates Khonighat from its neighbour Boropani, and with it, the past from the present and future. The contrasts between the two seem to be of polar extremes. Once, the lake was one of the two quarries that were dug to service the newly independent country's need for cement. Now, men wash themselves and their cattle and motorbikes in the waters that have collected here. Clothes, blackened and covered in coal dust, are soaped, rinsed and used to beat nearby rocks with. The water is kept as clean as possible, the only source for many. Women cook with it and children swim in it. Further eastwards is Boropani itself. At this hour of the evening, the bazaar is full of life and will continue to be lively into the night. One can see people shopping, eating and talking. On the Indian side of the demarcation, coal trucks whose paperwork has not been processed simply wait at the Zero Point until morning when the customs houses of both countries reopen. Under cover of darkness, people go back and forth between the two halves; many with the 'official' say so of the border guards.

THE FUTURE THAT DID NOT HAPPEN

Back on the hillock, conversations centre on subjects most young men everywhere are well versed in: new technologies, shoes, girls, boys, family life and hair. Often it is about the entity before us, the Project; what it did, what it stood for, its untimely collapse and its current state. Khonighat is a time-saturated landscape, where the past, present and future coexist and shape lives at the same time. Malik and Shorif are two young men who talk with an authority about these matters. They have the power of being able to recall from their own store of memories, when in fact this would be impossible as they were born at the precise moment in the early 1990s when the Project shut down. Stories about how full of life the Project was pervade the locality to the extent that for them it does not make any difference whether they were there or not. The stories are formative and connected to intricate emotional and empirical experiences. Maurice Bloch describes a similar experience with young informants in Madagascar who were able to recall an incident in the same detail as the adults who had been present during the event. He says that the attachment of powerful narratives to a 'history saturated landscape' ensures a long-term accurate transmission of it (1998: 120–1).

For older men sitting on the hillock who do have memories of when the Project was running, every building, tree, mark and person walking past below us carry significance. The bungalow where I have been temporarily put up, I am told by one such individual, housed an officer's family who had a daughter the same age as him. He attended a birthday party there once. The speaker, who is now in his thirties, was so scared of this officer that ordinarily he would not dare to walk near the house. As a result, he found the bash to be such an uncomfortable experience that he could not enjoy the games and the balloons that the officer's wife had organised. This kind of passing comment was frequent. Fernando Santos-Granero (1998) argues that such exercises are attempts at 'writing' history into landmarks. He says that the Yanesha of Peru, a non-literate Amazonian society, preserve historical memory by imbuing particular features of the landscape (trees, rocks, river bends) with meanings, connecting it to past events that are personal, historical or supernatural. Pilgrimages are made to them, underlying their importance, preserving and collectivising memory. For people in Khonighat, history is also 'written' on to the remnants of the Project, so that even those who were not present when it was running are able to recall stories and events from the past with the same visceral attachment as those who were.

Joshim's uncle is in his mid-thirties and is a *coila netha* (coal labour leader). He hires men and women to dig on the Bangladeshi side of the no-man's-land for low-grade coal which he then sells on to the larger import depots. Joshim's uncle's father was a Project labourer on the limestone rail-tracks for more than ten years. He had retired by the time it closed down, receiving a generous pension. Joshim's uncle recalls with pride how exclusive and exclusionary the Project was:

The entire area was completely different then, nothing like it is now. The officers all lived in those bungalows over there [pointing to them from the hillock]. Their wives would play badminton in the gardens and on the maidan [lawn]. No one was allowed to enter the Project gates without permission. Not even the BDR were allowed. Streetlights would be seen from the middle of the *haor*, they were that powerful. I remember three men would clean the outside areas, picking up litter and rubbish throughout the day. But look at it now. Cattle roam the maidan and eat the flowers off the trees. People [such as himself] transport coal through it. Even the NGOs who operate within Project territory would never have been allowed to do so then. Even you [meaning me], would not have been allowed to stay. It is nothing like it was ... People knew Khonighat before. Not anymore. The BDR just wander around whenever and wherever they want. The Ansar [the security force hired to protect the Project grounds] steal what they can and cut down trees that I grew up with, for firewood. One of the Ansar guards recently told me that they beat up a thief who was stealing cables and wires from the old machinery. This is the reality of what has happened here.

Malik and Shorif are best friends and have always lived in Khonighat. They are descendants of the dwindling numbers of the Project's old 'aristocracy of labour' (Parry 1999c): families whose patriarch held secure and permanent positions in the Project. I met them very soon after arriving in the area. They were playing football on the maidan in front of my bungalow and as resident sons of the soil, took it upon themselves to find out who I was. From then on, the two would come to my room most mornings (whether I wanted them to or not) and we would talk, swim and walk. Malik and Shorif are unusual these days in that their family members continue to be employed by the Project's headquarters which remain in Chhatak. There is only a handful of such people left, out of more than fifty or so remaining families. Malik's parents are considering transferring out of the area. His father, a PE teacher at the school, has been offered a teaching position in Chhatak. This would mean security, extra money and access to amenities. The family is however reluctant to leave the place Malik and his siblings have grown up and where the parents have spent much of their lives. His friend, Shorif, was raised by his older sister after both parents died. Their father had been an officer in the Project. The sister is now married to the current overseer of the Project, who acts as the contact between Chhatak and Khonighat.

Malik and Shorif come from slightly different social backgrounds. Malik's family trace their roots back to the neighbouring district of Mymensingh. His illiterate grandfather had been one of the hordes of landless peasants to migrate to the *haor* in the middle of the twentieth century in search of land. His father was born there, sent to school in Sunamgonj, found employment at the Project and worked his way up to his current teaching position. Shorif's father on the other hand was from a middle-class family in Sylhet. He had already been working for the Chhatak Cement Factory at its headquarters when he was transferred to Khonighat in 1965. During Project days, this difference in background may have meant that the two would have somewhat different life courses. With all areas of life, including social and intimate relationships being carefully managed, associating with one another across class and rank would not have been as easy as it is now. With the collapse of the Project, such distinctions of status and background no longer matter as much. United in identity by the legacy of the Project's decline, the two are able to be friends.

A shared experience of decline is evident for all remaining residents. Like the image of actual aristocrats whose kingdoms have withered away due to in-fighting and where heirs to the throne cut pathetic, melancholic figures, here too the old aristocracy mourn their glory days and complain about the 'utter dreadfulness' of the present. The condition of the Khonighat high school represents the frustrations of a bygone era in the most distilled way. Its current state of decay is indicative of all the other things that used to exist here and no longer do. The clinic closed down many years ago, the bank shifted its operations to Sunamgonj (the nearest administrative town) during the period of my stay and the electricity is now as intermittent here as it is in the rest of the country. Whilst sitting on the hillock and taking in the time-saturated landscape in front of us, I realised that there is a profound sense of anxiety and gloom about the present and future for all those who are connected to this particular past. As heirs to higher-ranking jobs, they expected to be treated with deference by subordinates and respect by superiors. None of this exists today, but people continue to mark themselves out as separate from other locals, in particular those in Boropani. Their lineages, they believe, are 'respectable, traceable and legitimate' compared to those involved in the neighbouring coal industry. Like the Anglo-Indians whom the anthropologist Laura Bear writes about as feeling slighted by history, they attempt to 'remove all suspicions of their bastard, illegitimate and low cast status' (2007: 9). Many residents still cling to the now defunct ideology of modernisation for which the Project stood. This has endured despite the disappearance of the kingdom. Old Project folk are increasingly insular, limiting their interactions with coal families, however wealthy and important the latter may be. What many Project folk dread more than being evicted from their quarters is slipping into the world of the coal cycle. Some have gone to the extent of refusing marriage proposals from coal barons who have done so well that they have acquired social standing beyond the region. It is now their children who go to the best colleges and universities in Bangladesh, even studying abroad. But this division is murky because some Project families have links to the coal industry themselves. Shorif's brother-in-law, the Project's overseer, is a successful coal importer, whilst Malik's sister is married to one. Without these links, many of these families would possibly be quite destitute.

When the Project closed down in 1993, anger and resentment was directed at the corrupt leaders who were in charge of it during its latter days. Nowadays the bitterness is aimed at Boropani, the coal industry and its own rising aristocracy, something Project residents are unable to disentangle from their own declining positions. The cross-border coal trade on the Bangladeshi side is monopolised by those men who were formerly limestone labourers at the bottom of the Project hierarchy. Many were discarded early in its decline by the factory in Chhatak, their fate no longer its concern. Several of these men have worked up from the very bottom and have today amassed huge wealth and respect. Project residents say that unlike the previous ideology of modernisation, the current dispensation is based on selfishness, market morality and greed rather than on national development, educational achievements or class. They consider coal people to be backward, illiterate and uncivilised. Their families and children are crude, ruthless and crass, representing a way of life antithetical to old Project ways. Malik once commented:

I don't like the people of Boropani. Those people are not good. Their society and culture is different to ours. If their children play on shit-covered ground all day, then that is all they will know.

THE FUTURE THAT DID NOT HAPPEN

It is little wonder why marriage proposals are refused. The richest and most influential person in the district is Chairman Babar. He is tall, dark and heavyset, permanently shrouded in pristine white *djellabas* and shawls which he buys whilst on pilgrimages to Saudi Arabia. Babar started life as a limestone labourer. After the Project shut down, he became the right-hand man of a successful coal importer in Boropani. When this man died, he married the widow, thus acquiring the coal import company. Babar is presently the chairman of the extremely powerful and influential Boropani Coal Importers Association. This is the organisation that all Bangladeshi coal importers have to join, in order to be granted a licence to import legally from Indian Boropani. Babar's ascent to the top is treated with suspicion, symbolising the contempt old Project families have for the coal industry. Some even maliciously attribute the death of his wife's first husband to Babar himself. Abed, a descendant of the Project who now runs a tea shop in Boropani, asks 'can you understand who we were and who they were and what we have all now become?' Some even imbue social meanings into the minerals that Khonighat and Boropani respectively specialise(d) in. As one of the men I sat with on the hillock explained 'limestone is white in colour, sophisticated and used for constructing buildings. Coal is black, used for fuelling brick kilns and gives you sickness and disease'. It isn't just the old aristocracy who mourn the Project's passing. People whose families were at the bottom of the Project hierarchy, with the reduced benefits and rights that came with that, also lament a lost time and place in equally emotive ways. They look back upon this period with rose-tinted glasses; the back-breaking work, hours under the scorching sun, hammering limestone for relatively small sums of money is considered honourable, good and worthwhile. This romanticising or relentless nostalgia reveals not just the grief of a world that has passed, but the shock of its simultaneous usurpation to its morally corrupt and disordered successor, Boropani.

* * *

Soon after the EPIDC took over the running of the Chhatak Cement Factory in 1965, the two limestone quarries began to be excavated besides the borderlands. Almost immediately, the physical, social and personal realms of those who came to live and work here, as well as the landscape itself, began to ring with the sounds of change. Land was allocated beside the border to assemble the Project colony. Quarters were constructed to house the employees arriving, following what had by then become a particular kind of design model for company townships. This was based on the earliest manifestation of British presence in the subcontinent and one of its most enduring images, the trading settlements, or factories. In the seventeenth century, the East India Company's factories were self-contained, fortified compounds with storehouses, barracks and living quarters for civilians (King 1984: 15). They were built away from densely packed Indian settlements. The view at the time was that such architecture would provide Europeans with an assurance of their own cultural identity and equally project their distinct cultural, economic and political presence (ibid.: 48). Throughout the eighteenth, nineteenth and twentieth centuries, the British built distinct towns and cities (New Delhi) with spatial distance between the civil lines and cantonments that housed colonial officers and the military and the so-called 'native towns' (Old Delhi). The 'white town' and 'black town' exemplified the urgency of social distancing, writes the historian of colonialism Thomas Metcalf (1989: 8). From the outset, colonial architecture embodied an assertion of conquest, simultaneously informing and giving meaning to the nature of the British Raj. Ubiquitous features included the church, officers' club and bungalow, the colonial residence *par excellence*. The wide, grid system of these planned spaces was to prevent disease and to promote comfort and coolness as much as it was about aesthetics.

The Chhatak Cement Factory's colonial antecedents continued in the programme that followed in the post-independence period. Nothing so starkly underlines this than the physical space that was created in 'white' Khonighat and in particular its relationship with 'black' Boropani. In keeping with earlier rules, the housing quarters in the Project were based on hierarchies of rank, salary and whether occupants were permanent or casual. The senior officers' colony, Grade 1—accountants, doctors, engineers—consisted of widely spaced brick bungalows with a large, covered veranda that ran along the length of the building, overlooking a garden at the front. Over time, fruit trees and flowering bushes were tended to by gardeners employed by the Project. The view from the main windows was of the large rectangular maidan. The backs of the buildings looked out on to the vast expanse of the West Khasi Hills now in India, that began a matter of metres away. Inside, there were two or three spacious rooms, a small kitchen and a bathroom. Officers were able to comfort-ably accommodate their families and a maid. The bungalows had access to locally generated electricity and indoor plumbing, including Western toilet and flush. The houses for the intermediate staff—administrators, teachers, nurses—were built along a grid system and were closer together. Though they did not have the veranda, the views, or large rooms, they too had electricity, plumbing and draping bougainvillea bushes. Again, wives and children would be expected to live here. The houses for the lowest grade and the majority of employees—labourers, explosives experts, radio/crane operators, security, foremen, contract workers, car-penters—built on the inside fringes of the Project perimeters were made out of tin. The barrack-like blocks were built to accommodate large numbers of working men, pragmatism outweighing comfort. They would share squat toilets and a well for water, but they too had electric-ity. There were no ethnic or religious enclaves. People of different back-grounds had to live with one another. Over time, the Project became more and more detached from its immediate surroundings. Roads and communication links to Sunamgonj and Sylhet were established. A school was built, as was a clinic, water supply, graveyard, post office, bank, guest house and a bazaar. A mosque was constructed as was a Hindu mandir (temple). Both were made using the same materials and painted the same green colour. Significantly, they were roughly the same size, in spite of more Muslims working and living here than Hindus. Whilst the officers had their club with weekly leisure activities to amuse them, the lower-ranking employees had an entertainments building with a *caramboard* set and later a television.

It was not just the built environment that was changing. Remaining residents talk about a new social order beginning to crystallise and an organised and regimented lifestyle forming. The distinct mode of pro-duction that the latest infrastructure required saw the very way people lived and worked having to adjust. This included needing a trained labour force, health and safety regulations, set wages, trade unions and fixed working hours. Modernisation was expected to incite an irrevoca-ble transformation of society and the individual in the same way it had done so in the West. These notions were considered to be vital for the new economy but also for the new society, eradicating poverty and 'backwardness' all at the same time. There were norms of civility and conventions that dictated interactions between officers and subordinates. This meant expectations of courteous conduct regardless of whether one was an accountant or a sweeper. Respect was not just paid to higher-ranking officers. Their relative wealth as well as perceived access to power and modern technology ensured that lower-level employees were also treated with deference from those outside of the system including people in Boropani. A former employee says that he remembers a high-level officer once slapping a labourer for having made a mistake in his work. This officer and his family were duly transferred to Chhatak by the management, apparently furious at what had transpired. Another ex-employee believes the officer was transferred to avert a potential strike the union leaders were threatening to hold in support of their colleague. Extensive provisions for workers were introduced, including set working hours, lunch breaks, a pension system, safety considerations, access to healthcare and the control of prices of goods in the bazaar. (Even today and despite it being run privately, if there is an attempt to raise the price of tea in the Khonighat canteen in keeping with general costs, locals threaten to boycott it and to write letters of complaint to the headquarters in Chhatak.) The Project became a coveted posting as employees and their families were well looked after. The security and safety nets provided were luxuries that lower-ranking workers would not have experienced in their rural villages or elsewhere.

In one of the moulding, old Project records that I found, the retirement papers of Fatik Chandra Sarkar, a 'store helper', are filed away in triplicate. Sarkar began service on 1 September 1967 and retired on 31 March 1978 ('afternoon'). The clearance certificate shows all the departments that had to sign him off. They were the mining section; workshop; stores; medical; civil; transport; administration; accounts; ration shops; and club. This was further signed off by the account staff, assistant accountant, account-in-charge and the manager. With 'nothing to declare' from any of them, Sarkar's own contribution to the provident fund came to 909tk. Provident funds were established to help employees set up small businesses when they retired. It was administered by the Project which retained a certain percentage of the wage every month. The accumulated amount was later handed back to the employee at the time of retirement. In Sarkar's case, the Project doubled the amount he saved and an interest of 226.80tk was added. The numbers of people needing to sign and all the many sheets of paper that one needed to gather in order to be 'cleared' indicates how bureaucratic the organisation was, as well as the large numbers of people it employed. Retirees such as Sarkar used their money to buy land outside of the Project grounds. Some started small businesses in Khonighat bazaar itself but also in Boropani which would have been less bureaucratic to function in. A number of them used their provident fund to establish themselves in the then relatively small cross-coal industry operating in Boropani.

Another badly decomposing record in the 1978 file is an application for a loan by a labourer who worked as a 'metal help' (up-grade) in the workshop department. Mohammed Abdul Maleque applied for a 900tk loan against his provident fund. The reason he gives is to provide 'treatment of my wife and myself as per advice of our medical section'. Mr and Mrs Maleque had been examined by the Project doctor and the money required was the cost for the medication that needed to be brought in from Sunamgonj. Maleque's provident fund, however, only amounted to 649.92tk. Hence he was awarded a loan of 400tk which he agreed to pay back in twelve monthly instalments. Although his application for the full 900tk was refused, the fact that he received medical treatment for himself and his wife, obtained almost half of the amount required for the medication (the remaining amount would have become part of the final sum he received on retirement), highlights the ethos prevailing at the time.

The Khonighat high school was established in 1966, a year after the founding of the Project itself. It was an incentive for officers and their families to take up employment and relocate to this remote part of the country. It was also necessary for the future needs of the company. Education was essential in producing reliable people with the skills, capabilities and pedigree to reproduce the upper echelons of the industry. This meant inculcating knowledge that enabled students to lead, manage and order large numbers of workers involved in the extractive industry itself. Furthermore, education was understood to be key to creating a modern, developed and democratic nation. Post-independence rulers in Pakistan and India used it as a means to create an indigenous middle class: new, upright citizens who would comport themselves in particular ways. Hand in hand with the formation of the 'national family', young people's loyalty and dedication to the Project and the school itself were seen in effect to be symbols of allegiance to the forging and strengthening of the national endeavour. Limestone after all was an essential building material and these young people were doing precisely that: building a nation

(Parry 1999c). Bear (2007: 89) shows that education was crucial in the creation of the Anglo-Indian railway community too. It was not something that simply existed, but was used to make people, guaranteeing social privileges and ensuring a particular kind of pedigree. Children would be taught not only to be workers in positions of authority, but also how to be 'respectable railway wives' and families (ibid.: 88), because 'intimate and public forms of life go hand in hand' (ibid.: 9). Though her work is tied up with ethnicity and the creation of biologically different communities, similar transformations were occurring in Khonighat.

The school was often described to me as a 'source of light in a sea of darkness' by local people. Even during the privations of the Liberation War in 1971, it remained open. Solely for the children of Project employees, it was generally the children of senior officials who would complete their full schooling before being sent to Sylhet or Dhaka for higher education. Many from Joshim's uncle's background were entitled to admission but decided against going because they needed to support the family financially. Not being able to get a job in the Project because of his lack of age, he simply drifted out of Khonighat into the world of coal extraction in Boropani. This was not because the system itself discriminated against the children of labourers by denying them access: it was simply that the practical realities of life took over. In other words, needing to eat and needing to support one's family. Arguably, the promise of modernisation for all was not even being fulfilled during the height of modernisation. It was not just the fact that the school existed where no others did that made the institution so valuable. The teachers and the education that was provided were believed to be of the highest quality. One has to remember that people of the highest calibre wanted Project jobs.

Standards at the school have not continued to be maintained with the closure of the Project. Joshim's uncle blames individuals for letting the system disintegrate:

The school was once very famous—though you wouldn't think it to look at it now. Out of every thirty students taking exams, twenty-nine would do very well and achieve high grades. Today the teachers take bribes to pass the students. Most students don't pass on the first attempt, but only on their third or fourth try.

The school is only minimally supported by Chhatak now. Only six of the teachers' salaries are provided for. The school is in limbo, it is neither a state school nor is it private. The remaining teachers as well as the costs to maintain the infrastructure and salaries are borne by more affluent parents, in particular the Boropani coal barons. For the latter, many of whose families do not even live in the area, doing so is a way to build up a public-spirited persona. With the state not providing, private entrepreneurs, individuals and NGOs carry out the roles the state, through the Project, once did. Chairman Babar is the most generous of such coal donors and is frequently the guest of honour at prize-giving ceremonies at the school. He also acts as a bridge between the contemporary coal industry and the old Project community, whose respect and admiration he seeks, having originated from its milieu himself.

Alongside the physical and social worlds that the Project took upon itself to intervene in, the personal worlds of its workers were also being transformed. The conditioning and shaping of the Project family in both symbolic and concrete ways was vital. Families were emblematic of the 'national family' *par excellence*. They were at the vanguard of Pakistani (and then later Bangladeshi) state attempts to create loyal citizens with the right middle-class values, aptitudes and morals. They were to be catalysts for change, altering everything and everyone around them. As a new generation began to be born, along with the high degree of security employment in the Project afforded, the workforce began questioning links with their birthplaces. Reluctant to revert to agriculture, workers across the hierarchy believed they had no chance of earning a living back home. For such people, life at the Project was considered better than the exploitation, instability and 'backwardness' of the rural life they had left behind. Visits to extended family members (and hosting them), partly because of the distance, became less frequent. Some stopped remitting money altogether. Khonighat represented the future and people began looking upon extended family ties and rural life with disdain. Having lost contact, later, those not transferred out upon the Project's closure, simply had to stay in the borderlands.

In other post-colonial countries, where industrial modernisation was also taking place, households became more 'nuclear' and for a while this seemed that confirm that development was actually happening. But this belief was quickly undermined when, as Jan Breman suggests, it was realised that for large segments of rural Indian society, for example, the extended family was never a common unit of cohabitation anyway (1999: 26). In this light, James Ferguson also writes that even though people in the Zambian copper belt knew that they did not have 'modern' families, the fact that an attempt was made in the first place shows the pervasiveness and attractiveness of such ideals (1999: 175).

Gender relations, domesticity and femininity were at the forefront of Project initiatives too. Female education was promoted and reproduction was maintained and controlled. Henrike Donner, writing about the creation of the urban middle-class Bengali woman, says that 'population politics', though mainly aimed at poorer women, by extension also impinged on middle-class women. Forged through notions of Western parenting practices dating back to the colonial period which produced certain modernist versions of motherhood (2006: 377), she writes 'it is the responsible middle-class mother who by planning birth control, proved herself to be educated and by extension capable of bringing up the right kind of young citizen' (ibid.: 372). In Khonighat, this included creating distinctions between 'desirable and educated mothers' of the Project and in particular the officer class and the 'deviant, undesirable motherhood' (ibid.) of the labourers and more specifically those in Boropani. The organisation of the home also became a battleground for modernist developments and transformations. Project wives and mothers, who did not have 'respectable jobs' as teachers and nurses, would seldom be seen outside of their quarters. Maids, usually adolescent girls or distant poor relations, were taken into their employment to carry out domestic tasks which were performed inside the Project quarters. Those lower down the hierarchy and/or from Boropani performed domestic activities outdoors. This is a feature of the locality that continues to this day. Even with its demise and the financial decline of many of its residents, middle-class women are not frequently seen in public. They continue to wash and bathe in their bathrooms. The anthropologist Katy Gardner (1993: 226) argues that such 'purdah' culture is an indicator of Islamic religious piety in Bangladesh, but in Khonighat it is both middle-class Hindu and Muslim women who continue such rituals and they are not specifically religious in character.

* * *

The transformations taking place within this would-be utopia were quite extraordinary. Firstly, immediately following Partition, the economic situation in East and West Pakistan was dire. People were dying of starvation. Tariq Ali says the dislocation from Partition had left an army of unemployed people in the cities. By 1955, in West Pakistan alone, the number of jobless people totalled 6 million (1970: 46). This was exacerbated by the newly demarcated borders which prevented people (legally) travelling to where there may have been the possibility of work (van Schendel 2001). But this was not something that arose simply after 1947. Even in the years leading up to the creation of East/West Pakistan and India, there was chaos in the industries. Production was at a near standstill due to political disarray and instability, particularly evident amongst artisans but also within large-scale industries such as the railways (Ali 1970: 43). With growing numbers of unemployed in the urban areas, coupled with the growth in population in the countryside and the lack of new job creation (Alam 1995: 134–5), wages in existing installations across both wings of Pakistan were extremely low. In light of this, the fact that the Project offered regular, paid employment with all of its concomitant benefits was exceptional.

Secondly, the Pakistani developmental state was always contested and fragile from the outset, especially so between the two wings of East and West Pakistan where the fault lines were particularly salient. In the first decade of the Pakistan project, the inherent disparities between them already questioned the viability of the new state. Rounaq Jahan suggests this was a manifestation of earlier inequalities from the pre-1947 colonial state that deepened with the policies pursued by the ruling elite, ensuring the concentration of economic and political power in West Pakistan (1972: 2). Ali argues there was political motivation behind keeping East Pakistan poor and dependent on the West. The military regime feared that if a national bourgeoisie was allowed to develop there, together with its potential economic and political power, this would make it the dominating force within the Pakistan project (1970: 61). So whilst one of the objectives of the Project was to create a new national middle class, much of East Pakistan was excluded from modernisation, simply becoming the source of raw materials used to finance developments in the West. Two-thirds of the country's foreign exchange, for example, continued to be earned in the East through jute export, but was diverted to the West. The widening gap existed in the country's politics too, where the participation of Bengalis was limited although they constituted the largest ethnic group in this multi-ethnic conglomerate.

Thirdly, in the whole period from Partition through and after the founding of Bangladesh, only a minority of people actually managed to find employment, security and relative prosperity in formal sector organisations. The majority were excluded from such jobs and benefits. Those who found employment in the burgeoning factories and mills in the informal sector experienced badly paid, insecure wage labour with none of the added bonuses which the workers in Khonighat were enjoying. People were vulnerable to being laid off at a moment's notice, working long hours with nothing to safeguard their health or safety. Legislation that existed to protect workers did not extend to them, with unscrupulous employers finding ways to circumvent them. Many had to continue with agricultural work in order to subsidise their industrial lives.

During the Project's heyday, Khonighat's neighbour refused to go into decline. Even when the Chhatak Cement Factory shifted to gas-powered furnaces in 1965, no longer requiring coal from Indian Boropani which it had until then depended upon, Boropani's fortunes did not wane. This was related to the ban on trade between Pakistan and India after the 1965 war. In fact the cross-border trade in coal continued illegally. The black market simply burgeoned. The ban on Indian imports just made the commodity more expensive to buy, which saw entrepreneurs from Sylhet town and further afield drawn to the area. There they joined labour migrants who were either unable (because they could not access the Project bureaucracy and aspirant numbers were always greater than the system was able to cope with) or unwilling (as they were possibly going to make more money in the unregulated, informal sector than in the formal sector) to work for the Project. The labourers would either illegally cross the border to work in the mines, or take up employment in one of the subsidiary roles on the East Pakistani side. Border policing at the time was lax and even more easily negotiable than today.

The physical segregation of the two places, expressed in economic, social, cultural and ideological ways, is comparable to the development of civil stations and cantonments in the colonial period whereby an 'unsightly' native settlement would grow besides the 'white' town. Boropani spontaneously grew into Khonighat's unsightly step-sibling. The view was that the Project exhibited order, civility and authority. It was a distilled symbol of the radiant national future that was being strived for. Its physical landscape, its working practices and the way of life it propagated affirmed these visions and values. On the other hand, changes taking place in Boropani after 1965 were equally intense, but took a very different form. This centre of the cross-border coal trade was perceived by those involved in the Project to be an archetypal emblem of backwardness, illness and disease, a past that would soon pass. Many of the migrant and seasonal labourers who turned up here from the middle of the twentieth century onwards had little idea of the benefits of healthcare, education, housing and electricity, all of which came with employment within the Project. But here was an inversion of the perceived colonial pattern, as well as of the overall master plan. Khonighat became increasingly dependent on Boropani, based as it was on the informal economy. This was not just for everyday goods from its bazaar (some of which were smuggled from across the border), transportation and also, according to one salacious informant, the clandestine flesh trade operating there, but also because many of its day-to-day services were performed by those in Boropani.

* * *

A number of things occurred for the Project to close down in 1993. All are significant and interrelated. With over-extraction, the limestone seams ran too low for the existing machinery to reach. As a result, production slowed down and losses mounted. At the same time, the liberalisation of the Indian economy meant that it became financially prudent for the Bangladesh Chemical Industries Corporation (BCIC), who after nationalisation in 1976 ran the Chhatak Cement Factory, to import limestone from India, rather than purchase new technology that extracted at much lower depths. This evaded the spiralling costs of the enterprise as well as the expansive labour force and all of its concomitant costs. Lastly, with the Bangladeshi state finding itself heavily dependent upon foreign aid, organisations such as the World Bank and the IMF had been forcing both democratic and military rulers to liberalise the economy and to accelerate privatisation projects and structural adjustment programmes. Whilst some of the infrastructure was dismantled and machinery sold off or transferred to other state-run installations around the country, most remain where they were left on the last day of operations. Cranes, railways tracks and carriages, large metal containers, earth diggers and tractors continue to litter the borderland to this day.

Closure was understood in personal terms by staff at all levels. People had truly believed in the project of modernisation and their intrinsic role in the future of the country. I met Tipu, the son of an ex-Project worker who grew up in Khonighat but is now a university student in Sylhet town:

My relationship to Khonighat is very complicated and will continue to be so. Finally, after many years of mismanagement, corruption and greed, I had to hear the last siren, calling the Project to an end. I was really sad when I heard that it is closing. Everyone that had been involved with it was speechless because even until the last moment, we knew how important the Project was and how much it had helped us all to survive. Now I do not live here, but when I come here, what goes through my mind is what we had and how that has become a disaster. I remember the golden times of my childhood, the things we used to do here, the friendly atmosphere, everyone knew one another, the nature, annual games competitions, my honoured elders, respected teachers and their lessons. If I can, I would be so happy to make it change to what it was. It will be a place where there is no corruption, no mismanagement, no more greedy individuals.

The sense of immense betrayal was also a result of the deep relationships that low- and high-ranking staff had built up with one another. Some had lived next door to the same neighbours for over thirty years. Kathryn Robinson's Indonesian informants say they felt 'sick at heart' at the mass dismissals from the nickel project in the locality she did her fieldwork in (1986: 143). The term captures how the people of Khonighat also felt and continue to feel today. Those who had been in service for many years expected more protection, loyalty and respect from the headquarters in Chhatak than was accorded them. It was the loss of a livelihood, the decimation of a community, a personal insult and the smashing-up of a dream. Today these sentiments are echoed in the ways people understand the reasons why India wants to fence the border to prevent Bangladeshis from crossing. In both cases localised discourses and experiences shape the way large, intangible issues are understood. That is to say, pragmatic, real life ideas and images are applied to the elusive workings of a global economic and political system. But that is not to say people are unable to understand that ethereal forces emanating from New York, London and Washington, or even Delhi or Dhaka, have a role to play in governing lives. Nor does it mean that their explanations for the closure of the Project negate the understanding of larger forces. Living in a borderland, people are all too aware that other places, 'places that matter', have authority and command over their lives despite their opaque presence.

The official reason employees were given for closure was that reserves of limestone had been exhausted. For Joshim's uncle and many others, closure is largely understood through the optic of large-scale corruption and mismanagement which became a feature of the Project when it was nationalised. This was something that was visible and obvious to everyone who lived, worked and had a stake in the Project. I was told over and over again that the quarries could be mined 'for the next hundred years and the limestone will not dry up'. I asked Joshim's uncle why he believes this. 'My father worked down there. He should know'. Abdul Matin, now in his sixties, is another long-standing Project resident. He is softly spoken and has a thick grey beard that adds to his years of experience. He believes the rot set in when West Pakistani officers left in 1971 and 'incompetent' Bengalis replaced them. For him, the Pakistani period of operations, which was when the Project was under private sector ownership, is associated with his own personal experience of social mobility, being able to work his way up from a 'runners' position at the age of sixteen in 1966, to security guard (earning 2tk per day). Working as a peon he was allowed time off to attend the school where he completed his exams, then as a clerk and finally ending up as one of the Bangla teachers in the school. He remembers that, at the time, the managers, high-level engineers and the management board were all from West Pakistan but there was no animosity between them and their Bengali subordinates. In fact, during the Liberation War in 1971, the West Pakistani officers surrendered themselves to Indian forces that came across the border, so sure were they that nothing untoward would happen to them as a result of their conduct in the Project. (Much later, when I spoke to Abdul Matin's eldest son, Tipu, he said that he remembered his father telling him that much of the infrastructure of the Project was attacked and destroyed by Bengali freedom fighters during the Liberation War.) The consequence of the departure of the West Pakistani officers was momentous, says Abdul Matin:

When the country became free and the officers left for Pakistan, people here were all over the place. There was no longer any order. The Project went into a bad direction and it never got any better. In 1969, we raised 120,000 tonnes of *chunapthor* [limestone]. That year all the employees were given two bonuses. In 1972, after the war, we raised 60,000 tonnes, half of what we had before. The Project authorities had to recruit people from outside. These people were not so cordial to the company, but to their own personal benefits. Lots of permanent workers who I knew personally were great shirkers. Even the highest level authority was not so cordial any longer. They just did their duty, always keeping their distance from lower-level workers. Few high-ranking officers wanted to stay here for long any more. The corrupt people also wanted to take out the honest officers by making scandals against them. The Project was in constant loss. There was a lot of theft. There was a lot of lying. The officers were wasting, the labourers were stealing. I didn't like it. Even today, they are stealing. This was wealth for the nation; it was wealth for us locally.

Abdul Matin resigned from the Project before it actually shut down, refusing to work in an environment that he believed had become immoral, steeped in greed and corruption, no longer standing for larger principles. The difference between the way the Pakistanis ran the Project and the Bangladeshis was like 'night and day'. This was a common theme expressed in conversations I had with people. Using the Project's old ethos to articulate his sentiments, another ex-employee says 'the work people did was not to become rich, but it was for something bigger, for the country. After Independence it was each man for himself'. The irony is that nationalisation at the time was argued to be for the good of the nation as a whole and not for private gain. Of course such collective views and memories are also very much antithetical to wider contemporary discourses on what transpired between the East and West wings of Pakistan between 1947 and 1971. One should recall that this took place against the backdrop of a conflict that would see 10 million Bengali refugees cross the border from Bangladesh into India, fleeing West Pakistani army brutality including mass rapes and killings. In fact, to voice opinions such as Abdul Matin's outside of the Project grounds today could attract accusations of being anti-Bangladeshi and pro-Pakistani. But these would be inaccurate descriptions of him and the many other Project residents who remember in similar terms.

* * *

It wasn't just on the Bangladesh–India border where the theory and practice of modernisation was arguably failing. All around the world, the myth of modernisation was proving to be just that. James Ferguson's work on the social experience of decline in the Zambian copper belt (1999) has become essential reading for social scientists examining the failures of modernisation theory and practice in post-colonial societies. He argues that it was not only planners, political theorists and policy and government experts who believed and expected modernisation to work, but Zambians of all socio-economic backgrounds too. This is not surprising as it was a convincing account of what was happening in

Zambia during the 1960s with the initiation of copper mining. The profitability of the extractive industry had turned the newly de-colonised country into a rapidly developing nation with all the enthusiasm, hope and confidence that seemed to echo the West's own path to modernisation '[a]nd everyone knew where that had led' (ibid.: 6). The urban population was apparently growing, wages were rising and social and cultural life was 'developing' in suit with everything else. This all came to a sudden halt with the crash of the international copper market, transforming Zambia into yet another 'poor African nation'. With the evolutionary trajectory proving not to be linear, since then there have been decades of economic and social decline, counter-urbanisation and deindustrialisation. Expectations of progress, status and prestige have been replaced with loss, despair and massive social problems. At the root of it is a theory which Ferguson believes is a myth, one which he says needs to be re-examined in light of the reversal of old linearities.

The belief in modernisation and development is also a point of longing for people in Khonighat today. It is the absence of hope that is most obvious and pervasive here, even more so than the lack of basic infrastructure missing in most parts of Bangladesh, indeed in Boropani too. Elsewhere in the country, where there is no history or tradition of modernist planning, one notices people's stoic optimism that 'expectations of development' will arrive at some unspecified future time. Here it is different: 'we once had it, it is now gone, what use is there in hoping that it will come back?' 'Abjection' is the term Ferguson uses to capture this emotion amongst the copper belt mineworkers in Zambia and it is apt for Khonighat as well. The word, he says, refers to a sense of humiliating expulsion, a process of being thrown aside, expelled or discarded (2002: 140). The doctrine of the linear progression of modernisation does not state that it has the potential to go backwards or even, in the most extreme case, disappear, as it has done in Zambia. He could easily have been writing about Khonighat and all of its old officers and their descendants when he says:

access to the first class things of the world—cars, suits, fine clothes, a decent necktie—was not something to look forward to, as an anticipated future but something to remember from a prosperous past ... history, as it were, running in reverse. How else to account for life expectancies and incomes shrinking instead of growing, people becoming less educated instead of more and migrants moving from urban centres to remote villages instead of vice versa? This is the modernisation through the looking-glass, where modernity is the object of nostalgic reverie and 'backwardness' the anticipated (or dreaded) future (ibid.: 13).

Ferguson's work accurately sums up the despondency felt by people who were swept up in modernisation's torrent and then dropped from a dizzying height. For the people of Khonighat it truly does not matter whether the doctrine was a myth or not. The predicaments they find themselves in today are a result of the fact that a power had once existed with the ability to transform society, individuals and dreams which persists in forming and shaping lives in the present. The Project, though very much an entity from the past, still pervades the everyday existence of its inhabitants, young and old. It ceases to work any longer, but what it represents is still real and lives on. It is not just the materiality of it that is found lying around that produces this. The belief that it was modern, developed, as were the people who lived and worked there, while everything else around it was not, shapes the way locals view the past, the present and the future.

* * *

Whilst sitting on the hillock and listening to the nostalgic revisionism of the old Project aristocracy, I often heard anecdotes that revealed other possibilities, alongside the formal narrative of how fantastic Project life was. Rather than simply seeing them as abnormal chinks in the unfurling of the grand master plan, what became clear to me is that even during its heyday and despite the overly wistful ways residents talk about what went on, the project of modernisation was never a complete one. It was in constant negotiation with multiple old and alternative ways of being. Moreover, it was far from being a seed of change that altered everything around it as traditional modernisation theory envisaged. Boropani was shut out from the 'developments' taking place within the perimeters, for example. There were other lacunas within the project of modernisation being carried out in Khonighat. It is prudent to see them as coexistent with and as integral to, or even products of, the formal doctrine itself. For example, Joshim's uncle once explained that his father was one of many low-level labourers to have bought his jobs at the Project. Unable to negotiate the bureaucracy in any other way, he paid a sum of money to an official employee for his job. So on paper and in all the records a Mr so-and-so was in fact a different person from the one who actually carried out the work and was remunerated for it. This way of gaining employment for industrial workers is common and remains so in the subcontinent. My point is that though the Project may have propagated a particular sort of modernity, one where patronage and nepotism was to be eradicated, this was not how it always operated. Arguably, multiple modernities existed even back then, alongside the meta-narrative of modernisation. This is in reality the sociology of the Project and its interface with the world around it.

Other sorts of contradictions which were not part of the formal, official system became part of everyday Project life too. It would have been the more privileged sections of the industrial labour force that were able to sever connections to rural homes and not those at the bottom of the hierarchy who would have been unable to afford to do so. Cleaners and gardeners, for example, were not permitted to live within Project grounds and had no rights to any of the benefits. Access to education, as we have already seen, was not open to everyone. Some regular Project workers moonlighted in the coal trade in Boropani. Corruption was ever present. The management (in particular, towards its latter years) would apparently sell off equipment to private businesses and individuals in Boropani. Having pocketed the money, they would then put in orders for replacement equipment 'making thousands of taka' in the process. I was told by ex-Project workers that anyone with any modicum of power and authority would participate in this, in the process of which they would lose the respect of their subordinates. Joshim's uncle believes that it was when the management in Chhatak became aware of what was happening that they closed the installation down.

There are a number of different ways one can understand the contradictions that were evident between the 'official' and the 'unofficial' as the watermark behind it. In his new book, *Seeing Like a State: How Certain Schemes to Improve the Human Condition Have Failed*, James Scott, argues that the history of Third World development is littered with the debris of monumental utopian, social engineering schemes that have failed: more than just failed, he says, they are among some of the greatest tragedies of the twentieth century (1998: 3). His argument is that this is a result of the exclusion of unofficial or 'local knowledge' by hegemonic, high-modernist planning. It is something that is found across the political spectrum from left to right. In Russia and Tanzania, for example, where utopian master plans were plentiful, those top-down, state organisations that managed to survive only did so because planners were forced to incorporate measures that were either not envisaged or else expressly prohibited by the original plan. For example, informal economies would develop next to the formal, supplying food and other essentials to those on the inside of the fencing. In the end, state officials had to tolerate, if not condone, many such informal practices that actually underwrote the survival of official schemes.

Another way of viewing the internal inconsistencies of the Project is through the discourse of uneven development, or rather, 'insufficient modernity'. The corollary of this thought is that modernisation was only skin-deep in non-Western societies to begin with and, in reality, they were still traditional. Such an argument assumes that there is only one teleological path to modernisation and all those who differ from it are not modern. However, the idea of multiple modernities asserts that the (Western, colonial) variant of modernisation runs concurrently with alternative forms and the effects are not homogenous from site to site. They evolve in very different ways depending upon existing social, historical, economic and political realities.

If history had not played its hand in the way that it did and the Khonighat experiment had continued, there would have been inevitable changes after the 1990s anyway, the result of economic restructuring of heavy industries in both Bangladesh and India. The Bhilai Steel Plant that Parry (1999c) writes about, for example, has reduced the number of regular workers it employs and has increased its contract workers, with the reduced benefits that come with that. Andrew Sanchez's (2009b) work on the Indian Tata Company is also applicable here. Tata had even attempted to purchase the remains of Khonighat after its closure in the late 1990s. To the dismay of Project residents who wanted the sale to go ahead, the Bangladeshi government refused. Nonetheless, for Tata employees, the rights they once enjoyed now exist for only a minority of people. Today more than 75 per cent of the shop-floor workforce is deemed 'casual'. The descendants of the company aristocracy are mostly on short-term contracts, earn less than their fathers' generation, and are no longer entitled to housing, healthcare, pensions, sick pay or even trade union membership. Sanchez writes 'Tata worker[s] appear more and more akin to the contract labourer from whom they have historically appeared so distinct' (ibid.: 5).

It was in the 1990s that the cross-border coal trade in Boropani finally became legalised, once again. As the commodity became increasingly lucrative, the Indian and Bangladeshi governments aimed to participate in the industry too. A Zero Point was created on both sides of Boropani where the coal was already being brought, thus legalising what had already been active in the hitherto black market. With this legitimisation, people were assigned new roles and titles. Rather than being known as just 'buyers' and 'sellers', those on the Bangladeshi side became 'importers' and those on the Indian side became 'exporters'. Up until then, traders were not nationally defined, with Bangladeshis working on the Indian side as sellers and vice versa. What this paradoxically did was to create a local distinction between 'Indians' and 'Bangladeshis'. Paperwork was generated, a bureaucracy emerged and infrastructure that had once been part of the Project on the Bangladeshi side was taken over by the newly created Bangladeshi customs office. Knowledge and expertise from elsewhere were brought in to systemise the two states' roles in the trade. The BDR and the BSF were assigned new positions. They were no longer just protecting the border from so-called infiltrators, but were now expected to make sure the cross-border trade operated with no disruptions. New groups of people started moving into the area, including businessmen, entrepreneurs and migrant men, women and children, all wanting their piece of black gold. This was the second time in the recent history of this borderland that there would be an influx of this kind.

2

EVERYDAY LIFE AT THE COALFACE

Over time, I understood that, even if the border zones are poor, one nonetheless makes big money there (Ngahoui, Cameroon, 2001).[1]

Bangladeshi Boropani is a ramshackle collection of blackened hutments and shabby buildings. It contains shops that sell basic essentials such as candles, soap and padlocks. There is a motorbike stand, godowns and workshops that fix trucks. It is filthy and overcrowded. Coal soot sits on everything. Unlike rural bazaars elsewhere teeming with people selling vegetables, seasonal fruit, writhing fish and squawky chickens, here little of that exists. Those who would otherwise be engaged in farming or fishing toil in the coal trade; the returns being more immediate and profitable. The lack of consumer goods is down to the shortage of demand from migrant labourers who aim to save as much money during their tenure to take back home. But with the cost of living as high as it is here, only a few are able to do this anyway. Single-storey houses, forged out of bamboo, corrugated iron, mud and wood, fringe the outskirts of Boropani, providing shelter to the majority of the area's inhabitants. Giving the impression of being temporary, the buildings are here to stay. Coal barons have started constructing multi-storey buildings (understandably) incongruous over the mud and tin shacks that surround them. They fund a large, new mosque, separate male and female madrassas and provide the upkeep for the Khonighat high school. Sanitation, healthcare and electricity remain aspirations for the future in other places, but here, however, in the backdrop of the master plan

51

enacted within the Khonighat Limestone Mining Project, they are remnants of a past. There is little hope that these facets of modernity will ever return.

From my Project bungalow, I would make my way to Boropani bazaar every day to eat. My chosen place was run by a Hindu *purohit* (priest). He was often not there, as according to the serving boy he would nip across the border to carry out rites for Hindus in Indian Boropani. In-between sorting out the overly complicated fish bones with my fingers, I would overhear conversations between the cook, the serving boy and customers. There was always talk of tit-for-tat arrests and people being beaten up by border guards from both side. At other times I would listen to tales of dacoits operating in the area. During such moments, someone would invariably make the comparison between the present and the past when apparently 'the Project was the safest place to live in all of East Pakistan'. One day, the topic centred on the image of Lord Krishna that was spotted in the quarry lake by bathers. The *purohit* who was there at the time refused to believe the story, arguing that the noxious fumes found in the coal mines were playing with the minds of those who say they had seen it. After lunch, I would ensconce myself besides the Zero Point that marks the divide between the two Boropanis as well as India and Bangladesh. I would sit in a shop belonging to a man who sold, in the main, phone credit. From the vantage point of the shop, the fluttering flag of India on the other side of the border was clearly visible. I could see the hundreds of trucks coming in and out of Bangladesh; the frenetic activity around the customs houses of both sides and the BDR and BSF posts and the banter exchanged by both sets of guards.

Since the closure of the Khonighat Limestone Mining Project in 1993, Boropani has grown in size, wealth and importance, a consequence of the liberalisation of the Indian and Bangladeshi markets as well as the insatiable rise in demand for coal across cities in Bangladesh. Today it is one of the largest landports between the two countries dedicated exclusively to the buying and selling of coal. Where once the Limestone Project, a product of a centrally planned economy, had attempted to carve its intractable mark on the physical and social landscapes of the borderlands, now the market-dominated coal economy follows in the same obstinate path. It too attempts to shape the physical, social and otherworldly realms of all those who come into contact with it. Having found themselves deserted, Project labourers moved into Boropani and took over the coal trade that operated between Sylhet and Meghalaya. Today, these men are the new elites. Their accomplishment was down to advantages the existing coal men did not have: provident funds, redundancy payments but, much more decisively, knowledge of large-scale industrial trade and how to navigate official state bureaucracy. Project labourers without the competences and/or money took positions as depot managers, bought up agricultural lands on which the depots were built or started businesses in the bazaar. Those who remained behind the perimeters, the fifty or so families of middle-ranking officers, were not senior enough to be transferred out of the area by the head-quarters in Chhatak or subordinate enough to try risking their reputations and relocate. Migrants from the districts of Mymensigh, Comilla as well as the *haor* began appearing to work in the trade. It was not some random decision to do so. The extractive industries in this part of Sylhet have been sustaining rural villages in Assam, East and West Bengal as well as further afield long before Partition. Sensing the potential for the commodity, Sylheti businessmen and entrepreneurs started investing in the area too. Very few would actually move here, to what remains, for them at least, a remote and distant blot on the border between Bangladesh and India.

The trade in coal begins its journey high up in the searing hot, dark and claustrophobic mineshafts scattered like honeycombs throughout the West Khasi Hills. Traditionally inhabited by Garos and Khasis, the hills are sparsely populated which means a scarcity of labour for the coal mines.[2] Young Bangladeshi men cross the line of demarcation every day to work illegally in them. Many also live in temporary coal camps in the hills, moving from one to another on a semi-permanent basis if and when an excavation project is completed. When large numbers of workers are required, the border guards of both sides are paid by the Indian managers of the mines to facilitate this. The Bangladeshi men are part of a larger group of migrant workers from other parts of the subcontinent, including West Bengalis, Oriyas, Biharis, Assamese as well as Nepalese. (Nepal shares an open border with India and it is legal for them to work there.) Some of these people will be part of a historically constituted tradition of seasonal labour migration to the region. Work gangs communicate in a mixture of Hindi, Urdu, Bengali and basic English. Many Bangladeshi men are also versed in some Mandi (Garo) and Khasi. The

Indian exporters for whom they work and will probably never meet tend to be West Bengali, Marwari and Assamese businessmen working with a Khasi or Garo shadow partner. As non-adivasis are prohibited from owning land or businesses in the state of Meghalaya which falls under the provisions of the Sixth Schedule in the Indian Constitution, outsiders enter into relationships of convenience with Khasis or Garos who do own land. The latter are paid a fee for which they become the figurehead for the application of a mining lease. Known as 'rat hole mining', a tunnel is punched into the side of the hill through which the miners crawl in one at a time. The coal seams may be anything between 5m or 100m deep inside of the rock. The entire process is un-mechanised and the coal is brought out using wheelbarrows. Amongst the Bangladeshi workers, the experienced ones may work as supervisors, the literate ones as bookkeepers. The majority work as colliers.

Sujon is in his late twenties and a descendant of the Khonighat Limestone Mining Project. His family now own a small clothes shop in the Project bazaar which they set up after the Project shut down. He believes the colliery maliks (owners) prefer to hire Bangladeshis because they don't drink alcohol as much as the other workers do (the Khasi men apparently 'drink whisky like it is tea') or get into fights and disputes. His family business is in fact where Sujon met the malik of the mine he worked for. Originally from Assam, the malik had crossed the border into Bangladeshi Boropani to do some shopping. He was also on the lookout for new workers. He had procured a temporary government lease to extract coal from a site around three hours north of Indian Boropani. Whilst on the Bangladeshi side of the border, he met Sujon and set about persuading him into working for him. Owing to the latter's slight frame, the malik promised a 'writing' job in the enterprise. Because of the dangers involved, Sujon's parents refused. There had been a row, but the young man had always wanted to go up into the hills and this was his opportunity to do so. He snuck across the border in the cab of a coal truck which had come to the Bangladeshi side to drop off its load. The border guards did not see him or the four other Bangladeshi interlopers hiding in it. Living in what he describes as a jungle, all day long, while the other workers hewed coal in the shaft with only a scarf over their mouths to protect their lungs, Sujon would sit outside the opening and record the amount of coal extracted, those men who had been remunerated and calculate debts that remained unpaid. When one truck was filled and drove off in the direction of Boropani, another arrived, needing to be fed. Sujon would spend much of the time trying to get reception on his mobile so that he could talk to his girlfriend in Khonighat. At night, all of the workers slept together on bamboo mats on the ground. In solidarity with his Muslim Bangladeshi workmates, Sujon, a Hindu, refused to eat the pork the Khasi men cooked, sticking to the fish and vegetables instead.[3] The 250 rupees a day he earned was a tidy sum of money by the end of the month, which is the length of time he worked as he missed his girlfriend terribly and wanted to see her again.

The slim-built, well-groomed young man is hardly typical of those who cross the border every day to work in the coal mines, risking dignity, life and limb. After all, the majority of the miners who do so are unskilled, illiterate migrants who work to supplement their desperate incomes in rural areas, where poverty, hunger and exploitation are everyday realities.[4] Sujon's family business on the other hand is reasonably profitable, bolstered by trade from coal depot managers and owners. His experience of working in the mines sounds more like a *Boy's Own* escapade, rather than the narratives that are generally associated with illegal cross-border labour migration. In particular, when he was retelling the incident about the young Khasi woman who approached him and asked if he wanted to sleep in her hut at night, it did seem a little fanciful. Very much a product of the Project whereby there is expectation that women behave with modesty, respectability and decorum, he was shocked by what he perceived as her licentiousness. But the reason Sujon rejected her, he says, was that he feared the wrath of the other miners who may attack him: the Khasi men because she was 'their own' and the Bangladeshis because they were jealous of the attention he received and would accuse him of 'rocking the boat'. This is not to say that amorous dealings do not occur. There are many men in Bangladeshi Boropani who have married women from the other side whom they met whilst working there. Some have gone to the extent of converting to Christianity, the majority religion of the Khasis and Garos. Alpa Shah's (2006) insightful account of adivasis from Jharkhand, for example, argues that despite the earning potential being the same if not greater in their homeland, it is precisely for the pursuit of libidinal passions that migrants travel and work in the torturous environment of the brick kilns of West Bengal. Sujon's experiences suggest that simple economic determination and material well-being (though crucial for most) are not the only reasons why young Bangladeshi men cross the border into India. Adventure and experience are also a rationale for both the desperately poor as well as the better off, as Sujon clearly is. I frequently met miners who said they preferred to work in the harsh environment of the mines even with all of their incumbent risks. An informant who had worked in coal extraction in India for a number of years explains it is because 'people there do as they say they will. We know when we will start, finish and even have a tea break. Bengalis do the opposite of their promise and we have no lunch break'.

Sujon's account is not intended to undermine the drudgery involved in such dangerous work. June Nash, for example, writing about the Bolivian tin mines describes it thus: 'every entry [into the mines for the worker] was like a burial and every exit like a birth' (1992: 80). Michael Taussig describes how miners in South America conduct sacrifices and gift exchanges to placate the malevolent spirit of the mines, *Tio*, who holds the power over life and death (1980: 143). Moodie and Ndatshe, chronicling the lives of gold miners in South Africa, state that 'underground they live like rats … trapped and harried' (1994: 11). They recall an informant stressing that 'one does not feel hunger underground because of the anxiety to come out once more to see the world again' (1994: 82). Working in dark, intensely hot, humid and cramped caverns, sometimes in pools of water for long hours in constant danger and uncertainty, for the Bangladeshi miners the experience is not too dissimilar from miners elsewhere. Many workers have malaria and back and chest problems. One cannot know the full extent of the disabilities, injuries and even deaths that occur in the coal mines in the West Khasi Hills. Around the world, underground coal shafts are more dangerous and claim more victims than all other underground mines put together. Risks come from mine collapse, methane explosions, carbon monoxide poisoning and the slow and debilitating effects of lung damage from rock and coal dust. The chance of dying is also four times greater for a worker in an Indian mine than in any other industry (Moody 2007: 74).

But here it is the more prosaic risks that miners fear most, such as drunken disputes with other workers, resolved through fighting. Sujon says that this is what he feared the most, that another worker who did not like him for whatever reason may stab him. This is not such an unreasonable concern. Alcohol plays a pivotal role in the borderlands both economically (with the large-scale trade in smuggled goods) as well as socially (public inebriation is widespread). Indian BSF raids are also something that Bangladeshi workers dread, their precarious position in India heightens the fear that naturally pervades the mines. Interestingly, writers on mining communities in other parts of the world also note that social and political conditions outside of the mines heighten the sense of fear workers have inside of it. In South Africa, Moodie and Ndatshe describe how the constant threat of violence from the (white) bosses as well as the general racial conflict outside made working inside of the mines quite intolerable (1994: 19). A Sylheti journalist, whose beat covered northern Sunamgonj, told me that many men die in the mines in the West Khasi Hills every month. Unable to bring the bodies back across the border, perfunctory burials are carried out on the hills by fellow colliers. Numbers are impossible to ascertain as they go unreported. In any case, as illegal migrant workers, whom does one report to anyway? Families are rarely informed, the nameless, illiterate victims having originated from the remote wetlands or even further away from isolated villages dotted across the country.

Once a truck has been filled by hand and shovel, it leaves the mine and joins the back of a raucous column of other vehicles all heading towards Indian Boropani. Many of these roads are old routes that were used in pre-Partition days, connecting the hills and the plains that have been tarmacked relatively recently for the coal industry. Decorated with the Christian cross and a variety of different national flags including those of the United States and Australia (an indicator of where the Christian missionaries who converted the Khasis and Garos came from), the Tata trucks wind along, bumper-to-bumper, over serpentine hilly roads. Despite the inevitable dangers, they also travel at night when their headlights are often the only thing one sees in the pitch dark after the electricity goes out. The drivers of the trucks are on the whole Garo and Khasi men. There is a long history of organising work along caste, religious, ethnic and gender lines in the subcontinent. Caste, for example, was most prominently utilised by the British, who took the feature and racialised it (the idea of the martial races/criminal tribes, for example). Ethnicity and religion in particular continue to play a crucial and active role in the extractive industries on the Sylhet–Meghalaya borderlands. In the pre-independence limestone industry that operated in the West Khasi Hills and even before the Chhatak Cement Factory was established, ethnicity was utilised to designate work. For example, the limestone quarries were generally operated and worked on by Khasi labourers whilst the boatmen and lime burners were 'local inhabitants of Sylhet' (Rizvi 1971: 249). Such divisions reinforced structures of employment but also the idea that certain groups were better suited to particular jobs.

The use of 'primordial' categories such as ethnicity to organise labour was attempted to be done away with by the project of modernisation enacted within Khonighat between the 1960s and the 1990s. This was promulgated by an institutional culture whose vision was to have transcended religion, ethnicity and caste, whereby an employee's identity as an accountant or a guard was to be more relevant than so-called atavistic stereotypes. But like other aspects of modernisation, the idea never gained the same potency outside of the Project perimeters in Boropani. Due to the precariousness of the coal industry, networks based on villages of origin, ethnicity and religion are used by migrants to find employment, accommodation and organise social and economic connections. But there is a further layer that interplays with them: nationality and citizenship. Dhaka and Delhi may wish for a neat division between the roles played by the borderlanders of either side, between exporter and importer, Indian and Bangladeshi, mine owner and coal labourer, but this is patently not being realised. As Sujon says, Bangladeshi workers are preferred by the Indian colliery maliks. This is primarily because, as illegal workers and migrants, they remain vulnerable and flexible: less likely to want a day off or complain no matter how terrible the conditions are, more likely to work hard to make as much money as possible and then leave once the work has finished. I met a number of men, originally from the Bangladeshi side of the demarcation who, having acquired experience and reputation, now work as coal exporters as well as managers on the Indian side. The existence of such men leads one not only to question the futility of the border but also the categories of 'Indian' and 'Bangladeshi'.

Laden with coal, the trucks arrive at Indian Boropani and wait at the chaotic and noisy Zero Point. A bamboo pole, the same one which I saw when I first arrived in the area, marks the divide between India and Bangladesh. It can take a matter of hours, or even a few days, for a truck to be processed so that it can cross the border and drop its load off to its buyer. The customs houses on both sides shut at 5pm every day. The border is formally closed on Sundays, a holiday in India which Bangladeshi Boropani also observes (the rest of the country has Friday off, the Islamic religious day). Depending on the size of the business, an exporter may deliver anything between ten to twenty truck loads per day to different import companies. They will rarely provide the entire expected amount in one go, taking up to a month or more to complete an assignment. A frustrated importer who had been expecting a delivery that is late believes that exporters hold back on purpose, denying the availability of coal, thereby increasing their selling price.

Conversations between buyers and sellers rarely take place face to face, though importers do often cross the Zero Point in the evenings to socialise and drink with exporters. Most discussions take place on mobile phones. This is how sales of the goods occur, dates and timings arranged, problems ironed out, Eid, Christmas and Puja greetings exchanged and news of BDR and BSF activity relayed. The Indian side of the border has no mobile phone networks that cover it. Importers told me this is because ULFA (the United Liberation Front of Assam)— the banned insurgency group waging a secessionist movement against the Indian state—would take advantage of the mobile network to plan possible acts of violence against it. Consequently, the Indian government has banned mobile phone towers in the borderland. The unintended consequence of this decision is that there is a massive black market in Bangladeshi mobile phones, sim cards and credit top-up cards that centres around the Bangladeshi side of the Zero Point. Indians and Bangladeshis alike both communicate with each other on 'Grameen-phone' or 'Banglalink', two of the largest Bangladeshi telecommunication networks.[5] The call is charged at a local (Bangladeshi) rate. Many businesses in Bangladeshi Boropani sell nothing but phone credit, mostly to Indian exporters. Even the Indian border guards are compelled to use Bangladeshi sim cards when in the area. A man who owns a shop on the Zero Point told me that the irony is that the wife of a BSF guard stationed in Indian Boropani calling from distant Maharashtra, for example, will be paying international rates to speak to her husband, whom the technology assumes is in neighbouring Bangladesh when he is actually in India. Certainly the sale of Bangladeshi sim cards and credit to Indians is illegal and there are intermittent raids carried out by the BDR to curtail this. (Mobile phones are not the only technology to question the viability of the border. Locals in Khonighat and Bangladeshi Boropani are able to view Indian television channels which means that both national channels—Bangladesh Television and Doordashan—can be watched on the same set.)

The customs house on the Bangladeshi side is a large, walled-in bungalow, the very one that was once the family home of the manager of the Khonighat Limestone Mining Project. From outside of its walls, coal importers and managers stand in anticipation, looking out for their truck, the registration number of which has already been texted to them by the exporter. Painted the same yellow as the buildings inside of the Project colony, the customs house is in much better condition than those within the perimeters of the Project. The upkeep of this official building continues to be maintained by the state. It was initially built here, outside of the Project grounds, due to its proximity to the quarries. But today, from the very location that it once oversaw the programme of modernisation, it overlooks and manages the market-orientated, cross-border coal trade between Sylhet and Meghalaya. The view from its veranda now is of the Zero Point, where through the thick plumes of soot and dirt, the blackened faces of the trucks are visible. Straggly children with unkempt hair, blond with malnutrition, dart in and out, bare foot, between the juggernauts, as if they are playing some death-defying game. They are part of the parallel unorganised informal trade, collecting coal that has spilt off the backs of the trucks on to the grooves near the massive wheels. Sharpened by life, they grab the coal as quickly as possible, constantly listening out for the whistles and boots of the border guards who shoo them away. The Khasi or Garo drivers have their paperwork stamped, pay bribes to the Indian customs official and any outstanding debts to the border guards. The truck is only then permitted to inch a few metres forward into the no-man's-land. The import manager drives a metal rod into the bed of coal which gives a rough estimate of how much coal has arrived. When he is satisfied, a labourer from the depot jumps into the cab to direct the driver to where the *mal* (goods) will be dropped off, passing the bamboo pole that officially demarcates the boundary of either country.

Bidyut is a thirty-two year old importer. Every day he is found sitting on his dazzling red, Indian Hero Honda motorbike waiting for his *mal* to arrive. Phone in hand, he is relatively new to the business but already has the conspicuous accoutrements of his position. Bidyut chooses to manage his own business to cut back on costs. There are two types of buyers he sells to: those who own brick fields and need coal to fire them and those who own coal depots and buy to sell. As Bidyut describes to me the workings of the industry, every few moments dirty children from the Zero Point walk past to buy bottles of soft drinks. They have been sent over by Indian exporters or the BSF to buy them on their behalf. Priced at 40tk, they are given 40 rupees which means a few taka profit. The system of Letters of Credit (LC), Bidyut explains, is what makes trade between the two sides possible and legal. In order for an importer to procure any coal, he requests an LC from the Pubali Bank in Khonighat, with the name of the exporter as the beneficiary.[6] The quantity of funds deposited will be noted on the LC and it is this that will buy the importer a corresponding amount of coal. The bank charges a fee, a percentage of the value of the LC. It then notifies the exporter's bank in Shillong, the capital of Meghalaya, that payment has been made. The LC is then submitted to one of the agents in Boropani whose offices line the bazaar alongside the phone credit huts. The agent rubber-stamps the form before forwarding it on to the customs house. It is at this point that formal taxes are calculated. Though slow and cumbersome, the system ensures that the trade is above board, exporters are paid for their goods and that taxes are paid by either side.[7]

Bidyut's business is now worth 50 lakh taka, which earns him roughly a lakh taka a month. For his first purchase in 2007, he had an LC for 100 tonnes of coal. This cost him just over 3 lakh taka. It took a month and thirteen trucks to deliver it all. Once it all finally arrived, Bidyut sold the lot for 11 lakh taka. 94,000tk was paid in government taxes and by the end of it he made a profit of 50,000tk, which he put back into the next acquisition. He explains that much of the formal trade happens in the 'black' and is the reason why countless importers go bankrupt as they don't learn the rules before investing money. Increased competition between depots also means that importers are less keen to share industry knowledge with each other. For example, for every 100 tonnes of coal noted on the LC, 200 tonnes will actually arrive. Understating the actual value of coal will mean paying less tax. But this means that the importer has to pay a separate, fixed and slightly smaller amount to the customs officer who pockets it. For every 200 tonnes of *mal*, there is some excess coal for which the importer has to also pay directly to the exporter at the Zero Point. This exchange happens in Indian rupees, which can be bought from the phone credit traders, who themselves are paid in the currency by Indian exporters and the BSF when purchasing mobile phone goods. The only people to get a bad deal at this stage of the set-up are the BDR who get around 50tk per truck that comes into Bangladesh. No one here, least of all importers who operate formally, believe any longer in the efficacy or the indefatigability of state bureaucracy, a sharp contrast to what people had hoped for and expected during Project days. Bidyut says the Bangladeshi customs official is greedy, making money on the side from a government job that officially pays a relatively good salary. To get the job in the first place the official would have had to pay a bribe which, by the end of his tenure, will be recouped many times over. When his contract ended and was transferred elsewhere, the official to replace him, local gossip dictated, paid 7 lakh taka to be posted to Boropani. His last position was at Shah Jalal International Airport in Dhaka. The developmentalist David Lewis argues that it is common for public servants in Bangladesh to use alternative sources of income such as bribes to increase incomes as they earn four to six times less than colleagues in the private sector (2010: 2). Anna Lowenhaupt Tsing refers to such civil servants as 'franchise entrepreneurs' who operate their own entrepreneurial schemes, thus creating a particular model of government which, as entrepreneurs, frees up resources for investors including themselves (2000: 124). Bidyut thinks the unpaid tax deprives the country of much-needed revenue which could be used to build roads, schools and medical facilities. None have been built here since the collapse of the Project. He acknowledges that there is no other way that one can operate here.

As the coal moves along the commodity chain from the hills, through the border and into the plains, travelling through different regulatory zones, controlled by diverse groups of people, the legal as well as the illegal is produced. Sometimes this will occur simultaneously and at other times one after another, depending upon whether the legal or the illegal will serve its purpose. To operate a legitimate business selling coal, wily Indian businessmen enter into illegitimate relationships with an adivasi partner whom Indian law will recognise as the only formal leaseholder but who will have no authority in the business. Illegal Bangladeshi workers are hired to work the mines. In order to communicate with the importer, mobile technology is utilised, though this is unlawful and contravenes national security regulations. Local taxes, traditionally called bribes, are paid to customs officials and the border guards. The payment of full official taxes is evaded with the complicity of the customs officials. Foreign currencies are bought and sold illegally. In short, the workings of the Indian and Bangladeshi states have created these contradictory conditions in that, to produce the formal/legal (i.e. trade coal legally), one has to operate informally/illegally. The key to being a successful coal trader is being flexible and knowing precisely when and how to do this. Moreover, whilst Delhi uses these examples of 'illegal movements', 'smuggling' and general 'improper activities' in the border areas as justification for its fence-building programme, in her work, Janet Roitman (2005: 165) rightly suggests that these networks in fact become part and parcel of the political logics of the state itself. Such transnational connections provide states with the ability to fulfil essential extraction and redistribution roles, the justification for having borders (and barricades) in the first place, as well as the prevalence of the border guards (providing them with remuneration).

To understand such linkages as a dichotomy between the pervasive image of the ('legal') state battling against ('illegal') criminal transnational networks is too simplistic and even misleading. Abraham and van Schendel propose a different way of conceptualising issues of legality and illegality. They write:

[F]lows of goods and people [are] invisible manifestations of power configurations that weave in and out of legality, in and out of states and in and out of individual lives, as socially embedded, sometimes long term processes of production, exchange, consumption and representations (2006: 9).

They suggest a third space of the (il)licit: legally banned but socially sanctioned and protected. (Il)licit takes into account the distinction between what states consider to be legitimate ('legal') and what people involved in transnational networks consider to be legitimate ('licit'). This space implies that certain transnational movements of people, commodities and ideas are illegal precisely because they challenge the norms and rules of formal political authority, though at the same time they are considered 'licit' in the eyes of the participants in these transactions. Though the term (il)licit is useful as a paradigm to understand various relations between importers and exporters as well as between importers and the state of Bangladesh and exporters and the state of India, it remains too rigid. Abraham and van Schendel's definition of the (il)licit posits the state on one side and local communities committing illicit activities on the other as if they are two separate entities with distinct or contradictory intentions. For example, van Schendel, echoing James Scott's *Seeing Like a State* (1998), writes about the 'limitations of seeing like a state' and instead privileging 'the perspectives of participants in cross border activities' (2006: 3). The problem with this dichotomy is that it continues to reproduce the idea that the workings of the state are legitimate (licit) and those of the borderlanders are illegitimate (illicit). What one finds on the Bangladesh–India border on the other hand is that the state apparatus, in this case represented by border guards and the customs officials, are implicated and in collusion with local people in the creation of the (il)licit. States are not after all just a distant, academic idea attempting to do good. In places such as borderlands, states have legs, name tags and the ability to look away, permit and sanction. What the coal trade demonstrates is that states, as much as local people, are structurally organised to break the law. As Bidyut repeatedly said, even if one wants to do anything by the book (if such a codified set of laws existed), one simply could not do so. There are no other possible avenues to operate here but the (il)licit and the particular rules that govern them.

* * *

In total, there are around 250 coal depots in Boropani, organised on a grid system. Dirt tracks run between the rows, allowing trucks, motorbikes belonging to the import managers as well as thousands of labourers' pushcarts to pass through. Each depot, an independent business, with names such as 'Rony Enterprise' and 'Babul Brothers', consists of a lot of land that is cordoned-off with bamboo fencing. Inside, towards one end of the enclosure and beyond the heaps of coal is a rectangular corrugated tin shack. This contains a kitchen, sleeping and office space. The larger depots have a squat toilet and water pump. Most have no electricity, but with the aid of small loans offered by NGOs the use of solar-powered lighting is increasingly prevalent. The land the import depots are built upon were once rice paddies. With the legalisation of the coal trade, locals began leasing and/or selling their land to businessmen who needed somewhere to store the coal they had bought. To rent land today for a depot costs over a lakh taka per year. Entrepreneurs have already bought much of the agricultural fields in the vicinity, knowing that the demand for coal is ever increasing and that the industry will continue to expand.

EVERYDAY LIFE AT THE COALFACE

Having negotiated the bureaucracy at the Zero Point, trucks arrive at the depot where the *mal* is unloaded by the armies of migrant day-labourers. As they go about shovelling, soot flies everywhere. It can be tasted in one's mouth, felt on eyelashes and is buried in-between toes and fingernails. In the monsoon it turns to thick, squelchy mud. As the heavers unload the truck, the driver waits in the office, watches television, gossips with the managers, drinks whiskey/tea, makes suggestive comments at the effeminate hijras who work in the kitchens or otherwise roams the bazaar outside. The numbers of people working in a depot at any given time depends on the size of the business and the season. Small businesses will buy a finite amount of *mal* to sell throughout the year. They hire heavers on an if and when basis. The larger companies, with more funds, able to take risks, purchase greater amounts continuously throughout the year and hence need labourers most of the time. Nonetheless, the monsoon season is the busiest period for the entire industry when the opportunities to make money and the need for labourers, for small and large companies, increases dramatically. Boat-loads of migrant families with all their possessions in bundles turn up at the start of it, staying for the four- to five-month period. The flood waters throughout the country ensure the furnaces of brick kilns cannot be lit, which is when the demand for coal increases from owners as they restock their raw materials. This is coupled with the fact that it is much easier to transport coal on boats and barges when the wetlands are full of water.

Kauser is a cook in 'Shyamol Enterprise'. I meet her towards the close of the monsoon season when the waters of the *haor* are finally in retreat and the land below begins to reveal itself again. The senior managers of the depot had gone to Sylhet to give the owner a breakdown of how the business had fared during the busiest period. There is no coal left in the compound, a good sign. Like most outsiders who own coal-import businesses in the area, the owner rarely comes to Boropani, considering it to be dirty, dangerous and uncivilised. In particular, its people are thought to be antisocial and their personal lives uncouth. Kauser's responsibilities include buying groceries, cooking for the senior staff and keeping the office/home shack clean and tidy. Kauser calls herself a hijra, which for her means having 'the body of a man, but the heart and mind of a woman'. Hijras are employed in most of the depots in Boropani. 'Why hijras and not "real" women?' I ask her. 'Because the moment a *nehrun* [female, in *ultapalta*, the hijra slang] steps into a depot, she will become pregnant', Kauser replies. 'In order for a depot not to be brandished with a bad reputation, they employ hijras'. The large community of hijras work in various roles in the coal industry. Most are cooks, traditionally a male occupation in the subcontinent, but many also do other work. Their significant presence is explained by the roles they play in the wider social order that has grown around the coal industry. In-between talking about her newest love interest and carving out her latest dance moves, Kauser says part of her work involves making sure coal does not get stolen. There are various scams and ploys in place. Young boys creep in through the fencing in the middle of the night carrying water jugs which they fill with *mal*. Another is when 'labourers will say they have dropped off 100 sacks and you yourself have counted 100, but in fact there were only 90 that were delivered'. Even the managers 'have a sideline'. 'They drive around on motorbikes, smoke Bensons and Hedges cigarettes and talk to their lovers on their mobile phone', all of which, according to Kauser, costs more than the 3,000 to 4,000tk they officially earn per month. The security guards employed by the Coal Importers Association are involved too. 'There is a lot of *dui nombori kaj* [number two work, meaning illicit] here, but it would take you a lifetime to work out all the ways people do it', she says.

* * *

One of the preoccupations of Third World modernisers was to expand the formal sector of newly independent states. The Project itself was a case in point. This would occur, it was thought, with growing state involvement and with increased control over the uses of capital, labour and other resources. Breman (2003: 199–200) says it was felt that informality was a temporary phenomenon that would shrink with the expansion of the formal sector. This would lead to technological modernisation, agricultural expansion and the productivity of services. Nevertheless, the categories of formal and informal are problematic and contain enormous diversities between them but also within them (1994: 18). He defines the informal sector economy as having no explicit written or oral contract stipulating rights and obligations, where there is no legal protection for the conditions of employment and where activities are sketchily recorded in government accounts if at all (2003: 196). Adding to this, MacGaffey and Bazenguissa-Ganga say such activities may take place outside or on the margins of the law, thus depriving the state of revenues. Some may even break the law whilst others are legitimate but avoid taxation (2000: 2). One may deduce that the formal sector economy is the opposite of such explanations. However, Breman is sceptical of an immediate parallel being drawn, because often there are no clear or consistent distinctions. Whilst keeping Breman's caution in mind, the formal generally guarantees specific legal protections such as job security and stability, a system of social security, working conditions, periods of leave and wages (1994: 18), very much akin to what had previously existed under the Project regime.

The example of Khonighat and Boropani suggest that since liberalisation, the informal economy has expanded as the formal sector declined here and across the Third World generally and indeed in the First World. In the borderlands, too, what is abundantly clear is that the formal trade in coal is integrally connected to the informal economy. The formal economy describes the actual cross-border trade itself which includes the system of purchasing coal by Bangladeshi importers from Indian exporters. For it to be possible legally, paperwork is required, taxes are paid and customs houses, border guards and local association boards have to be negotiated. This, however, is in contradiction to the actual extraction and processing of coal which is carried out by the informal sector. The majority of long-term, seasonal and short-term migrants to the area who work in the coal trade are involved in this part of the border economy. There are no laws protecting their rights, wages, safety or health. Labour in the border economy is required to be cheap, exploitable and expendable; they are to be 'usable and disposable subjects who are not citizens' (Brown 2010: 99). There are no trade unions here. So, whilst the liberalisation of the Bangladeshi and Indian economies has resulted in the freer movement of capital and goods, this simply protects the interests of the new coal barons, those once at the bottom of the Project hierarchy.

There are two caveats to this argument. Firstly, it is not just the world of the informal labourers that the formal economy here is dependent upon, but a myriad of different inbuilt components, what Abraham and van Schendel (2006) refer to as (il)licitness. Without this, the formal cross-border coal trade simply would not be possible. Secondly, those who work in the informal coal industry are not an undifferentiated mass. They are divided between those who do organised informal work and those who do unorganised informal work. The two groups coexist and overlap with each other. Labourers involved in organised work in the day, for example, work in the parallel unorganised one at night. Family groups are also divided between those who work in the organised informal sector and those who work in the unorganised informal sector. However, the salient difference, and the reason why I distinguish between them, is to do with who is permitted to do what and where. The organised informal sector is mostly made up of men. They have a general rate of pay and work a rough set of hours placed by the import depots employing them. Many of them cross the border illegally to work in the mines. On the other hand, women make up at least half of the unorganised informal sector (children and old and disabled men make up the remainder). They have no fixed rate of pay, timings or even work. They make up loose networks of work gangs, are not employed by the importers and much of their work is illegal.

Coal heavers begin their day at sunrise when the temperature is most bearable to work. A straight line of dust and the faint sound of deep groaning accompany the thousands of men heaving over-burdened pushcarts from the coal depots towards the direction of the riverbank. From here, it is taken out by boats and delivered to larger barges that transport the goods throughout the country. These are the people who work in the organised informal trade. On closer inspection, the workers, all male and below forty years of age including boys—wariness, sleep and physical exhaustion still in their eyes—haul anything up to eight sacks of coal. Each weighs roughly 25kg. The physical toll means that the old, infirm and disabled are disqualified and have to find work in the unorganised informal sector, alongside women. As one pulls the wooden cart along the unpaved path, panting and sweating, trying to navigate past the pockmarked paths which could overturn the load, another pushes with all his might, making sure the sacks don't topple over. They are dressed in shirts and cotton trousers, the fashion of early morning city workers. Most are barefoot or wear frayed rubber sandals. None of these labourers wear scarves around their mouths as it makes breathing impossible. The French ethnographer Gerard Heuze also observes that coal heavers wear such attire in the Dhanbad coalfields in West Bengal. He understands this to be a particular kind of local modernity amongst status-conscious workers (1996: 126). The people I spoke to, however, give a more pragmatic reason for their choice of dress: it is a (futile) attempt at covering as much of their skin as possible from the itchy soot.

The perspiration on their sun-blackened faces this early in the day, with the temperature not so high, and even in the winter when they are all swathed in scarves and jumpers to ward off the cold, is a testament to how unforgiving a job this is. They earn by the amount of times they ferry the sacks from the depots to the riverbank. Taking a day off for illness, pain or physical wariness means that they do not earn. It is around 80tk per drop. The fit and healthy can expect to make around 300tk per day. Those depots further away from the river pay a little more. What they take home is much less, as they have to buy or rent a *tella ghari* and the costs for fixing the wheels every week or so come out of that amount. In a country with such high population density and chronic unemployment, there are always people desperate enough to work long hours in harsh surroundings for relatively little money. Consequently, there has been little incentive to improve health and safety conditions, raise wages or to provide any social benefits such as accommodation, health or educational facilities; strategies used elsewhere to retain workers. The sole purpose of the Boropani Coal Importers Association is for the owners of the import companies to air their grievances and to rally behind if/when exporters, the BDR or the BSF make unreasonable demands on the industry. It is not for the labourers who actually work for them. These workers could be said to be very much 'locked into a total system' (Moodie and Ndatshe 1994: 11), the aim of which is the exploitation of resources and labour.

The coal industry remains largely un-mechanised as labour is cheaper than technology. Higher wages need to be paid to those with machine knowledge along with the maintenance costs, thus making importers and depot owners wary of change. But there has been an attempt to introduce tractors recently to the transportation process. It makes light work of the loading, carrying and unloading that thousands do every day. A tractor driver, recently returned from Dhaka, was sent there by his manager to learn how to operate and fix the machine. He earns 200tk more per day than the pushcart heavers. Actual resistance to the mechanisation of the industry, however, has come from an unlikely source and not from the coal depots themselves. The overseer of the Project has been refusing to allow coal tractors to pass through Project grounds, which in effect brings any nascent ambition to mechanise to a close. His reason for doing so is that the tractors are apparently dangerous and make too much noise for the residents of Khonighat. The paradox is that in its heyday the Project was the most technologically advanced installation for miles around, procuring the latest machinery from around the world. Furthermore, the equipment used inside the quarries and the dynamite used to blast the rock would make a thunderous sound, reverberating off the hills, amplifying many times over.[8] This apparent nimbyism on the part of the Project residents is an example of the fortress mentality which prevails now amongst the old aristocracy of labour. The soot, the noise and the uncouth people that the coal trade has brought with it remind them of their own fall from prominence. Their past is now inscribed on the landscape of the decaying industrial site and any interference with the physical impinges on the fragile memories of the past.

I soon realised that there is a massive disparity in aims and practices between the ideology underpinning the marketised coal industry and the previous state-run limestone industry. For the coal barons, the resource they buy and sell is aimed at making a profit—providing a continuous supply of coal for the development of the cities elsewhere, something that is essentially of benefit to their own class of people who live in the apartments and shop in the malls for which the coal plays a necessary part. Beyond this, there is no further overarching ideology. For coal heavers and labourers, their aspiration is not too dissimilar. Their goal is to make and save money, in particular during the busy monsoon period. Working hard then means that they can rest a little during the slack months, repay debts, organise marriages in their villages of origin and become a source of earnings for those even less well off than they are. The labourers know the work they do is for the benefit of others, for managers, coal depot owners and traders. The use of the commodity further along the chain makes little difference to their peripatetic and chaotic lives. This sense of separation from the commodity they work with is in contrast to how workers connected with the Project talk about limestone and the work they once did. Acceptably, such nostalgia is due to the harshness of the coal industry, nonetheless, many Project residents across the hierarchy, for a period at least, truly internalised and believed in their integral position in the larger master plan and the role limestone extraction played within this. Project labourers not only had regular work and salaries, but were recompensed by the greater ideological aims of what they did, which was building a modern nation state. For the officer class as well, their patriarchal role in overseeing the Project was synonymous with their position as the vanguard of a new breed of citizenry. This was not merely management rhetoric. Berman, for example, says that such meta-narratives were inspiring for people across the socio-economic spectrum who produced the modern. He says they found meaning and excitement in work that was physically gruelling and ill-paying as they had a 'vision of the work as a whole and believed in its value to the community of which they were a part' (1989: 300–1).

Other than the work they do, there are certainly many differences amongst the organised informal coal labourers. In the main, they are seasonal, short-term landless migrants. But there are long-term and permanently settled migrants too. For these men, the precariousness of the coal trade means that it is prudent to continue links with villages of origin and the rural economy. During religious and national holidays, they make visits to their ancestral village homes and do grave prayers. Remittances are sent back as are expectant mothers. Deterred by the deterioration of rural life, they refuse to move back. The connections and knowledge the older settlers have of the industry, its people and the border area generally ensures that they and their family live a little better, that their children go to the Project school for at least a short period and that they earn a little more and work a little less than the recently arrived and the temporary migrants. Nonetheless, the long-term settled have complex connections with the short-term and seasonal migrants. Many are distant relatives, have a patron–client relationship or their ancestral home is in the same district which means that they have obligations towards one another. Labour leaders, for example, supply and organise workers for depots, giving priority to people from their own region when it comes to recruiting for a job. This way they help fellow countrymen and in return are ensured loyalty, an important commodity in the borderlands.

Kuhn (2003) argues that, in other parts of Bangladesh, rural to urban migrants use social links and patronage to secure jobs and accommodation too. Access to credit is also a facet of this relationship in particular for newly arrived migrants. In the absence of formally organised trade unions, networks of support, for the new and the temporary in particular, mean that they have a degree of leverage against any possible excess of coal depot power. During the dry months, landless migrants work in agriculture in their home districts, growing paddy and other crops for a landlord. In exchange, they keep half of the produce. During the wet season, when the waters claim these lands, men, women and children migrate en masse to Boropani, travelling by boat and walking long distances to begin their four- to five-month campaign. Men live with men and women live with women in cramped and crowded shacks that they rent privately. The more there are, the cheaper it is. Those lucky enough live with extended family members or friends they have made when previously here. Sanitation is primitive: particular hillocks on the borderlands are designated toilets. The quarry lakes serve as the main source of water for washing and bathing. The seasonal labourers work through the monsoon, until the waters dry up and they slowly drift back to their villages to continue the cycle again. Breman describes such people as 'labour nomads' and as enduring 'a living hell': constantly on the move and paid wages often below subsistence levels, they have lives that are characterised by heavy work, physical exhaustion and the odium of untouchability. 'Rapidly worn out by the production process, when their productivity decreases, they are discarded as so much waste' (1999b: 418–19). Such migrants are increasingly termed 'climate change refugees'. Swollen rivers claiming entire villages mean people move from low-lying areas to drier, higher areas such as Khonighat and Boropani. The burning of coal and other fossil fuels are at the root of this contemporary phenomenon. The sad irony of course is that though poverty ensures that these migrants have a very limited carbon footprint themselves, they are entangled in the unequal global relations which cause global warming in the first place.[9]

* * *

Alongside the organised informal work where labourers perform unquestionably exhausting work is that of the equally excruciating unorganised informal work. This is something that is generally carried out by women, children, the old and the infirm. Women in Boropani cannot work in the formal trade let alone the organised informal one. They are banned from working in the mines themselves. This latter exclusion is a colonial law passed in the 1920s as part of a raft of liberal legislation that continues in Bangladesh and India. The ban, one may argue, reflects social and cultural mores which restrict women to domestic and child-drearing roles, a pervasive argument used to explain their exclusion and part of a wider discourse that attributes them to the repository of tradition (Chatterjee 1989). However, Samita Sen's (1999) work on the Bengal jute industry contradicts this sort of arguement. She says that the first jute mills in Bengal were established in 1855. By the 1880s they employed 30,000 women. As the numbers of mills grew and the work-force became more heterogeneous in terms of caste, ethnicity and religion, the numbers of women dropped. By the 1970s, women were a negligible 2 per cent of the industry. This trend was not isolated to jute alone. In the Bengal coal industry there were twelve women to every eleven men in 1901 and by 1921 the number went down to thirteen women to every thirty-four men. Sen believes the exclusion of women from the industries was an economic strategy and not a result of a cultural or social prohibition which it is widely thought to be. After all, the position of women in the subcontinent is far from homogenous and varies according to religion, caste, class, age and life experience. Sen says that as wages and working conditions improved through collective political struggle for men, these very forces contributed to a more rigid exclusion of women. The reason why this occurred and is also the most convincing explanation for why women continue to be excluded from the formal and organised informal sector in Boropani today is the fear that their presence would erode the bargaining power of organised male labour as well as undercut their wages.

As the rains begin, thousands of female migrants arrive in the border-lands as part of a family unit or individuals who attach themselves to larger groups as fictitious kin. They are primarily women who have fallen on hard times, have been widowed, whose husbands have taken another wife, who have been accused of infidelity, unable to bear children or are escaping familial or social persecution. Much of this is in keeping with the received wisdom that the mining industry impacts more heavily on women than on men and that the process of migration makes them as vulnerable as the initial ordeal they are fleeing. Roger Moody, for example, says that women around the world are forced into mining because of displacement, loss of access to resources, lack of livelihood options and as land-based economies shift to mining economies (2007: 84). Feminist critics of neo-liberalism argue that social and economic transformations have a clear gender dimension and that the experience of female labour migrants is part of a broader system of exploitation and oppression (Phillips 2005: 251). In line with this thought, those involved in this work then are considered to be the most desperate out of an already marginalised group with their precarious position reflecting this desperation. They carry out the most dangerous jobs, earn the least and work the most.

However, whilst gender may be one of the most crucial fault lines along which encounters with neo-liberalism are felt, the effects are complex and not equal. As with the case of Sujon earlier, one needs to be cautious of easy generalisations. While neo-liberalism does indeed impact in specific ways on women, including what has been termed the 'feminisation of poverty', there are alternatives to this too, some even allowing women to become active agents in their social and economic lives. For the Darana women in Jaipur that Unnithan-Kumar (2003) writes about, migration has engendered greater physical freedom, allowing them to break out from desperate economic relationships of indebtedness and constrictive extended families. But on the other hand, whilst in the city, they experience greater workloads than men, even though they have a more equal relationship with their husbands and menfolk. As Annu Jalais says, in the backdrop of growing structural gender inequalities, there are greater opportunities to challenge pre-existing patriarchal norms compared to an earlier generation of women (2010: 27). This is the irony of neo-liberalism in which empowerment and its opposite, disempowerment, can paradoxically go hand in hand.

Most days, female labourers line the route of the formal trade from the Zero Point onwards, scavenging for bits of coal that have fallen off the back of the trucks. Outside of the depots, women squat on the dusty ground, sweeping dirt up into a pan which they then sieve for bits of coal. Along the path the pushcarts take to the river, women and children zig-zag in-between them, collecting stray bits that have tipped out. Amidst the hardship, there are moments of subtle opposition. It is the boat men's responsibility to ensure that the *mal* gets to the barges moored out in the *haor*, from where the coal is loaded and then shipped across the country. Sacks are often open and others torn, with coal seeping out of them. Someone may nonchalantly tie the sacks back together again. The haphazardness with which this work is carried out helps female labourers who brush up the sprinkled coal. Scott (1985) describes such acts of symbolic rebellion (i.e. pilfering), as 'everyday forms of resistance'. This is the prosaic and constant struggle between the worker and those who seek to extract labour, food, taxes, rent and interest from them, but which stops short of total defiance (ibid.: xvi). Such pathetic actions occasionally disrupt the designs of a system that has all but reduced everything, bodies, labour, reproductive capabilities to the level of a commodity.

During the monsoon a stream formed behind the bungalow I live in, heralding a constant traffic of labourers with fishing nets, wicker baskets and other agricultural utensils that have been adapted for coal collection. Night and day, women in sodden, brightly coloured sarees, collect, dig, screen, load, sift and sack the black stuff. Organised by long-term labour leaders such as Joshim's uncle, the low-grade coal, known as *Bangla* (as it is found on the Bangladeshi side of the border), is sold on to coal depots where they mix it with higher-grade (Indian) coal. Based on the numbers of sacks filled, workers earn between 200 and 300tk per day. Paid by the number of sacks they fill, there are numerous children, 'helpers', also involved in the work. In the unorganised informal industry, women work alongside men. Some are related to them, but not all. At night I hear their chatter, occasional laughter and cries of babies as they go about their work. Once I heard a woman shouting, presumably at her husband/lover. She had a baby on her hip and a naked, toddling one following behind. 'He [lover? husband?] just hit me on my hips', she cried to no one in particular. 'This is why I am living away from him. If he doesn't want to look after them [meaning the children], then I can do it very well myself. I can work and feed them'. Once the sacks are filled, heavers carry them through the Project grounds on their backs and pile them by the road, before transporting them to the depot area. This form of coal collecting is illegal because they are operating along the border, on the prohibited no-man's-land as well as the fact that there is no paperwork involved or taxes paid. However, in the evenings, one would see high-ranking BDR guards come to the stream to extract payment from the coal *nethas*. This form of 'local tax' collection permits, or rather legalises, what would ordinarily be illegal.[10]

As the evening settles in and all the boats leave, the depot area is quiet. Most of the coal men are in the bazaar, drinking tea, socialising and gossiping. The hijras begin preparing supper. Project elders promenade along the quarry lake, gazing benevolently at the heavers who wash their pushcarts and then themselves in its waters. A few coal depot managers potter around the Zero Point talking to their Indian counterparts on their mobiles. It is the women who remain in the depot area, continuing to sweep up the remnants of the day's spillages. They remain the most vulnerable out of all the migrants who flood into the area to feed the trade with cheap and expendable labour. Some of them are in the river, the water as black as coal, fishing out chunks. They work the longest hours, for the least amount of money. Most are filthy, their sarees torn. Work does not end when they get home, where they will do the cooking, washing and other domestic and caring responsibilities expected of them. I notice a woman, a regular in the depot area who has a skin disease around her legs. She collects coal soot with her six-year-old daughter. The woman has small gold earrings on, probably her only assets. At least she has something that gives her some self-respect, I think. These are all people who are part-time farmers and fisher folk. They come to the borderlands for money and as a result have radically transformed their connection to a cycle that had once given their lives a semblance of meaning: the land, the water, loved ones, seasons. Now they have become a reusable, disposable part in a large, dirty, industrial machinery where they process coal in order to fulfil the hopes and desires of a growing metropolis elsewhere. What of their hopes and desires? Living a life free from illness and hunger? Their deaths in the mines go unnoticed. The labourers are simply replaced.

3

THE SEXUAL LIVES OF BORDERLANDERS

Marriage is a serious matter on which rest the security of the family and the stability of the state. But marriage can only maintain its authority if extra-conjugal relations are not only tolerated but sanctified.[1]

Mohammed is in her twenties and one of a number of new tractor drivers in the coal trade in Boropani. She[2] spends most nights transporting coal sacks from the depot area to the river bank where in the mornings they are shipped out to buyers across the country. The work Mohammed does is hard and dangerous. She starts her shift at 6pm, finishing just after the *fozor azan* (early morning call to prayers) from the mosque around 5am. The Project overseer, who had been preventing tractors from going through the perimeters, eventually reached an agreement with the Boropani Coal Importers Association, allowing them to drive past Project fencing only during the night when the chances of causing accidents were apparently lessened. During the daytime, the loading, unloading and transporting had to continue to be carried out manually. Taking it in turns to drive with the man she calls her husband, Mohammed says she enjoys the work she does. Needing to stay awake, they talk to each other all night, telling stories, reciting poetry, singing Bengali pop songs, gossiping and making plans for the future. The winds from the West Khasi Hills help cool her mind, she says. A few years ago, Mohammed was a well-known hijra in Dhaka:

I called myself Julie. I had gold jewellery, beautiful sarees, status and a rented apartment. I earned a living by doing *hijragiri*, which meant going from shop-to-shop collecting money from businessmen, sleeping with whoever could afford to pay and dancing at weddings and birthdays. I did this for many years and people knew me. A lot of other hijras were jealous of my success. I can speak well and men liked me. This all changed once I was raped. People, in particular this one businessman, would come to the apartment and force themselves on me.

Out of curiosity, I asked if the men paid her afterwards. Annoyed by my question, Mohammed replies: 'If you don't like someone, it doesn't matter how much they pay, they cannot change your mind. But if you like someone, then you can even do it for free'.

She continues:

My mind was bad from the experiences and I left Dhaka. Other than my gold and sarees, I sold everything else and moved to Sylhet. I lived there for a while, again doing *hijragiri*. One year, I went to the Shah Arfeen *mazaar* [shrine of a local saint] to pay my respects. I met another hijra there. It was from him that I first heard about Boropani. Afterwards, I left Sylhet for my home village where I spent time working on the family rice field. My mind was still bad from what had happened in Dhaka. One day I had enough of working on the fields and decided to come to Boropani where I met Abed. He took me as his disciple, gave me food, a place to stay and found me a job as a cook for the then officer at the customs house. I've been here for two years now. I am a hijra, yes, but I don't want to do *hijragiri*. Though driving is hard, I prefer it to who I used to be.

The hijras are an integral part of the human and social landscape the coal industry has carved out for itself and is thoroughly interwoven with the need for a particular public and private life. The majority are semi-permanently settled migrant workers from other parts of Bangladesh who work as *babuchis* (cooks) in the coal import businesses. Hijras here say '*amader shorir purusher, kintu meyerar mon*' (we are physically men, but have the hearts and minds of women). With their overt and garish caricature of femininity they are very distinct in appearance, behaviour and presence in comparison to other manual labourers in the area (male and female). Sauntering through the bazaar while on the quest for provisions, they flirt with sellers as they haggle over prices, wink as they coquettishly twirl scarves at rifle-yielding BDR guards and fend-off advances from motorbike drivers who courier coal merchants to and from Sunamgonj. The hijras are attracted to the area for the abundance of work and the well-established community. As Mohammed articulates, she is able to earn a living here by doing jobs other than *hijragiri*, the role traditionally expected of people such as her. They say there are over 140 members who work as *babuchis* alone. (The total number is many more, as not all hijras work for the depots). Other than cooking, they manage the upkeep of the coal depot office and living areas, officiate security, handle petty cash and deal with coal traders. In addition, hijras work as coal heavers on both sides of the border, labour *nethas*, truck and tractor drivers, serving staff in tea shops, (il)licit coal miners on the Indian side and servants in the BDR camp stationed in the locality. There are also some (literate) hijras who are managers of coal depots. The range of work they do here may come as a surprise compared to what hijras elsewhere in the subcontinent do for a living. In reality hijras generally work in a variety of different occupations. The anthropologist Serena Nanda, for example, says that a hijra she knew delivered milk on a bicycle, while one was an electrician and some worked in construction, which in India is a woman's as well as a man's job (1999: 17). Sharma says he also spoke to a hijra who worked as a porter at the Bombay Railway Station (1989: 54). However, such routine jobs are usually side-lined by researchers for the more attention-grabbing *hijragiri* work.

Abed is Mohammed's guru (teacher). He is the most senior of the Boropani hijras and has around ten *celas* (disciples) and twenty-five *nathi celas* (*celas* of his own disciples). All are based in Boropani and most are involved in various aspects of the border economy. The guru-*cela* relationship is the defining characteristic of hijra culture and society. It designates formal membership within the hijra community and delineates the lineage of an individual. It is through the guru-*cela* network that information, gossip, news and knowledge are transmitted across time and space, placing an individual into an established hierarchy of seniority. The guru-*cela* system is not unique to the hijras and is the basis of other trans-relational connections too such as Sufi brotherhoods. All hijras in Boropani are connected to the house of Beauty Hijra. She is apparently a middle-aged hijra, who lives in Dhaka and is spoken about in revered tones by Boropani hijras. The *rit* (the formal marker of an allegiance to a hijra lineage) between the Boropani hijras and Beauty was established in the 1990s. Abed is unsure precisely when this occurred, but it was after the Project closed down. Having lost his job as a porter in the Project, his father had relocated the family to Boropani where, with the handsome provident fund he received, they started their first business. The closure of the Project is crucial to the formation of the hijra community of Boropani because before then no one I spoke to could remember any hijras living in the area, in particular inside of the Project grounds. Abed found out about Beauty from one of her Sylhet-based *celas* who had gone to the same *mazaar* Mohammed would many years later. Soon after learning of her existence, Abed went in search of Beauty in Dhaka and was accepted as one of her disciples. Beauty's networks of hijras span the country, from Sylhet to Dhaka and Chittagong as well as across the border in Calcutta. With hijras from Boropani increasingly marrying Indian coal men who live and work in Meghalaya and Assam, the network is spreading into the Indian north-east too.[3] During his hijra initiation, Abed learnt to speak the hijra slang (known as *ultapalta* 'upside down'),[4] the rules and codes of being a hijra as well as the stories and myths of the hijra *bongsho* (origins).

It is through this traditional network that hijras hear about jobs in Boropani, the whereabouts of friends and those who have been arbitrated, excommunicated and/or fined by the hijra courts.[5] When an unknown hijra arrives in the area for work, the lineage and the name of their guru are sought. It is this that places them and makes them knowable. If the guru is someone recognised by the senior hijras in Boropani, and importantly liked, then the new arrival will be taken into the fold, helped to find a job and a place to live. References for individuals are crucial. A place of much transience, it is not easy to find suitable places to live and jobs that aren't too arduous. There are no all-hijra communes here as there are in urban centres. Permanent hijra locals such as Abed live with their natal family. Long-term hijra migrants live in the depots and shacks that employers have set aside for labourers. Short-term, seasonal hijra migrants live in barracks with others who do similar work. In this sense, there is very little difference between hijra and non-hijra workers. If the guru is disliked then it is practically impossible for a *cela* to find a job in the Boropani coal trade. He will be shunned by the community as well as by the wider non-hijra population. Some hijras have no gurus. This is either because they are new to hijra society or because they have broken a previous *rit* with a guru. In such circumstances they are considered to be almost 'without caste'. It is inconceivable that a hijra be alone without a guru, and one is assigned them. Gurus have immense power and control over *celas*. They expect to be given a part of a *cela's* earnings, gifts during special occasions, moral and emotional support, as well as defended during disagreements with other hijras. *Celas* are expected to be trustworthy, loyal and devoted. In turn they are 'looked after by their guru as a mother would', taught hijra knowledge and customs, helped to find jobs, lovers and supported if they commit hijra misdemeanours.

Mohammed and Abed's experiences indicate three important points. Firstly, most migrant hijras in Boropani work in some capacity in the cross-border coal trade between Meghalaya and Sylhet and do not make a living from *hijragiri*: the traditional source of living for members in cities and towns across the subcontinent which includes sex work, begging for alms and granting blessings. Secondly, it sheds light on the networks along which hijras hear about and come to Boropani that places them within a wider social context that goes beyond their immediate identities. Thirdly, despite its general unpleasantness and the overwhelming difficulties for most who live and work here, since the demise of the monolith that was the all-embracing Khonighat Limestone Mining Project, Boropani and the coal trade has become a site of possibilities for various groups of 'marginalised undesirables' to be able to make a living. This is because the Project's singular vision of modernity entailed promulgating an organised and stable social and intimate life, based upon heteronormativity, patriarchy and reproductive controls as the basis for an ideal citizenry. With its collapse and the fragmentation of such ideals, alternative forms of modernities have been able to gain ground.

* * *

The informed reader will appreciate that the hijras of Boropani are markedly different from how hijras have conventionally been represented in the finite number of anthropological works on the community. Written about and situated within contemporary literature as the personification *par excellence* of the third sex/gender, hijras are understood to be 'men' who wear 'women's' clothing, who sacrifice their penis to the Hindu goddess, Bahuchara Mata, in return for the power to bestow blessings on baby boys and fertility on newly-weds. The ideal type the literature establishes, and which has entered the popular lexicon, in practice creates a regulatory image of what a 'hijra' is, though this in itself is a patchwork of diverse forms. The effect of it is to exoticise and essentialise a social group, which for all intents and purposes are like any other social group within society. Nanda's seminal work in the

1990s on a community of hijras in 'Bastipore'[6] and Bombay challenged long-standing sensationalist accounts of the community. She argues that as an institutionalised third gendered social actor, hijras are not only interesting in themselves, but also for the wider academic study of gender categories and human sexual variations (1999: ix). This is particularly so, she says, as many former third gender roles in non-Western societies have become subsumed within the 'cultural imperialism associated with colonialism, modernisation and westernisation' (ibid.: xi). Nanda explains that the fact that hijras were not eradicated by such forces in India is due to the supposed multifarious nature of Hinduism. According to her, Hinduism is able to accommodate gender variations, ambiguity and contradictions, within which hijras have managed to carve out a 'distinct place in Indian society as a viable and recognised third gender'.

Gayatri Reddy rightly questions Nanda's understanding of hijras and says that like any member of any community, hijra identities are shaped along a multitude of axes, including kinship, religion, class and caste and cannot simply be reduced to an analysis of sexuality and gender alone (2005: 2). Her work on a hijra community in Hyderabad attempts to rectify this representational discrepancy. The hijras she works with live together in tents and shacks on government land. The majority work as sex workers, while the older ones grant blessings. By historicising the hijras in Hyderabad, Reddy shows that the sexuality and gender categories are not consistent lenses through which hijras have always been viewed. What is most interesting about her analysis is that by distinguishing between pre-colonial, colonial and post-colonial representations, indicating changes in attitudes and status that have been assigned them over time, she questions the timeless, static paradigm by which hijras are currently viewed. Extensive debates in ancient Hindu, Jain and Buddhist texts situated 'third sex' individuals within a larger framework about the nature of sexuality and the differences between biologically and socially constructed notions of gender.[7] From the eleventh century onwards, and with the arrival of Islam and later of the Mughal Empire, the word 'hijra', an Urdu word, began to be widely used. Much of the literature from that period refers to their political, religious and slave status. Hijras rose to prominence in the royal courts (as did eunuchs in the Chinese and Ottoman empires) and became a crucial 'instrument of imperial power'. Unable to impregnate and procreate, their bodies were inscribed with 'honesty and fiscal responsibility' (2005: 22). In the religious sphere, societies of eunuchs guarded the tomb of Prophet Mohammed in Medina and at the Ka'ba in Mecca: societies that have endured from the twelfth century to the present day (Marmon 1995). This had inevitable bearings on the way they were viewed in the subcontinent and questions Nanda's overgeneralised and rather naïve view that the tolerance for alternative forms of gender and sexualities is specific to Hinduism. It is later, during the British colonial period, that hijras become associated with deviancy, likening the phenomena to sati or infanticide, when they become one of the several hundred tribes and castes of India and included in the Criminal Tribes Act of 1871. Act 27 calls for the 'registration, surveillance and control of certain tribes and eunuchs', thus effectively criminalising their bodies. In the post-colonial period, academic debates that begin to sexualise hijras for the first time 'created a separate domain for the analysis of hijra sexual practice as distinct from their religious/ritual practice' (Reddy 2005: 30). It is also then that hijras were situated within a larger discourse of Western versus non-Western sexualities, gay and lesbian studies and discussions on 'third gender' categorisations.

From purity to profanity, respect to disrepute, once the pivotal actors in royal and religious intrigue to outright social, economic and political marginalisation, today hijras across the subcontinent are perceived as social pariahs because of their apparent transgressive behaviour. The hijras of Boropani do nothing to simplify these contrasting and often contradictory understandings. In fact, if anything, Abed, Mohammed and their fellow hijras complicate further what has come to be the accepted representation of hijra identity. They do not, for example, even fit into the most traditional understandings of them. To call the hijras of Boropani the 'third gender', as it has become commonplace to do so, would be convenient but inaccurate. They are not castrated, saree-clad individuals. They retain their penis and wear male clothes (trousers, *lunghi* and shirt) in public. They do not beg, cajole and threaten to expose their genitals unless they are placated with alms. They all have jobs and some even own businesses. Though they take part in and practise Hindu rituals, they are on the whole Muslim, and they do not bless babies or couples.

Boropani hijras may not fit neatly into the established categories, but these very 'common characteristics and practices' are themselves not wholly agreed upon. Confusion amongst the general public as well as academics still abounds as to whether hijras generally are hermaphrodites (i.e. born intersexed), castrated (i.e. 'man-made')[8] or just homosexual transvestites. Nanda for example argues that a key defining criterion of a hijra is that he undergoes an emasculation operation, thus 'neither man nor woman' (1999: ix). This is what Reddy's Hyderabadi informants also tell her (2005: 55). However, both anthropologists provide examples of individuals, who though self-define and are known publicly as a hijra, have not undergone the operation. Whether they are 'incomplete', 'pre-operative' (Cohen 1995b: 285) or happy as they are with no intention of surgically altering themselves, is left unsaid. It seems then that castration, though understood in the public imagination and in much of the literature as the undeniable signifier, is not necessarily the norm. In failing to carry out the procedure, Reddy's informants suggest that the least one can do is to get circumcised. The hijras she works with are in the main born Hindu who, in accordance with 'hijra rules', become Muslim after joining the group. This means that they undergo the less extreme procedure of circumcision, consequently changing religion and orientation (2005: 57). None of the hijras in Boropani are castrated and other than one, they never expressed an interest in the subject either.[9] One of Abed's *celas* did once expose himself to me, trying to prove that he was a 'real' hijra. He simply tucked his penis and scrotum in-between his legs to make it look like he had no male appendage. In fact, I was told by Abed that out of the thousands of hijras throughout Bangladesh, there are very few who actually are castrated. Even their main guru, Beauty Hijra, is not castrated (though her own guru was). This could be due to a lack of expertise and *dais* (midwives) to carry out the procedure, or because initiates—the majority of whom are born into Muslim households—are already circumcised, thus obviating the need altogether.

It is generally believed that hijras are sexually impotent with regards to women. In fact, an insinuation of having been married and fathered children is one of the worst accusations in the hijra community. In Boropani, many hijras, including Abed, are married to women. Their marriages were arranged by their families. The father of Mohammed the tractor driver, at the time of fieldwork, was seeking a wife for her. Towards the end of fieldwork, Abed's wife even gave birth to their second daughter. One can suggest that societal, economic and familial pressures force individuals to marry with the expectation of reproduction within it. From all my conversations with people who define themselves as hijra, they say they marry because they themselves choose to do so. 'How else do you expect to have children?' they ask. 'Whom will you pass your property on to when you die?' and all importantly, 'who will look after you when you are old?' (These questions are more salient here than they would be were they to be living in a hijra commune.) Even for these people, heterosexual marriages remain an ideal for social and economic reproduction and procreation both for a mixture of emotional and structural reasons. Companionate relations with men on the other hand are for individual (emotional, corporeal) fulfilment, rather than (or in addition to) reproduction. In fact, for many, it is particularly after marriage that they are able to take individual risks that they are not able to do before it. As Khan, writing about Pakistan, says, 'if a husband takes care of his family's security needs and sires many children, what he does for personal sexual satisfaction is uninteresting to everyone involved, so long as he is discreet' (1996: 277).

According to the literature, the hijras of Boropani may be termed 'zenanas' (Nanda 1995; Reddy 2005) or 'jankhas' (Cohen 1995b). Zenanas and jankhas are essentially effeminate men who have rits with gurus but are not castrated. They can marry women, dress like them and dance like hijras (Cohen 1995b: 276). There are many differences/ divides as well as similarities/alliances between them and hijras. The castrated, saree-wearing hijras dislike zenanas/jankhas vehemently for supposedly 'mimicking' them and stealing their business. In Boropani I never heard these terms being used by hijras or non-hijras. Other than 'hijra' the only other term used on the very rare occasion was 'kothi'.[10] However, to make these categories more distinct and analytical than they are has the danger of flattening-out something, which at its core is fluid, overlapping and contradictory, where individual identities and behaviours spill outside the boundaries attributed to them. A person may cross-cut with more than one of these types without even publicly/ personally knowing/acknowledging that they do so. Despite her attempt at explicating the differences between the various hijra subcategories, Reddy concedes that 'fluidity of perceived self representations … precludes any easy reading' of these individuals (2005: 77). Cohen also says that his informants would frequently collapse boundaries and play with terms. They would describe themselves as one thing to one set of people and another thing to another set (1995b: 288).

Rather than assuming that the hijras of Boropani are ill informed with respect to what they are supposed to be, my view is that these are all contested terms and that there is no easy reading of non-heteronormative desires and behaviours. In effect, there are diverse groups of individuals, practices, experiences and explanations that make up a spectrum of non-heteronormative identities in the subcontinent. On one extreme is the (publicly) visible, castrated, saree-wearing hijra who has become a mainstay of urban fantasies from the colonial period onwards. On the other extreme are 'out and proud' gay men, akin and aligned to global gay movements, increasingly the nightmare of the political and social right. The two are juxtaposed not just in terms of corporeal and sartorial differences, but also class, language, jobs, geography, wealth, worldviews and power. In-between these two porous, shifting and unstable identities are a myriad of other possibilities. Some come with names, many others don't. MSMs (men who have sex with men), for example, is a term created by NGOs and attributed to all kinds of different (often clandestine) behaviour. Like *kothi*, it too is an entry point for HIV prevention and public health workers and NGOs. While a few may be castrated, others are not. Most are horrified by such practices. Some live in communes and are endowed with spiritual, ritual and other-worldly powers, others live with their wives and children, natal families, husbands and/ or partners.

What existing works on hijras are firmly united upon is the idea that they are figures of disrepute within mainstream Asian society. Cohen refers to them as the 'most marginal of social beings' (2004: 184). Nanda believes that 'as in the case of marginal and oppressed peoples in many cultures, very little of what has been written on the hijras gives them a voice of their own at any length or on a wide range of topics' (1999: xi). Such ideas are united by the notion that it is the enduring difference of hijras that propounds their positions, locating them outside of the mainstream. In Boropani on the other hand, that very same difference is what situates them in prime position, very much at the centre of mainstream society. In recent years the community has increasingly become visible and undoubtedly an independent entity in its own right. This is an unintended consequence of their presence: one which the coal depot owners never envisaged. It is not due to the work they do. Generally occupying the lower sections of the labour hierarchy, they are considered to be as replaceable as any other manual worker. It is partly owing to the intimate relationships they have with men from the 'labour class', as well as the more influential sections of society, which normalises such relations. Secondly, and linked to the first point, their increased visibility within public life sees their explicit affirmation as figures of respect and reputation within coal society. This is distinct from the wider gentrification of the 'hijra movement', part of the general politics of identity and human rights, visible throughout urban centres in the subcontinent. Some hijras in India, for example, are standing for elections in local, state and even national office and are increasingly vocal in the media.[11] Though implicitly and very loosely connected to such hijras through the extensive hijra network that spans Bangladesh, India, Pakistan and Nepal, there are no actual interactions between the 'politicised and socially aware hijras' and the Boropani community. In fact, the Boropani hijras would probably be looked down upon for being rustic and parochial by their more urbane sisters.

* * *

Abed is obviously a potent local force wielding both power and authority. He sat regally on the veranda of a house in the bazaar the first time I saw him. The large white shirt he wore stretched tight over his generous belly. At his feet lay a thief whose face and body were dark and swollen. Dried blood encrusted his vest. He had been apprehended earlier in the day whilst attempting to steal two cows by forcing them on to his boat. The rightful owner of the animals had taken the thief to the BDR camp, the highest authority in the area. Since the cattle were not being taken across the border the BDR were not interested in dealing with the case.[12] The BDR commander's advice was to take the complaint to the nearest police station located in the headquarters of the district subdivision a couple of hours away by boat. A *panwallah* explains that if the owner was to do that, he would have to take the culprit, as well as the two cows and any witnesses, along with him. All of this at his own expense, which includes costs for tea, biscuits, *paan* (betel leaf), grass and boat fare. The victim would then have to bring them all back and if the court case came up, the process would have to be repeated again. It was easier (and cheaper) to enact the local process of dealing with the offender than have to go through the logistics of the formal legal procedure. Therefore the thief had been tied up and beaten in front of onlookers who swore and made fun of him. Importantly, there were respected local persons present. The latter were crucial so as to bear witness to the course of action taken and to ensure that no excesses against the accused took place. It had to be a measured response. Abed was one of these esteemed people who had been called to carry out this role. Others also bestowed with this responsibility were a local imam, a leading personality from the Boropani Coal Importers Association, as well as respected coal depot managers. Eventually the cow thief was let off with a warning that he was not to be seen anywhere near the bazaar again. Later, Abed tells me that he felt terribly bad for the crook. He was only a boy, barely fourteen years old.

As a *murrobi* (respected elder), Abed is frequently called upon to carry out such civic roles. He regularly attends meetings to resolve disputes between the informal work gangs who want access to the same coal sources on the hills. He intervenes in domestic rows whereby a husband/ wife is threatening to leave, arranges marriages, and he also participates in negotiations between traders and the BDR. In the absence of adequate state presence, 'respected persons' tend to exert disproportionate amounts of power in public life. It is not just the tea shop and the import depot his family own that provide him with legitimacy. Abed is a member of the bazaar committee, overseeing the smooth operation of the marketplace, as well as being on the board of the *mazaar*. He organises the annual *urus* (death anniversary of a saint), a significant fixture in the local religious calendar. The son of an ex-Project worker, having been born and raised in that rarefied world gives Abed an edge over other coal men, even those more prosperous than he is. He continues to revere everything associated with the Project. But like the lax yet passionate follower of a religion, this does not mean that Abed continues to live by its strictures any longer: the lived experience differs very much from the ideal. Along with other descendants of the Project who left for Boropani, he circumvents the principles and codes of conduct that they were raised in if and when it suits. Even so, such people transgress not only the inherent physical boundaries between Khonighat and Boropani but also the two distinct ideological spaces that they constitute. The fact that Abed is a hijra guru is very much intertwined and integral to everything he is and does. It is not a hindrance to his public position and respect ability. Far from it, most locals from Boropani and Khonighat are aware of his multiple identities. With the ability to command authority over a large constituency of people, it is a major reason why he is held in high regard. This is reinforced by the fact that Abed's current husband is the manager of a bank in Sylhet. Previous lovers have included influential coal depot managers and owners and a high-ranking officer of the BDR who was once posted to the area.

In his role as a senior guru, Abed spends much of his time ordering, badgering, consoling, joking, comforting, counselling and shouting at the streams of people who come every day to the kitchen area of his family's tea shop in the bazaar. There is a mixture of hijra and non-hijra staff who work for him, hurrying in and out, serving tea and samosas to labourers, managers and depot owners. Here, in 'public', Abed's gestures are not what one would associate with an archetypal Bengali masculinity, but neither are they the product of an archetypal Bengali femininity. They are a conspicuous caricature of both. Even the way he looks, the use of cosmetics, the plucking of eyebrows for example and smoking in public (which women generally do not do) subverts distinctions between the feminine/masculine. Abed refers to himself and the other hijras in both masculine and feminine terms and makes lewd and bawdy comments, despite the presence of non-hijras. 'Most people have two names. We have three', he explains during one of our conversations. 'The first is the name given to us at birth by our parents. The second is our worldly name, which is the nickname everyone knows us by. The third and this is what differentiates us from everyone else, is our *"kolom kinthu kali nai"'* (pen without ink) name. Abed's *kolom kinthu kali na* name is Abeda, a feminised version of Abed. But Abeda does have ink in his pen. He is far from sexually impotent which is what the adage insinuates. He of course is not alone in this. Many other hijras too are married and have children. He then tries a different course in attempting to explain who the hijras are and what differentiates them from everyone else. 'We are not just men and we are not just women. We are both. We have the body of a man, and the heart and mind of a woman'. This definition is crucial for an understanding of the hijras. In Boropani, hijras consider themselves to be phenotypically men. Outwardly in self-presentation in public life they have 'male' jobs in the coal trade, wear 'male' clothes and have 'male' relationships with women. However, privately—both on the insides of their bodies (that is, their hearts and minds), as well as behind the privacy of walls—they are women. Here they wear 'female' clothes, think and feel 'female' thoughts and emotions and have relationships with men in which they will take on feminine roles.

This is of course a critical variation to Nanda's assertion of 'neither man, nor woman' (1999). Her understanding assumes the features (both physical and behavioural) that make up a 'man' and a 'woman' are absent in hijras. The result is an altogether altered character that is physically and behaviourally distinct, that is neither man, nor woman. It is this understanding that represents hijras as truly transgressive and outside of the bounds of mainstream society. Shah says it is precisely this 'abnormal[ity]' that makes them 'socially powerful' (1961: 1329). In Abed's understanding that 'we are both' man and woman, however, the hijras are made up of both (physical and behavioural) qualities attributed to men and women. Whereas in Nanda's understanding, the qualities of men and women are not present, in this explanation, they are together and exist at the same time. It is precisely this ability to be '"within, rather than outside" the binary gender framework' (Aggarwal 1997: 292) that allows Boropani hijras to be socially active and prominent within the private domains of intimate lives and the public worlds of civic, religious and political life. This is because hijras here are much more selective than Nanda's hijras with regards to social circumstance, choosing to wear male and female clothes and taking on 'appropriate behavioural norms' depending upon context.

It helps to explain why they rarely if ever wear sarees in public. Only once did I see them do so, when around thirty of them put on a show for their *panthis* (lovers) and I was invited along to it. They dressed in sarees and put on make-up and then, one by one, did a solo dance performance. One can argue that this is to do with the industrial environment itself which is not conducive for them to walk around in public in extroverted ways. Heuze, however, alludes to the presence of 'eunuch transvestites' in the Dhanbad coal mines in West Bengal who dress in sarees (1996: 201) which suggests this may not be the case everywhere. In Boropani, hijras actively negotiate both male and female personas, using names, dress, manners and sexual relations. This is contingent upon whether they want to stress the masculine and/or feminine subject position.

In private, with *panthis* and *pariks* (husbands),[13] gurus and hijra sisters, individuals wear sarees, use feminine kinship terms and exploit general feminine cultural symbols. This is when it is expected that they will play the 'feminine role' and where they gain social and erotic capital from doing so. In public, where being a man attains greater power and authority, they perform the 'male role'. They have short hair, wear *lunghis*, trousers and shirts, as all men here do. This includes relations with actual kin, so Abed says 'during sex with my wife, I am a man. During sex with my *parik*, I am a woman'. This binary distinction, however, is not always consistent because hijras wear 'male' clothes (in effeminate ways) and 'female' clothes (in masculine ways). The way they tie their *lunghis* as one would a saree with pleats at the front and the cut, fit, colour of their shirts and trousers more than indicate a traditional femininity. It is further problematised by unpredictable and contradictory gestures, behaviours and the switching of male/female pronouns. Were they to take on the full-blown hijra transformations *à la* Reddy and Nanda, or to try and take on a stable feminised subject position, then their status in Boropani society would be compromised and not as assertive as it is.[14] They would be socially and economically subordinated. Not giving up the privileges of being a man (one of the major reasons why they are not castrated), is a crucial aspect of their relatively secure lives in Boropani.

* * *

With such a tautly organised industry, as the coal trade is in the borderlands, opportunities for violence and disputes are always very near. This is exacerbated by the uneven sex ratio, soaring alcohol use and the lack of basic facilities in the area. As a result, depot owners employ hijras for what they consider to be pragmatic reasons and this is why there is the significant presence of the community here. It is considered less risky and more prudent to exclude women and systematically institutionalise the employment of hijras who cannot get pregnant during relations with labourers, thus protecting the trade and businesses. This, alas, does not prevent some hijras from believing that they are able to conceive. Boropani hijras take contraceptive pills in order not to get pregnant. Those who have sexual relations with men take the tablet once a month on the night of the full moon which they believe prevents a baby from forming in their bellies. One of Abed's hijra sisters (married to a woman with whom he has five children) is convinced that he recently had a miscarriage. Were women employed by coal importers in the formal or the organised informal sector to work alongside men, the concern is that they would become pregnant. Not only do depot owners not want a succession of expectant female labourers who are unable to do their jobs, it is also to do with reputation. If it was discovered that female workers in their service had become pregnant (nearly always understood in the language of rape due to patriarchal notions of female sexuality based on the maintenance of virginity before and chastity after marriage), then shame would be brought upon the owner, the business and his family. This would adversely affect trade. Questions over the costs of looking after the baby would also be raised. Women in this way are considered to be a veritable 'ticking bomb' (Mody 2008: 32). This understanding does not deny they have sexuality, but that sexuality is potentially dangerous and needs controlling. Importantly, this exclusion of women is not to do with the safety and sanctity of women themselves, though of course such discourse is often paid lip service to. Were it to be, the fact that they work outside of the depots in the unorganised informal coal trade in worse conditions than men would be a point of concern. During Project days, on the other hand, the existence of large numbers of single men and the social tensions that that potentially created was mitigated against by the presence of families and the concomitant resources for their upkeep, including leisure activities, days off and health facilities.

Amin was born in Boropani to parents who work as coal labourers on both sides of the borderland. She now works as a *babuchi* in the coal depots. Though she usually dresses in the distinct fashion of most hijras, she says her parents and brothers don't suspect anything. I doubt this. They probably do know but as long as it does not question her marriage-ability to a woman, it is tacitly condoned. Amin's *parik*, Basir, is a Bangladeshi labourer who works for an exporter on the Indian side. He comes to Bangladeshi Boropani a few times a month, when he and Amin spend a night or two together as '*shami ar stree*' (husband and wife). Basir brings gifts for his wife from India. He is originally from Sylhet, which is where his female wife and children live. He seldom visits them, but often sends money. Like so many long-/short-term and seasonal migrant labourers, Basir is a young man who is away from home for long stretches of time. Such men create fictive kin as soon as possible, favouring people who are from their home districts. For such migrants, anyone who knows their way around Boropani claims to be able to steer newcomers away from the 'evils' of the place and assist them in finding jobs and a place to stay is a great boon. Many hijra-*panthi/*

parik relationships begin by such associations and the hijra networks are used to support them. The friendship, affection and love, as well as the more practical knowledge the hijras have of the coal industry, the border and of Bangladeshi-Indian Boropani ensures their influential position. Basir describes how in the first week of arrival, his mobile phone was pinched as he slept in the depot office. Obviously still upset by the theft, he suspects one of the labourers to have taken it. Phones are considered so valuable for these migrants, the only way to keep contact with loved ones in village homes, that culprits are treated the same way as cow thieves, despite the animals being monetarily and symbolically more valuable than phones. Through Abed's coal contacts, he managed to persuade the Indian exporter to replace Basir's phone.

Amin shows me a picture of the two of them taken at the local photographic studio. Basir is unexceptional and looks like all the other labourers in the area. He is in his late twenties but is prematurely aged by the sun and hard work. In the picture, he clumsily stands on the edge of Amin's blue silk saree. Amin's left hand holds the *anchal* (end of saree), the right hand is flung over Basir's shoulder in a rather masculine manner. The photo was taken when they married. Basir had to give gifts to Amin's guru. He also gave his new wife a saree, blouse, petticoat and some jewellery, which Amin wears in the photograph. Had he not done so, Amin would have been prevented from marrying by the hijras. Even in marriage, the guru asserts rights over his *cela*. On the night of the *durani* (sex, in *ultapalta*), hijras came together and sang and danced at the depot Amin works in, giving the couple their blessings. Basir's role in wider hijra society is very much ascribed though he is not a hijra himself. No one from his side was present at the wedding. Amin says Basir is planning to take her to India where he has his own quarters in the export depot he works for. Having told me this, she mutters that there is another Bangladeshi coal man who lives on the Indian side that she is flirting with. They haven't yet had sex because the *panthi* is busy excavating a new mine in the hills. 'But what about your husband?' I ask. 'We hijras are all the same. When it comes to *panthis*, we have to have one in the hand and the other one loose. If one leaves us, then we have another to fall back on. If we just have the one, then we will be alone if he leaves'.

It is common knowledge that men who have intimate relations with hijras are lonely and transient migrants with wives and lives elsewhere and so relations with hijras are considered acceptable locally if they are kept discreet. This is particularly so for the labouring classes who are generally regarded by middle-class South Asian moralists, including the old Project residents and the recently arrived NGO staff, as exceptionally licentious. Whilst most assignations between hijras and their *pariks* and *panthis* are fleeting, alongside their heterosexual lives (for both hijra and male lover) which may include marriage to women, some are in regular, long-term relationships with each other. There are many long-term settled men as well as respected and wealthy coal barons (some who have family in Boropani) who take hijra lovers. Such relations are also overlooked. The reason for this can be explained by the general recognition of male sexual needs and even promiscuity, an attitude that is prevalent throughout Bangladesh and across the subcontinent. Khan goes as far as to say that male sexual release is considered to be of the 'pragmatic' variety which assumes that males need release before (or in addition to) marriage. Such needs are frowned upon, but accepted (1997: 280).[15] Parry's work on family life in the public sector steel plant in Bhilai furthers this point. He says that whilst the first, or 'primary', marriage is nearly always within the caste and community, the chances are that it will end. The rates of marital breakdown are apparently extremely high. However, the 'secondary' marriages that are conducted are able to cut across caste and community lines (provided that they belong to one of the Hindu castes) (1999c; 2001). In this way, primary (public) marriage to a woman for both the hijra and her/his lover is the ideal and is what most strive to carry out. The secondary (private) union between a hijra and her/his lover is, on the other hand, for companionate and sexual reasons. Such relations are considered less risky for settled husbands to have because there is no chance of pregnancy or that even greater threat that he will leave the wife and children for the hijra.

Importantly, none of this is to suggest that *panthis/pariks* do not have desire and attraction for hijras, a fundamental basis for such interactions. As with why some Bangladeshi men cross the border to work illegally in India, desire, choice and individual personality are also motivating factors. A lack of appreciation for individual desire is the problem with Evans-Pritchard's (1970) classic anthropological analysis of same-sex relations amongst the Azande tribe. The privileging of structure over desire also shapes Moodie and Ndatshe's (1994) otherwise illuminating account of male mine-marriages in the South African gold mines. Here workers take young and new arrivals as 'mine-wives' under an organised and structured system that is policed and regulated. Both the Evans-Pritchard's and Moodie and Ndatshe texts are reductive and time-honoured in their explanation of non-heteronormative relationships, understood as attempts at replicating male/female relationships. Exploring the works of Foucault and Kenneth Dover on this very subject (the latter whose works on ancient Greek homosexuality heavily influenced the former), James Davidson reminds us that same-sex relations are not 'quasi-sexual', as it is specifically other males that are chosen for sexual relations and not females (2001: 13). What Evans-Pritchard's and Moodie and Ndatshe's analyses lack are prospects for personal agency and individual desire, and the argument put forward of there being a lack of women may simply be a ruse to draw attention away from the obvious.

Panthis and *pariks* are not just Bangladeshi heavers, depot managers, importers and BDR guards. They also include Indian truck drivers, labourers and coal exporters, as well as BSF guards. In keeping with the schemes of racial/caste classification perpetuated by the British and which continue to be potent today, brawny, fair-skinned North Indian ('martial race') border guards, believed to be courageous and virile, are particularly sought after and considered more prestigious by hijras who are all Bengali by birth. This is in contrast to what they believe are 'effete, sexually weaker' and dark-skinned Bangladeshi border guards.[16] Once the traffic in lorries dropping off coal in Bangladeshi Boropani stops in the evenings, it is the human traffic that begins. Amongst the importers and exporters crossing the border are hijras, wearing make-up and their hair puffed up, setting themselves apart from the other inter-lopers. Rendezvous take place as close to the Zero Point as possible because if the lovers were to be caught on the wrong side of the border (rather than being in the company of a hijra), such encounters could become an international affair.

Nearly all sexual relations between *panthis*/*pariks* and hijras involve a monetary transaction. Earning cash in such a way can be financially rewarding though I do not know of any hijra who describes him/herself as a sex worker. They have their own sources of income, often earning more than the men they have relations with. The question arises as to why they require recompense for such trysts. These exchanges lie partly in the hijra's own desire to fulfil personal sexual pleasures. But it is also to do with a specific sartorial performance of femininity. Playing the 'female role' in sexual transactions includes having to perform the role of being sexually unspoilt and pure. The penetrative male, having had his 'wicked way', is then expected to forfeit a payable cost for doing so and compensates the 'innocent and virginal' hijra for the violation. Were they to be 'real' women, the men would have to do the same. Astonished by my question about money, a hijra says 'why would I do this for free? Why wouldn't he pay? If he takes something precious from me, I expect him to give me something in return'. For the hijras, it is important not to appear to desire sexual encounters, as this would lead to allegations of being fast, open and lessen one's desirability. By playing this role, a hijra puts on a 'veil of virtue' (Mody 2008: 145) similar to 'real' women. Were they not to charge, they would be considered base and immoral by *panthis/pariks* and by wider hijra society. The extreme of such polite fiction is that some hijras describe their sexual encounters as *dhorshon* (rape). Individual women do provide commercial sex, though it is not widespread and is much concealed. But were they to exist in larger numbers, this would not affect the desire for hijras, because the latter are not just substitutes for the former, but desired for what they are. They are adept at performing the desired feminine sartorial styles in ways in which 'real women' here do not and cannot. The hijras are at the very least able to pretend to be demur and passive when needs be—considered locally to be ideal feminine qualities—even though it is an abstraction of such traits. They spend much of their spare time preening and beautifying themselves in preparation for such liaisons, which involves precious money, time and resources that women, who work scavenging for coal and as mothers, do not have.

* * *

The Project, in its capacity as the exemplar of modernisation and the state in microcosm, had once provided healthcare, education and electricity in the area. Today it no longer exists, nor does much of what it had once stood for. Commercial companies, individuals and private organisations have stepped in, including a number of NGOs. It was a local NGO worker who had initially informed me of the existence of the hijras after they had approached him to help them set up a formal hijra *shomithi* (committee). He thought it would be an 'interesting experience' for me to meet a 'strange group' of people. I accompanied him to the first meeting they had together. Shomithis have become a 'tool for poverty reduction interventions' in Bangladesh. NGOs form clusters of them in so-called 'poverty stricken areas', the aim of which is to empower, intervene and develop the livelihoods of the poor. The fifteen or so hijras who came to this initial meeting explained to Sam, the NGO worker, that they wanted a shomithi that enabled them to fight for better protection in the coal import depots and which exerts greater influence in the cross-border trade. Furthermore, they wanted lubrication jelly. They had heard from their hijra sisters in Sylhet that foreign NGOs distribute packets of them and they wanted some too (they were led to believe by Sam that I may be a foreign representative of one of these NGOs and would hand them out). Condoms they were less interested in. It was obvious the hijras wanted a shomithi. It was not so obvious that Sam was willing to help them achieve it. He was motivated by prurient curiosity and asked whether they had penises or not, what sexual acts they perform and about the hijra religion which he had heard about. They answered his questions frankly, shocking him even more. The NGO worker's attitude towards the hijras (and also those involved in the coal trade more generally) is reminiscent of a colonial era, paternalistic stance towards those they are supposedly developing. Ann Stoler reminds us that participants in the European colonial enterprise had a voracious interest in the sexual lives of the 'natives'. There was probably no other subject that is discussed more than sex, she says, something which was frequently 'invoked to foster the racist stereotypes of European society' (1989: 635).

Nothing came of this meeting between Sam and the hijras and later, every time I met the individuals who attended, they would pester me about it. I would in turn refer them back to Sam, who showed little interest in taking it any further. It seemed his aim in having the meeting was merely to impress upon me how sexually deviant and debauched a place Boropani truly is, not too dissimilar in this respect to how the old Project aristocracy feel about their neighbours. Regardless, it was obvious that the hijras are already well organised. Their aim in meeting Sam was opportunistic, attempting to exploit the resources that the NGOs promise, something they see other so-called groups of poor also do. None of the hijras present at the meeting were senior gurus. Expecting it to be unproductive, younger *celas* were instead instructed by Abed to attend the meeting. Their actual abilities to organise, exert vigour and energy became evident during the 2008 Bangladesh national elections. Though none of the senior gurus stood for positions, some of their *panthis* and *pariks* did. The hijras played a decisive role in the victory of a number of people including senior members of the Union Parishad (local council). During rallies, they went door-to-door, handing out leaflets and adding colour, music and laughter to the proceedings. Some of the younger hijras wore sarees and made a ditty for their chosen candidate, whose political marker is a tiger. 'The tiger will give, give, give to you', they chanted. 'Why support him?' I ask Abed. 'He is an old *parik* of Kamruls [one of Abed's hijra sisters]. We had to support him. He came to me and said I don't have any help but yours. You must help. So I sent our *celas* to help him'. The returns for such assistance are opaque. At the very least, the hijras have a number of *panthis* and *pariks* that are politically influential. What is apparent is that with friends and lovers in positions of such power, the hijras of Boropani are anything but marginal.

Hostility towards the hijra community comes from a predictable source. The Bangladeshi NGO-wallahs based in the area refer pejoratively to them as 'half-women' (in English), taking the community's visible and assertive presence as well as their 'unorthodox' sexual and living arrangements with other male workers as indication of how depraved the area is. Unable to recognise nuances between Project families (some who share similar attitudes) and coal people, they are vehement in their contempt of Khonighat and Boropani. The coordinator of one NGO, overly fretful about my safety when he discovers I live alone in a Project bungalow, explains that he believes the area to be a magnet for criminals on the run from other parts of the country. 'From here, it is only a hop, skip and a jump to India where our (Bangladeshi) police have no jurisdiction'. Educated up to master's level, the men of development have career ambitions but have (unfortunately for them) been posted somewhere so remote as to be distant from all signs of what they consider to be civilised society. With the growth of mosques and madrassas in the area funded by coal money, imams from other parts of the country are also moving into the area. They are as itinerant as the labourers. Still a relatively new transformation to have occurred in the area, the men of cloth are, as yet, unopposed to the population. As Mohammed the truck driver happily confirms, many of the hijra's *panthis/pariks* include imams and religious school students who live and work in Boropani. '*Era amra ke khub pochondo kore*' (they like us very much). He also says that, not so unexpectedly, NGO staff make up a significant proportion of their lovers. Is there absolutely no opposition from the imams, I ask Mohammed. 'Even if there was, we would say to them that we are also human. Allah made us as He made you', he replies. 'Anyway, if they didn't like us, what can they do? We are from here, they are not'.

It is actually the devotees of a worldly paradise that are most troubled by what the hijras represent: the descendants of the Project aristocracy. In particular, it is a section of that group, people who had left Khonighat for greener pastures after its closure in 1993 and who occasionally return to visit family members and friends, that are most vehemently critical. What this implies is that though the remaining residents have a proclivity to romanticise the glory days of the Project, to remind themselves that though the coal industry and everything it represents reigns supreme, it was not always like it is. However, their actual interaction with the place is robust. They may have disdain for the present, its development and many of its people, but they have reluctantly (and some with their own commercial interests in coal) learnt to accommodate it. Those who left Khonighat on the other hand simply have memories to fall back on. They, like transnational, diasporic migrants, actively remember only a (mythical) past/place/people where they and everyone else were comfortable, healthy and morally good. Their memories do not tally up with present realities. There may even be an element of guilt involved in that they did not remain to prevent such decline. For them, the hijras are the epitome of the moral and physical decay that has taken root in the area over the last thirty years. I am not suggesting that the area was previously unfamiliar with hijras and that they are historically unprecedented. None of my Khonighat friends or neighbours remember hijras working for the Project or even being in the vicinity at all during its roughly thirty years of operation. This is not to say anomalies or even overt or direct challenges to the Project ideology did not occur during its height. Alternatives to the master plan were veiled, so much so that they were probably unseen or unknown outside of a group of like-minded people. The point is that the Project regime had introduced a radical rupture with what had previously existed, that the hijras could not have publically existed and it is only with its fragmentation that they are able to see the light of day.

According to Attik, for example, a social worker who now lives in Dhaka and whose father worked as a clerk in the Project, the area suffers from social problems more akin to those in a city. 'Alcoholism, drug use and violence are on the increase', he says. 'The area has simply degenerated'. I meet him and his friends outside the Hindu temple located on the inside of the Project enclosure. It is Durga Puja. He is telling me his thoughts on the similarities between Bengali Hindus and Bengali Muslims and the importance of brotherhood between them. Two hijra friends from Boropani approach to say hello. Attik is visibly disturbed by their presence. He begins interrogating them. He wants to know how many of them there are, what they do and whether they are married. The hijras reply eloquently to his questions. After they leave, Attik, referring to them as a 'disease', says he has heard that since the closure of the Project the hijras 'have taken over the area'. One of his friends is not convinced that they are 'real' hijras. If they were, he believes they would be 'more shy, coy and feminine' than the ones we just met. A third friend jokingly says that he wants to cut their balls off. 'They have no regard for society or their family'. I was struck by their comments. A few minutes earlier these men were propagating the importance of tolerance and now they are troubled by the presence of difference. Yet Attik and his friends do not represent common sentiments and are in fact in contrast to how Malik and Shorif, Project teenagers who still live in the locality, for example, talk about the hijras. They know individuals from the community, allowing their views to be contextual, based on personal relations. Normally antagonistic when it comes to coal people, they are unfazed by the hijras, considering them to be a part of local society as much as anyone else.

4

A STATE OF RELIEF

The presence of the Bangladeshi state in Boropani and Khonighat is represented by the customs house at the Zero Point (presided over by one official), the rotating contingent of Bangladesh Rifles guards and the Ansar brigade (stationed to protect the Project grounds). The concentration of these categories of employees/institutions in the area indicates the state's concerns and interests at the border: primarily to generate profit from and gain its authority through sanctioning cross-border activities. This feature of the margins of Bangladesh and India has not altered since the formation of the new states at Partition and, if anything, has been exacerbated from then onwards. In addition, there is also the intermittent presence of other state characters in the locality too. During the monsoon months, a district magistrate bases himself at the now decrepit Project guest house from where, each morning, he patrols protected parts of the wetlands to prevent the poaching of fish and birds. Each evening, after setting fire to the fishing nets that he confiscates from illegal fishermen, he listens to complaints brought to him by locals. The magistrate adjudicates on matters that range from issues to do with itinerant children, wastrel wives and alcoholic husbands, to disputes arising from the informal coal trade. Most of the complainants are recent or temporary migrants who work as labourers on either side of the border. Long-term Project residents never take their problems to such a public forum. For them, it offends their bourgeois sensibilities, with some even grumbling under their breath that such proceedings should not be held on Project grounds. Vote-garnering political candidates make visits too. Between elections, they are not seen in these parts again. The nearest bank, police station and health facilities are some hours away in the headquarters of the district subdivision that Khonighat and Boropani are located in. Sunamgonj town, the district's main administrative centre, is around six hours away by boat during the wet season and at least two by motorbike when dry. Locals forced to take their ill family members on this arduous journey may have to go to Sylhet town, a further two hours away, due to a shortage of facilities in Sunamgonj. It is usually the more affluent and most desperate who carry out this expedition.

The reasons for the lack of the state here are more complicated than Aihwa Ong's assertion that there is a 'thinning of state power at ... border zones' (2005: 95). Across Bangladesh, the state is thinned out. In this regard, there is little difference between border and non-border areas. However, in Khonighat and Boropani, present realities are in contrast to what had previously existed during Project days, when, within the perimeters at least, the 'corporeal presence of the state [wa]s potent' (Roy 1994: 105). Project workers and their families had exceptional access to healthcare, housing, electricity and educational facilities. Although it was, at one level, a microcosm of what the state was hoping to become on a larger scale, those who did not work for the Project, or lived outside of it in Boropani, were unable to access the services it provided. These people had to make the long journey to Sunamgonj and so, for many, little has changed over the years. It is no wonder that remaining Project residents feel an acute sense of abandonment and rejection when recalling the past. To be sure, Bangladesh (or the Pakistani state previously) was never a welfare-heavy state as were/are the UK, the former USSR or the United States, for example. Neither was it ever in a position to provide services for the majority of its citizenry. To argue then that, in the neo-liberal era, the Bangladeshi state has retreated, as many observers have, is inaccurate. Modernisation schemes such as the Project were always exceptional. This is what made the Project so extraordinary and its visions so powerful for the people who came to live and work here. Today the single, unitary idea of the state has become a rumour for Project residents (who thought they knew better) and recent migrants alike. Many people here have little to do with the reduced icons of the state that do exist. While these are generally people at the very bottom of the social and economic hierarchy, coal importers and depot managers also complain about the lack of facilities in the area. The argument they put forward (of wanting greater state presence) justifies their evasion of taxes on the coal they import. One such businessman explains:

The government makes lakh lakh taka from us [the coal industry] but would you be able to tell what they have provided in return? The answer is no, nothing. There is no school, no pucca road, nothing. I can afford to go to Sylhet when ill and send my children there to be educated. But, tell me, what about the poor? What are they to do? Tell me, what is the point of paying taxes?

Around the world, there has been a general weakening of the theory and practice of state-led development. Today, local, national and international NGOs carry out roles once expected of the state. Operating with funds, ideologies, instructions and support from national and intergovernmental donor organisations, NGOs are more visible and their works are often more pervasive and diverse than that of the state they operate in. In Khonighat and Boropani, NGOs delivering services include BRAC (Building Resources Across Communities, previously known as Bangladesh Rural Advancement Committee: the second largest employer in the country after the government [Lewis 2010: 9]), ASA (Association for Social Advancement), Sancred (a Norwegian organisation closely related to the Lutheran Church) and also a smattering of very small, grassroots, locally focused organisations that specialise in the wetland region. Sancred members are seen by a doctor for a 20 taka fee for which they are examined, given advice and provided prescriptions. The cost for medicine is extra and more complicated procedures are sent to Sunamgonj. BRAC offers loans to purchase solar-power facilities as well as general business loans. One organisation brings a vet from Sunamgonj a few times a month to treat livestock belonging to members. All of them specialise in microcredit programmes which is how they fund the services they provide. Locals do not remember precisely when NGOs began arriving in the area, but some say Sancred was the first to set up its offices outside of the perimeters of the Project. A neighbour remembers seeing a white woman whom people believed to be a Christian missionary. Apparently her presence was not welcomed by locals who would throw stones at her. In any case, the arrival of the NGOs in the area in the 1990s coincided with the closure of the Project, the opening up of Bangladesh and India's markets and the beginning of the abdication of what many in the borderlands had come to expect of the state.

All over the country, NGOs have become a pervasive sign and symbol of a contemporary modernity. The logos belonging to Oxfam, World Vision and CARE are as omnipresent as any other commercial brand. This is a development which many contrast to their ideal of the top-down state, which plans society and the economy. From bustling towns and cities to the remotest of villages, there are signboards, buildings and processions that attest to their virtues and increasingly their drawbacks.[1] NGOs provide a diverse range of services including healthcare (both rudimentary and more sophisticated requirements), protection from natural hazards, electricity, credit, safe drinking water and education. They carry out programmes on agriculture, animal husbandry, forestry, horticulture, the environment, human rights and social justice. They aim to improve physical infrastructure as well as institution-building and/or create altogether new employment opportunities and ways of living for recipients.

In the 1990s, with international donors feeling that the government had little or no capacity to process the aid coming in efficiently, the rise of the NGO phenomenon began. Donors believed their funds could be spent less wastefully through such private organisations. NGOs also fit into donors' 'new policy agenda' of stressing good governance as well as the wider, long-term ideology of economic and social reforms. Sarah White, author of *Arguing with the Crocodile: Gender and Class in Bangladesh*, observes that on one extreme are the massive projects of multilateral and bilateral donors who strengthen or extend the national infrastructure (roads, bridges or electricity) and on the other is the multitude of smaller organisations using foreign funds for the welfare or development of disadvantaged groups (1992: 12). Today some of the latter organisations are in charge of neighbourhood development projects whilst others run massive enterprises and have (inter)national ambitions and reach. Some observers celebrate the roles they play, seeing them as a crucial force for improving the quality of life of countless Bangladeshis. With the inability of consecutive governments to provide services (whether due to ineptitude and/or lack of resources), these endeavours, it is claimed, contribute to the state's viability and stability, halting the slippage of many more into desperation (White 1992: 12–13).

Critics say that the optimism that NGOs may help to decrease poverty has not proven justified. They argue that the industry has propelled sections of the middle classe into prosperity by providing jobs and access to resources whilst the majority continue to languish at the bottom. Some also claim that their expansion has advanced the 'retreat' or 'rolling back' of the state (Sobhan 1997; Rahman 1999), have 'cut away ground from beneath a still-weak state', eroded public accountability and provided the international aid community with the opportunity to intrude upon domestic policy (Lewis 2010: 10). Geof Wood (1997), for example, believes Bangladesh is moving towards a 'state without citizens', in that, as a result of patronage relationships and structural adjustment policies, it has 'discarded' its responsibilities to its citizens for service provision. Rahman Sobhan, a prominent Bangladeshi academic, writes:

the sovereignty of the Bangladesh nation state, in its prevailing social configuration, is therefore likely to remain a polite fiction which is perpetuated by the courtesy of the donors as long as Bangladesh does not challenge their current strategic assumptions and ideological preconceptions (1982: 226).

* * *

The current formation of the neo-liberal state operates by working alongside non-state actors (e.g. aid organisations, NGOs, volunteers, private companies, entrepreneurs, consultants, security companies) who together bring about and produce state-like effects. In this way, the 'state' in its 'multiple incarnation' continues to be a powerful object of encounter even when it cannot be located as a unitary structure, says Aretxaga (2003: 398). The idea of multiple governing agencies challenges the idea of the state as a single centre of power and can be seen as an extension of 'governmentality'. This is a concept first introduced by Michel Foucault that goes beyond the more simplistic 'weakening' or 'eroding' of the state argument, and is a useful tool to employ in analysing transformations to the state and how various, multiple forms of power are exercised. Foucault put forward the suggestion that power has to be analysed in a multidimensional form taking into account factors such as economy, politics and history. The eighteenth century saw the rise of a new type of sovereign power where the practices of government became 'multifarious and concern[ed] many kinds of people' (both internal and external to the state). This included a multiplicity of differing techniques of domination, discipline and regulation of bodies and populations, leading him to suggest that 'we find at once a plurality of forms of government and their immanence to the state' ([1991] 2006: 134). Foucault questions the notion of the (European) state (the archetypal model) as ever having been a unified, supreme container of power, or ever having 'this individuality, this rigorous functionality, nor, to speak frankly, this importance'. He describes states as 'no more than a composite reality and a mythicalised abstraction, whose importance is a lot more limited than many of us think' (ibid.: 142).

James Ferguson and Akhil Gupta extend the term and formulate the idea of 'transnational governmentality' (2005: 107) to view the contemporary changes being wrought to the state system. The core feature of this idea places the 'governing-practices' of subnational, supranational and other non-state institutions and actors within a single analytical framework. This means exploring the workings of the state alongside those of deterritorialised institutions of global governance such as the World Trade Organization, the International Monetary Fund and World Bank, as well as systems of transnational alliances forged by grassroots activists, NGOs and voluntary organisations. Corporate, globalised media and 'international public opinion' are also amongst this multiplicity of governing agents, all of which work alongside existing, localised actors. Rather than describing these global entities as being 'below', 'above' or even outside of the workings of the state, Ferguson and Gupta say they are in fact 'integral parts of a transnational apparatus of government' and components of an emerging system of transnational governmentality (2005: 121). The fusing of the local and global, they argue, does not replace or necessarily challenge the older system of nation states, but it does transgress, disregard and 'decentre' previous understandings of the developmentalist state framework.

So what roles do states continue to play and, in particular, how do they govern what is happening within their territorial borders? There are two ways to explore these questions. The first is the bureaucratic route which proposes that states in fact facilitate transnational movements. For example, Philip McMichael argues that states remain integral to creating the very conditions needed by transnational capital to operate (2009: 23). Ferguson also says that they are key to providing the contractual legal authority that legitimises the extractive work of transnational firms and 'neither political instability not even civil war threatens such sovereignty' (2006: 207). Sharma and Gupta take the example of the outsourcing and call-centre phenomenon in India to argue that the state itself provides the larger macroeconomic and the critical infrastructure for outsourcing to be possible (2006: 7). Such powers include providing tax and duty exemptions and (subsidised) training and education for Indian graduates who work for multinational organisations. States themselves also benefit from such relations. Graduate employment in call centres helps increase the tax base, boosting domestic spending and provides white-collar employment for educated youth.

A second direction to take in answering how states control their territories in an era of multiple governing agencies is that of increased militarisation. This can be seen both within national territories and also along national borders which interact and combine with existing social and historical factors. In the case of Bangladesh and India, this manifests itself through the heightened securitisation of the Bangladesh–India border, most acutely symbolised by the fence-building programme and the rising number of deaths along the margins of both countries.

* * *

In the borderlands, the reconfiguration of the state has indeed changed from its older, developmental paradigm, involving large-scale infrastructural and social change and resource redistribution (which gave birth to the Project), to its current neo-liberal avatar, with its reduced presence, focusing upon extraction and as a facilitator of multiple agencies that have power to act upon the territory. The state is now merely one of many other multiple governing agents that produce 'state-like effects'. Sometimes these are in competition; often they work alongside one another. As opposed to some of the writers cited above (both supporters and critics of NGOs), neo-liberalism alone has not fractured the link between nation states, sovereignty and territoriality. Instead, post-colonial countries such as Bangladesh have always had fragmentary powers and mediated sovereignty. This is a phenomenon that has simply continued to the present, whereby international donor agencies and regulatory authorities have almost as much authority as states themselves. In this light, Sobhan's forewarning above about international aid 'eroding' Bangladesh's sovereignty is misconceived. The truth is that Bangladeshi sovereignty has always been at the whim of many centres of power. Even before 1971, when the country was established, none radiated from the territorial entity that is contemporary Bangladesh. Sudipta Kaviraj argues that in traditional Indian society, political power was often distributed between several layers of authority stretching from the village, through regional kingdoms, to empires (2000: 142). From the Mughals, through to the East India Company and the British imperial state, power lay elsewhere in Delhi, Calcutta and London respectively. During the Pakistan period, economic and political clout resided in Karachi and Islamabad. Through and beyond the cold war, Washington, Beijing and Moscow were crucial sites for the realities of East Pakistan. The Middle East is also key to this argument, with the majority of the country's population being Muslim but also because a large amount of aid comes from Saudi Arabia today. This, though, is not particularly new; what is, is the myth of wholeness itself and the idea of the unity of the country's sovereignty.

The economic chaos that Sheikh Mujib (head of the Awami League Party and who led the revolt against the Pakistani state in 1971) inherited when he became prime minister was a consequence of the systematic advantaging of the Western wing of Pakistan. The struggle for independence aimed to bring this disparity to an end. But the civil war and the resultant humanitarian crisis made the difficulties of the new country worse. Over 80 per cent of the population lived below the poverty line (van Schendel 2009: 221). Critics on the left insisted Bangladesh implement state socialism and wide-scale land reform. Those on the right saw the solution in economic liberalisation and state support for the private sector (ibid.: 193). In keeping with its declared socialist principles of state capitalism (it received aid and support from India and the Soviet Union), the Mujib government began to nationalise industries, banks and commercial companies (Alam 1995: 95). However, these polices failed to make the industries profitable or pull the country out of a financial quagmire. The strategy further created divisions between social classes, in particular between the government and the business elites. Mujib increasingly responded to the discontent with draconian measures, reliance on a paramilitary force, the Rakkhi Bahini, the amendment of the Constitution to create a presidential form of government and the institution of a one-party state. Soon political stability collapsed and crime and disorder soared.

In this situation, the lure of international aid was powerfully felt and the 'narcotic of foreign aid was injected into the veins of the economy' (Sobhan 1982: 7). Dependence on international funding had already begun to grow in the 1960s when Western aid became easily available for newly decolonised countries. Institutions such as the World Bank and IMF became closely connected to the military dictatorship of the Ayub Khan regime, which 'conceived and underwrote Pakistan's development strategy' (ibid.: 168). Despite concerns that foreign aid might compromise Bangladesh's new found independence, the Mujib government realised that it was key to its survival. Aid revenue grew massively in the early post-independence period and the country became a celebrated 'case of aid-propelled development'.[2] Cold war logic also stated that aid-dependent countries would not turn allegiances to communism. The social and political implication of this period continues to be far-reaching with the professionalisation and institutionalisation of the development sector. Thousands of foreign consultants, volunteers and diplomats descended on Bangladesh. Jobs were created for the new indigenous bourgeoisie in emerging NGOs and myriad development projects across the country. If the Pakistani elite had been aid-dependent, van Schendel writes, the new and much poorer Bangladeshi elite were even more addicted (2009: 220–1).

Following Mujib's assassination in 1975, which the economist Mushtaq Khan attributes to his economic mismanagement (2000: 581–2), the country entered a long period of consecutive military dictatorships. During 1975 to 1990, foreign aid dependence went up still further. This helped to prop up the dictators, but more saliently, brought about fundamental shifts in the country's economic policies, heralding the move away from its founding principles. Hulme and Edwards are correct to suggest that in the area of 'development', 'he who pays the piper, call the tune' (1997: 8). International organisations such as the World Bank and the IMF induced the regimes to liberalise the economy and to accelerate privatisation and structural adjustment. The development strategies that were pursued under the regimes of General Zia and then later General Ershad saw the unpicking of policies laid down by the Mujib government and the increased role to be played by the private sector. Large-scale disinvestment and denationalisation programmes were initiated and industries were returned to former owners. It saw the gradual opening up of the country's economy to foreign capital, an emphasis on export-oriented industries through private enterprise, the promotion of agricultural production and the granting of fiscal and monetary incentives of various kinds (Alam 1995: 90). Neo-liberal reformers envisaged that such steps would resolve the symptoms of the post-independence crisis. The country's elite believed the private sector to be more efficient in directing economic development and the public sector was wasteful, making it even more dependent on foreign aid than it already was. Some disinvested industries registered a decrease in performance and many reduced the number of production lines. A few even closed down (ibid.: 92). The increase in foreign aid had little or no bearing on the poverty situation in the country.

It is at this point that the growth in NGOs began. There was real optimism that they would solve many of the country's problems. Here, a comparison with the past is illuminating. There were many international NGOs carrying out relief work in the country during the crisis of the early 1970s, but relatively few indigenous ones were established. This is because, as Hasan says, there was an anticipation that the government would look after rural people ([1993: 94] Lewis 2004: 307). This point is crucial in appreciating what was anticipated of the state at the time. The state gradually became unable to deliver rural or urban development and the hopes raised first in 1947 and then in 1971 became unrealised. Consequently, as Lewis (ibid.: 307) observes, activists and social entrepreneurs began to search for new organisational structures with which to address public problems (as well as to build personal careers) and the boom in indigenous NGOs began. This is particularly so during the dictatorship period when people were unwilling or unable to enter formal political institutions.

The programme of economic liberalisation initiated under generals Zia and Ershad's dictatorships has accelerated since the establishment of democracy. The first democratic government in 1992 also continued the denationalisation of the public sector, lifted market restrictions and integrated the national economy with the world economy. Institutions that were seen to distort market outcomes, facilitate collective action, centred on a planned economy, labour relations and social policy were targeted and dismantled (Taylor 2009: 29–30). It is during this period that, unsurprisingly, the Project closed down. Ferguson, writing about African states but applicable to Bangladesh, says that the promise of democracy was held out to the citizenry at the precise moment when crucial issues with regards to the economy were taken out of the hands of national governments. Democracy, he cynically argues, became a way of attributing blame to national governments (and by implication to voters themselves) for the failures of national economies and of structural adjustment programmes. At the same time, matters to do with the policies of donors were taken out of the realm of representative democracy (2006: 12). Bangladeshi economist and public intellectual Anu Muhammad states that regardless of whether the government has been a military dictatorship as in the past, or the democratically elected governments of Khaleda Zia (the Bangladesh Nationalist Party) or that of Sheikh Hasina (Awami League), there is little difference in policy with regards to the economy. This is because they all share the same 'class and imperialist interests as that of the international agencies that run the country' (Pegu 2010).[3]

* * *

During the monsoon season I am invited by Tariq, my NGO friend who initially introduced me to Boropani and Khonighat, to accompany him on a 'Relief' that is to take place in the *haor*. I was very keen to observe this most defining of NGO rituals. Crucially, it is from isolated villages such as the one we are to visit, strewn across the wetlands, that the majority of the seasonal and temporary coal labourers in Boropani originate from. During the monsoon, when the waters take over their rice fields, the men and a number of women and children migrate to Boropani and devote their time and bodies to coal. At least some of the money earned in the cross-border coal trade between Bangladesh and India comes back to villages such as this. Tariq has been working for the large European NGO, which I shall call 'Hands Together',[4] based at its regional office in Sunamgonj, for four years. Hands Together runs a number of programmes throughout Bangladesh (one of twenty countries it works in). Its website says that it helps to improve the livelihoods of poor farmers, creating a national market for their products, 'empowering partners to help themselves' and encouraging people to take responsibility for their own development. It was Tariq's visits to Hands Together's many local partners in the Sunamgonj region that had acquainted him with Boropani and Khonighat in the first place. In 2007, an unexpected flash flood destroyed large numbers of homes in a particularly isolated part of the wetlands. The devastation caused was far-reaching even a year later for many of the inhabitants of this geographically precarious region. The 'Relief'—NGO jargon for the distribution of aid materials—was a one-off event to be carried out in a village where one of Hands Together's local partners, which I shall call NAT, had been working in for some years. NAT is a grassroots, community-based NGO that specialises in development projects in the *haor* region.[5] The schemes it runs include setting up *shomithis* (committees) to which it provides ideas and logistics for income generation. But it is microfinance that it is principally concerned with. Over a period of time, affected villagers whom NAT works with were to receive building materials, as well as ducks and goats, all funded by Hands Together. Tariq is in charge of coordinating the programme and I join him on the day corrugated tin is being handed out. Houses here are in the main made out of bamboo and mud, but tin is believed to be more hardwearing. This makes it more desirable even with its drawbacks including being boiling hot in the summer, freezing cold in the winter and deafening when it rains during the monsoon.

On the back of Tariq's Indian Hero Honda motorbike, we follow the now disjointed and broken railway tracks that lead from Khonighat to Poschim bazaar, from where we are to take a boat to the village. As we drive past the BDR camp, I hold my breath and pray that we won't be stopped by the sentry posted at the main steps. I continue to be frequently stopped and asked who I was despite the camp commander's assurance. Sentries would be on rotation from other parts of the border and would not necessarily know anything about the area or its inhabitants. Eventually the ritual just became an annoyance rather than something to fear, though, coupled with all the rumours about beatings and arrests that flew around Khonighat and Boropani, this was always topmost in my mind. When quizzed by the armed men, I would, in my best Bengali accent, say that I was from Dhaka and worked for one of the NGOs based in the area. I would thus confirm what many in the area already suspected I did. This time, however, we were not stopped. During Project days, the limestone from the quarries in Khonighat was transported to Poschim bazaar, uploaded on to barges, and sent to the Chhatak Cement Factory. No longer with a role to play in the moderni sation of cities elsewhere, today Poschim bazaar looks forlorn and stranded, not too dissimilar from the Project itself. As well as being historically and economically marooned, in this season it is also physically so. Other than the one road that leads to it from Khonighat, built upon a high embankment, it is all but surrounded by water. Since the rains began and the bloated rivers overran their courses, water has been steadily collecting in the *haor* around it.

Tariq and I wait on the embankment for a boat. It begins pouring with heavy rain. Winds from the West Khasi Hills accompany it, causing waves to form in the water and lash up against the high ground. I notice a patchwork of squares and rectangles buried in the water. These are ordinarily the demarcations of fields that are planted with rice during the dry seasons. This water does not constitute a flood in itself. It is expected and what makes the region so fertile and is crucial for its agricultural cycles. But increasingly, with the build-up of silt—a consequence of trees being cut down higher up in the hills—the water stays for longer, causing havoc to those in the plains. The rainy season is a boon for the coal trade and is its busiest period. Out in the waters, an armada of engine-driven barges laden with black gold beat their way through the elements, heading for Dhaka as well as other parts of the country. With no sign of the boats that ply people around the *haor* during the rainy season, Tariq confides that he is nervous about the distribution. Heated words have already been exchanged between Hands Together's regional office in Sunamgonj, NAT and the villagers expecting relief. The list of names that was originally drawn up of people who are to receive the building materials and the livestock, supposedly the most severely affected by the devastation in 2007, had to be redone. According to Tariq, NAT employees had filled it with names of their own relatives and clients, arguably denying those who are the neediest. The Sunamgonj office had learnt of this through informal channels and instructed NAT's staff to redo the list, threatening otherwise to deny it of any future project work and funding. The second list that was drawn up had a different set of names, but, as Tariq explains 'there is no way of checking the validity of the revised list. We just have to go on trust that what they say is correct. But personally, I am not convinced'.

What adds to Tariq's troubles is that Hands Together's country head office in Dhaka has ordered the regional office in Sunamgonj to ensure that the distribution goes ahead without any glitches. This is despite the problem on the ground with the lists, something that would take time to iron out, if at all. The source of this dictate is Hands Together's main donor office in Europe. The European head office is answerable to their own national government, tax payers, international and corporate donors it receives funding from and (to a limited extent) the Bangladeshi government; but not to those the policies it implements most impinges upon. This draws attention to the uneasy fit of the multiple governing agencies, policies dreamed up in global cities and multinational institutions and practices that are rolled out on the ground in developing countries. Tariq says this sort of thing happens frequently, where:

[the European capital] and the Dhaka office expect field staff to carry out programmes following their schedules and timetables. This may be good for them, but may not be appropriate for those we are working with ... Sometimes they don't know or care that what they want us to do makes no sense here.

As if to underscore the nervousness he feels, as we wait for a boat, Tariq receives a phone call from his staff still expecting us at the village. They have been sworn at by people whose names have been erased from the original list and who will no longer be receiving aid. With no alternative way of getting to the village, Tariq talks about turning back and cancelling the distribution. The recipients will have to go empty-handed and the barge hired for the day to transport the corrugated tin will return to Sunamgonj, its cargo intact. This will mean added costs which officials in Dhaka will invariably complain about and the donor will disapprove.

Suddenly, a tiny rowing boat appears on the horizon, steered by two soaking wet little boys. They look like they have barely passed their tenth birthdays. One tries to keep the boat on course, the other paddles vigorously. Despite my inevitable reluctance about getting in, I am persuaded that the journey to the village is not far and that everything will be well as the boys have already been doing this for much of their short lives. However, Tariq warns me (not very reassuringly) that if we capsize the trick to surviving the waters is not to swim against the current but to go with it when one will eventually reach land. The waves beat the vessel, threatening to overwhelm us. The boys avoid the coal barges along the way. Their sides, garishly painted with images of buxom Dollywood actresses and lotuses (the national flower), are incongruent in the scene. The nervousness on my face becomes a source of entertainment for the boys. 'We have experienced much worse conditions, older brother', they say. 'What will happen to them if we do capsize?' I ask. 'Don't worry', Tariq consoles. 'They are survivors. They will be fine'. At such a moment, wondering what the European donor office and their earnest tax-paying patrons would make of our dependence on child labour and their, albeit implicit, proximity to it, does nothing for my fears.

The boys eventually row up to the village. One can make out that it is situated upon raised land in the middle of the water. Surrounding it are lush green trees and vegetation that hold the soil (now wet mud) in place. The only pukka building is the one school, which also serves as the flood and cyclone shelter, occasional administrative office and now, relief distribution centre. Other than this, there is no physical presence of the state here. There is no electricity, bureaucracy or health facility. The women and children follow Tariq around as if he were the Pied Piper of Hamelin as we ungracefully squelch into a classroom with mud-sopping sandals, disrupting the lesson taking place. The select group of sixty or so villagers that are to receive aid have been waiting for us since daybreak. By now it is mid-afternoon. Boredom adorns their gaunt, rain-sodden faces. Nearly all are women. They are skinny and possibly part of some national statistic that states that they only have access to one or two simple meals a day. The men of the village of working age are either in the mines in India hewing coal, or else in Bangladeshi Boropani labouring in the transportation-end of the trade. This is the busiest period in the year for them when they have the opportunity to make extra money to relinquish at least a little of their indebtedness to village moneylenders as well as NGO microloans. The coal trade has little use for the few men who are either old or physically and/or mentally infirm, reliant on brawn as it is. Some able-bodied men have been called back to the village to help mothers and wives with the sheets of tin they will receive. Being here brings into sharp relief how dependent people in the border region are to the cross-border coal industry not just for economic reasons but also for social reproduction. Nonetheless, whilst the industry has invariably benefitted some, in particular those with previous connections to the Project, the liberalisation of the economy has not financially or materially improved the lives of the majority of its workers.

Tariq holds court in the classroom. His two staff members stand behind him. He begins the proceedings by impressing upon the villagers that his staff should be able to work in the area without being harassed. At this point, a woman, sensing I may be the weak link in the official show of force, beseeches me. She has already received the bamboo poles which NAT and Hands Together had distributed previously but will not be receiving any of the tin. 'I was on the first list of names, but not on the second. What am I to do with just a bunch of poles?' Tariq though continues undeterred. He looks slightly anxious but also extremely authoritative as he talks. Though he is only in his late twenties, his university degree and the backing of the foreign NGO give him the confidence to do so. The villagers refer to Tariq as 'officer', addressing him as 'sir'; terms of deference traditionally used to address government bureaucrats, illustrating how boundaries between the state and the NGO sector are blurred. Tariq is one of increasing numbers of bright and energetic young Bangladeshi graduates in recent years to have opted to work for NGOs, who in an earlier age would have hoped to work for the government. 'Hope' being the operative term, as public sector jobs were always limited and difficult to get hold of without connections and/or leverage. There is a widespread perception that there are more opportunities and better pay and conditions working for NGOs (especially foreign ones), than there is within government employment. Nonetheless, public sector positions are still held in high regard despite (or because of!) being associated with corruption, sloth, ineptitude and patronage. Tariq says he would prefer a stable, permanent government job, even with less pay, than a better paid NGO one. With the emergence of flexible labour markets having entered all areas of work, he also has to reapply every couple of years for his position and is hence unable to plan for the future in case he is made redundant or the programme he works for folds. He aims to make the switch to the other side once he has put in sufficient time working for Hands Together. It would be extremely difficult for him to get a government job had he not done so in this way.

Lewis too finds that the boundaries between governmental, business and civil society are extremely ambiguous but nonetheless continue to be constructed and maintained by the agents themselves, as well as those on the receiving end of their resources and services. The 'three sector model' has been created on the basis of a supposed structural separateness between them. Maintaining their clear identities is essential to the idea of 'synergistic partnerships' between government, the marketplace and NGOs which form a central component of widely adopted policies of 'good governance'. Lewis argues that the myth of institutional distinction is oversimplified and at odds with everyday experiences and that, once constructed, there is an ongoing need to police the boundaries between them (2010: 21). Professional movement between the govern-

ing agencies, for example, is common during careers as are social interactions (2010: 1/5). Furthermore, in Bangladesh the blurred boundaries
between the different agencies is a contentious matter that has in the
past flared into violence due to the politicisation of NGOs and the
patronage between NGOs aligned to political parties.

One of Tariq's two staff members is Sam, the prurient NGO-wallah
who had initially introduced me to the hijra community in Boropani
bazaar. The other is a woman. It is she that the irritated villagers had
been particularly abusive towards. Needless to say, her sex made her a
soft target for their frustrations with her chasteness being called into
question. 'She has come all the way from dry land to this wet land to
help you. She doesn't need to do this', Tariq chastises. 'She is also someone's daughter, someone's wife. She should not have to hear bad things
said about her'. Tariq attempts to talk to some of the group representatives of the *shomithi* to appeal to what, he believes, are common gendered aims and sympathies. These are a handful of women from the
village who have been elected by the rest of the *shomithi* to represent
them in all matters relating to NAT's work. They have experience of
labouring in the coal industry, and with it all of its concomitant issues
as working women. Having group representatives is not only for pragmatic reasons, but in the discourse of contemporary development they
are part of an emerging social agenda which supposedly improves the
public 'visibility' and status of women, encourages 'participation' and
'democratic decision-making' and contributes to wider 'community
development' and 'empowerment'.

Sharma and Gupta (2006: 21) argue that initiatives such as group
representatives attempt to teach people, in this case women, how to
build their 'capacities' and become 'self dependent, responsible citizens
who can take care of their own welfare and govern themselves'. This they
say is a further example of the 'neoliberal unloading' of public services
on to 'empowered and responsibilised selves and communities' and must
be seen in the framework of the global circulation of neo-liberal discourses of good governance, the strengthening of civil society, privatisation and the roll back of the welfare state. The outcome of this varies. At
this precise moment and in this precise place, the success of the group
representatives seems questionable. The women simply huddle next to
one another on the bench allocated them, not saying a word. They chew
on the ends of their sarees in trepidation and seem very uncomfortable

at being called to speak in public by Tariq. This is in particular because they may find themselves at odds either with their own neighbours or with the authority (and prospective resources) of the NGOs. The group representatives, it seems, do not consider the female development worker to be one of their own, or at the least, not one worth defending. Her education, class, job and language are more effective dividers than her gender is a unifier. These women seem a world away from those Aminur Rahman writes about, members of the Grameen microcredit bank, who he says are 'more vocal and articulate compared to other women in the village who are not … members' (1999: 95). In fact, here, it is women not receiving and who have nothing to do with NAT and Hands Together's development work who are the most vocal in expressing their disapproval of the erasure of names off the list.

At this point, a self-appointed village representative, a man with traditional social capital as opposed to the group representatives who are in effect slates for the development workers to work on, begins to shout about the lists. He is angry and demands to see the original, accusing Tariq and his staff of cheating the recipients. It becomes obvious that the villagers cannot, or, rather, do not, differentiate between the representatives of Hands Together and those of NAT whom they had, up until then, been dealing with. It is not too surprising that this is the case. Tariq's two colleagues were previously employed by NAT. Furthermore, with the majority of the funding and project work that NAT does coming from Hands Together, all taking place conveniently under the banner of 'partnerships', the institutional separateness between the two is only notional. Is NAT a grassroots organisation? Is Hands Together an international organisation? Ferguson and Gupta argue such entities not only do not fit easily within the 'state' versus 'civil society' grid, but they cannot easily be labelled 'local', 'national' or 'international' either. They at once embody a significant local dynamic and are at the same time a product and expression of powerful national, regional and global forces (2005: 117). But the myth that they are independent is something that both NAT and Hands Together attempt to maintain, though it is at odds with everyday experiences, leading to the evident tensions.

Tariq warns me that the last thing he wants is to get involved in a long protracted argument with the villagers, in particular because he fears a physical altercation over the lists may be likely. He suspects that some of the people on the original list may have paid *goosh* (a bribe) to NAT representatives (not the two assistants) to be on it, hence why they may be particularly cross at being struck off. The fee may have been a few hundred takas, but nonetheless would still have been cheaper than buying tin on the open market. The practice of charging a fee for services that should be free for users is generally morally condemned in mainstream Bangladeshi society, but it is in fact extremely common when dealing with official government bureaucracies. In the borderlands, this includes paying the border guards to sanction illegal mining in the border zone, to ensuring paperwork is processed by the customs official, the 'greasing of the palms', so to say, allows things to happen. It is plainly a bureaucratic working practice that has seeped into the privatised realms, further collapsing the distinctions between the various governing agencies operating here and their behavioural practices. Importantly, the distribution is taking place just before the 2008 Bangladesh national elections and Tariq's concern is that local 'big mouths' may use the issue as a platform to garner support for their campaigns. He tries to take charge of the situation, telling the accuser that if he so wishes, he is welcome to go to the Hands Together office in Sunamgonj where they have copies of the first list. 'But for today, I have been instructed by my managers to distribute tin only to people whose names are on the second list'. The man responds that if he were to go to Sunamgonj, it would mean losing a second day's wages. He works as a coal labour *netha* in Boropani and has already lost income from having to stay in the village that day. Tariq says that Hands Together will be happy to refund his journey if he can provide receipts for it. This is of course a cheap trick, a receipt being a commodity that no one in the wetlands deals with. The distribution finally begins, overcoming any nascent attempt at resistance against the NGO staff by aggrieved villagers.

Tables are taken out of the classroom and set up on the veranda and the captain of the barge and his assistant haul out the dull, metallic sheets on to the deck. Despite them all being officially known to the local NGO staff, there is little trust between the givers and the receivers with an implicit fear that the villagers may storm the barge. The poor are inherently distrusted in this country of poor people. I have become accustomed to this and would experience it frequently and in a variety of ways. They are thought of as being dishonest, dirty, carriers of disease and peddlers of social ills (perhaps not too dissimilarly from the way international donors view Bangladesh and the people of the Third World generally as the particular programmes directed at them show). It is not just amongst the wealthy and influential that this attitude is pervasive, but amongst those of more modest means, as well as the 'poor' themselves. During the many lectures I endure from NGO staff stationed in Boropani, the importance of my safety and of not mixing with locals (i.e. the coal labourers) is always at the top of the agenda. The NGO-wallahs are on the whole young, university-educated men, ostensibly liberal, secular and open-minded individuals who put high value on female education and emancipation. However, when it comes to ideas about the *ghorib* (the poor), their comments and ideas seem to be a familiar blast from the colonial past. But rather than the topic of criticism being 'the natives', here it is their own countrymen. This attitude is clearly a remnant of the colonial state, where distrust underlay the relations between the governed and the governor, a discourse and practice which entered the workings of the post-colonial, developmental and now the neo-liberal state.[6] As one NGO man, his face firmly in a newspaper, scanning adverts for a new job (dreaming of the day he can move to Dhaka away from 'un-civilisation') once explained to me:

You have to be careful. Imagine if one of them leaves a gun in your room, calls the BDR and gets you arrested. Or even, you are invited to one of their homes and find a girl in there and the family force you into marrying her ... You know Boropani used to be a jungle and these people came, cut it all down and took over the land. They are all criminals. You can tell who they are from the kind of lives they lead. It's in their blood. You have to be careful. It's taken me three years to work out the people here. They are not good. None of us NGO staff mix with them.

It seems that the very work they do in 'development' exacerbates the suspicion and lack of trust. Fear and stereotypes intermingle with the feelings of superiority and the burden of responsibility to 'civilise and develop' the unfortunate. It is worth noting that such attitudes among government-employed development workers were one of the things it was hoped that funding through NGOs would overcome. The fact that the *shomithis* they organise in the border region on the whole make a living not from agriculture and fishing (as the deserving poor) but in the quasi-legal cross-border coal trade intensifies this attitude. This is regardless of the fact that their organisations benefit financially from the regular microloan repayments made by coal labourers, with added bonuses and commissions. But instead of attempting to better the working and living conditions of their members, the men of development take a morally superior stance against those they work with and do nothing.

Before the actual distribution can begin, Tariq makes a further announcement. Rather than receiving six sheets of tin, as previously pledged, everyone on the list will be getting five. Some groan, but these are desperate people; they are used to broken promises and disappointments. This is particularly so during election time, when 'everything under the sun is promised us, but nothing is ever delivered', as one villager explained. Tariq does not publically announce why this is, but he tells me later that it is because NAT, as well as having responsibility for drawing up the list of receivers, had been in charge of procurement. Senior members of the organisation had embezzled funds, meaning fewer sheets were eventually bought. Not just this, but the sheets were in fact '*dui nombori*' (second rate).

Tariq's colleagues had already handed out chits of paper to the recipients which had their and their father's names written on it. When a name is called out, the recipient goes to the table where Sam matches the chit to the official list. He/she then either signs or prints their thumb indicating that they have received. They then show the ticket to Tariq who stands on the barge and five sheets of tin are passed down. Older men and women are able to sign their names. Not having held a pen in their hands for some time, their signatures are child-like scrawls, but nonetheless, they are able to sign. One woman, offended by the assertion that she may need the ink pad, states 'I want the pen. I know how to write my own name'. Some youngsters, collecting on behalf of others, cannot do what the old woman is able to and stamp their thumbs. The difference between the two is indicative of a time not so long ago when it was believed that education would help people and the nation itself out of poverty: an aspect of the modernisation theory that has lost the sway that it once had. This is not to say that everyone in the past knew how to write their name. The ledgers I discovered in the Project quarters show that the majority of labourers put thumb prints on payment sheets and did not sign. This of course does not indicate whether they were literate or not, but what it does reaffirm is that the benefits of modernisation were only for a few and not all. Furthermore, across Bangladesh today, literacy rates and the numbers of children attending state schools, in particular girls, are on the rise and is something that is internationally recognised and praised.

Chits and sheets of tin are exchanged, counted and dispensed. Women carry them on their heads. Some cut their hands on the sharp ends of the metal. The wind pushes a piece over on the ground, narrowly missing a child's face. There are constant complaints and grumbles from villagers, almost like it was expected of them. It seems to be the customary way of behaving towards authority, in the same way that it is Tariq's to look commanding and official towards them. 'What is the point of five sheets of tin? You can't even build a toilet with five. You need eighteen in total to build a house'. Someone else retaliates 'when you go to a wedding, you don't expect to eat all the food, do you? So why complain so much?' I meet a coal labourer in the throng. He has been called back from Boropani by his aged mother to help her with her allotted tin. He earns roughly 300tk per day by lugging coal sacks from the depot area to the river. Each sheet of tin on the other hand costs 400tk. What will you do with the tin? 'I will strengthen my house with them', he replies. 'Half of my mud house was washed away in the flood'. Tariq believes some of the recipients will go on to sell their donations. Despite NAT's chicanery, what is abundantly clear is that those who have been struck off the first list seem as poor and needy as all whose names are on the second list. By denying aid to the first listers, Hands Together believes it is taking an explicit moral stance against what it labels 'corruption'. It expects to wipe clean such ingrained cultural and operational practices and exercise its own 'organisational culture' (Lewis 2003: 214).[7]

Corruption, one can deduce from this line of reasoning, is at the root of social, economic and political impediments. In cases such as this, the consequence of such explicit practices (i.e. Hands Together denying certain villagers aid and then later terminating its relationship with NAT altogether over their combined 'aberrant behaviour'), is that by neatly sidestepping the messy business of community development and village-level politics, one lot of poor are simply dodged over for another. There are no real challenges made to the more engrained structural reasons that cause the payment of *goosh* in the first place. The cause of the villagers' frustration is not just to do with them handing over money—which is no small matter—and the incumbent uncertainty over whether they may get it back, but because of the confusion, inconsistency and ambiguity created as to how they are to operate in the public realm and with the multiple regimes of power. If the payment of *goosh* (as requested) does not materialise or create the intended aim and attempts at negotiating for these services fail, then the system they have hitherto known and operated within is simply ineffectual and inadequate, further highlighting the villagers' own sense of alienation.

Back in the classroom, youngsters who have not been inside one for a while though still old enough to have been at school, commandeer the chalk and doodle on the blackboard. 'We don't go to school', they say, smiling, exposing iron-eroded teeth. 'Can you read and write?' 'No', they say nervously. 'We work in Boropani as day labourers. We don't need to know how to read and write to do that'. They laugh. 'If you are not careful', I say, frustrated, 'then soon, you too will be waiting in the rain for tin'. 'What are we to do, older brother? We have to eat and feed our families. If knowing how to read and write would do that, then of course we would. We are not stupid'. I watch people tend to their freshly cut wounds as arguments over the lists as well as the rain continue unabated.

More accusations and counteraccusations of corruption are hurled when a member of the Union Parishad arrives. His belated appearance in the village coincides with our preparations to leave. All the tin has been distributed. The member is furious at Tariq for not consulting him before the distribution occurred, implying that as a publicly elected state official his authority is greater and has been called into question. According to Tariq the member was told about it. The man conflates Hands Together and NAT, insinuating that the staff of both organisations have been cheating villagers. With the impending elections, his opportunism is obvious. He plays on the increasingly generalised views of NGOs in Bangladesh as simply being interested in the material well-being of their staff and not the people they are supposed to be helping. This also draws attention to the practical knowledge of the multiplicity of governing agencies that the villagers have. They are willing to accept the resources of the NGOs, but when they feel aggrieved, turn to others within the conglomeration that produces state-like effects, even (un)consciously pitting one organisation against another. The member threatens Tariq, telling him not to set foot in his constituency ever again. One is left thinking that if he is exemplary of the quality of representative democracy in Bangladesh, there is little doubt why the country's poor suffer so much.

On the deck of the barge back to Khonighat, it all seems so futile. By the end of it, the only sign of relief is on the faces of Tariq and his staff, glad to be leaving the area. The villagers look as disgruntled and unsatisfied as when we arrived, their experience of the various governing agencies leaving them none the wiser on what to do, or whom to turn to next time an unexpected flash flood destroys their homes. Regardless of who or what the state is and even in its multiple forms, it has abandoned these people, its citizens. The floods will return, simultaneously a need and a tragedy for the people who live and work in the cross-border coal trade. The multiple governing agents will go through the motions, giving the impression that 'something is being done' to alleviate suffering (in the extreme cases) and 'development' is being carried forth to those who require it in the everyday sense. The system that causes poverty, alienation, exploitation or marginalisation is not tackled, the status quo remains unquestioned. It is no surprise why the dwindling number of residents of the Project, as well as many others in Boropani who simply live and work alongside the decomposing public sector installation today, hanker for a future that was never delivered.

5

TEMPLES OF BELIEF

It is Ramadan, the month of fasting for observant Muslims culminating in the Eid festivities heralding its end. Even though they are dictated by different calendars, it is a coincidence that Durga Puja (the worship ceremony of the goddess Durga, the most revered out of the pantheon of deities for Bengali Hindus) is to follow Ramadan/Eid. There is excitement everywhere; tailor shops are full and sweet and toy stalls spring up for the period. Family members of Hindu and Muslim Project residents who live in other parts of Bangladesh trickle into Khonighat. This happens as migrant coal families, managers, labourers and all of the industry's ancillary workers begin surging out of the area to spend Ramadan/Eid and/or Durga Puja in their villages of origin. These population movements are unequal in size. The people arriving are simply a hundred or so, whereas those leaving the borderlands are literally thousands upon thousands. It is impossible to tease apart which festival those remaining in Khonighat and Boropani are most enthused about. The uncomplicated rationale would be that Muslims are slightly more excited about 'their own' celebrations of Ramadan and Eid whilst Hindus are equally so with Durga Puja. To be sure, there are indeed people here who are only interested in 'their own' religious celebrations, though this is not necessarily the case for everyone. Many Hindus and Muslims—those who practise, are nominally sympathetic and those who are altogether (non)observant—seem equally as thrilled by the prospect of both celebrations. There is little or no exclusivity between the two events.

Similar to the way national allegiance and citizenship works in the borderlands, religious affiliation operates in equally opaque but pragmatic ways. Most people know whether they are Indian or Bangladeshi (as in by birth) as they know whether they are Muslim or Hindu. Though in spite of this—or rather, as a result of it—at times they function by traversing the borders between the two areas as if none exists and at other times circumnavigate away from the so-called margins as much as possible. With two religious holidays taking place back-to-back, breaks from work, visits home and time with family and friends are longer than usual. As a neighbour explains, people are 'twice as happy'.

But it is not just the Eid and Puja festivities that cause this excitement. The rituals for operating around the border area change during times of religious celebrations when the very people with responsibility to protect the lines of demarcation, the border guards, show the most 'leniency' towards those they are ordinarily 'protecting' them against. The border is made '*kula*' (open) and the BSF, as well as the BDR, allows Indians and Bangladeshis to visit either side without restrictions. This suggests that it is not just the borderlanders who live and work here who see the landscape in more complicated ways than in just binary opposites. The locally based state apparatus, in this case the border guards, are able to do so too. In reality, there is nothing physically different about the border area during such moments of relative relaxation. It is simply that crossing the line of demarcation by ordinary citizens is permitted without harassment from border guards. Bangladeshis are able to go '*bhitore*' (inside), as locals refer to India, take photographs of themselves on the hills, shop in Indian Boropani and needless to say, openly drink alcohol in the shacks there. Indian visitors to the Bangladeshi side partake in equally innocuous activities that are normally policed against: they watch Bengali films in cinema-huts, visit friends and relatives and shop for mobile phone accessories in the bazaar.

During Ramadan, I discover that most of my friends from both Khonighat and Boropani, who self-identify as Muslim, have a variety of different approaches towards fasting and in particular their religious beliefs and commitments. Abed, the hijra guru, does not fast at all. He explains that because his wife and mother do, he considers this to be sufficient. I heard this rationale from other male informants. Abed's behaviour during the holy month does not change in keeping with the occasion. He smokes, has sex and drinks alcohol, activities that are forbidden during the period. A note on the door of his tea shop bears the injunction 'WE REMAIN OPEN FOR OUR HINDU BROTHERS'. Inside, anyone would be forgiven for thinking that there are no restrictions against eating, drinking or smoking during daylight hours for Muslims. For that is what they are in the main and not Hindu. Most are locals and have not been travelling, which exempts one from fasting. All are men so neither are they menstruating, another source of exemption. (Women who work in the coal trade do not generally frequent the tea shops, which are on the whole male-only spaces.) There are more customers here than usual because the owners of other tea shops in Boropani have left for their rural villages. Those who ordinarily eat at home are also here as their wives and mothers are preparing *iftar* (the meal that breaks the fast) and on whom there is greater societal onus to fast. The majority are manual workers for whom it is impossible to go without food or drink in light of the physically demanding work they do.

One day, as I am having my lunch, a brawl breaks out in Abed's tea shop. The disagreement is over how much money one man owes the other. Abed warns the fighting duo and their quickly assembling entourage to end their raucous behaviour but it nonetheless continues. Abed goes over to the main door, pulls the curtains apart, thus exposing the people inside. In a flash, the entire space is cleared of customers lest they are seen by those outside as openly disregarding the rules of fasting. This level of piety and praxis is in marked contrast to how Ramadan is performed elsewhere. Samuli Schielke's work on Egypt, for example, describes how all forms of prohibited behaviour, including entertainment deemed 'immoral' or 'un-Islamic' stops during the month. For his Egyptian informants, Ramadan is more than just about fasting. It is a 'social, moral and pious commitment' and a 'spiritual exercise in disciplining carnal desires' (2009: 26). He says people discuss in detail the correct forms of prayers that need to be made, the consequences of not observing Ramadan and the exact details and ways to maximise the rewards gained. Rather than this being the norm in Muslim societies generally, one can argue that the reason for it in Egypt is the very specific Islamist revivalist movements that have taken place there, giving rise to puritanical understandings of the faith. This is something which, as yet, is generally not a common feature in Bangladesh, though with increasing inroads made into society by Islamism and with the pressure to homogenise as part of a 'global Islam', it is becoming so.

There are many in Khonighat and Boropani, on the other hand, who do take the month seriously and who I speculate are in the majority, but they too negotiate how and what they do. Habib, for example, is a coal depot manager. He not only fasts but goes to *terrabi* prayers (the special prayers following the breaking of fast) in the evenings. He attempts to persuade friends to do likewise. With all sorts of distractions, one has to be truly committed to go as it can last anything up to an hour and a half. A migrant from the south of the country who has been resident in Boropani for fifteen years, his parents did not deem it necessary for him to learn the Quran when he was young so he performs the prayers by mimicking those around him. (Here it may be prudent to understand Islam not as a religion of beliefs, but one of praxis [(Cantwell Smith 1957) Reddy 2005: 46].) Habib never goes to the mosque or prays outside of Ramadan. Always with a convenient excuse for why he is unable to do so, he is on the whole irreverent towards outward displays of religiosity, flouts Islamic doctrines and norms (his dream is to drink French champagne) and is suspicious of the power that imams wield. 'Hell will be full of men who spent their lives on earth with Allah's name on their lips', he would often say. He tells the anecdote of an imam to illustrate how morally corrupt he believes them to be:

an imam wanted to change the name of Boirob [an area outside of Dhaka] because he considered it to be Hindu in origin. He wanted to change it to one that is more Islamic sounding. The campaign is successful and succeeds in changing the name. Afterwards, he says we [Muslims] have to take over the bazaar. We need to bring Islamic decorum to it. We have to take over and occupy each and every shop. That is, every shop, except the one that belongs to a specific Hindu shopkeeper.

Habib explains that this is because the imam knows the shopkeeper has a beautiful daughter who he desires. 'All he wants is to have the skin of a Hindu woman'. In exchange for his daughter, the Hindu shop-keeper is able to keep his business.

The moral of the story is that men of religion abuse their power and are motivated by lust, power and greed. So, for some in Khonighat and Boropani, Ramadan is treated with indifference. It is a period of elaborate ploys and subterfuges, their lives continue as normal, managing the potential pitfalls when asked loaded questions. For others who rarely pray, have no totalising approach to religion and where ambivalence is part of the normative order, Ramadan is an opportunity to repent, spiritually cleanse and commune with Allah, something they have possibly evaded the rest of the year. The point to keep in mind is that there is no unified or agreed upon way of being a Muslim here. They are cross-cut by a variety of factors, including the region of Bangladesh they originate from, the work they do, their class and education. But more fundamentally, it is the relationship they have to the past. Project descendants, Hindu and Muslim, are more likely to have more in common with each other than their religious counterparts in Boropani.

A relatively new way of being Muslim in Boropani is summed up by the chairman of the Boropani Coal Importers Association. Chairman Babar was a labourer in the Project until it shut down. Afterwards, he, like many others, turned to the coal industry and over the years he has amassed wealth and respect. Today he is very influential in the region. One of his social responsibilities is the role he plays at the Khonighat high school, which he funds. Frequently the guest of honour at ceremonies there, he is treated with respect by teachers and students alike. Having originated in that particular milieu, it is their respect he seeks, acting as the bridge between the new coal barons and the old Project elites. As the last working facility in Khonighat, the school is central for the remaining residents, acting as a touchstone to the past. It remains a bastion of secular modernism that the Project as a whole had once instigated, continuing to propagate its values in the present. The overwhelming majority of the students and staff are Muslim, but the current head teacher is Hindu whose family have been resident here since the Project started in 1965. In the classrooms are framed photographs of the writer Rabindranath Tagore, the national poet Kobi Nazrul Islam and General Osmani (head of the army during the War of Independence in 1971), figures which secular Bangladeshi nationalists have propagated as their prophets. Such images are common in government schools across the country and represent Bangladeshi nationalism devoid of religious sentiment. Military drills are performed weekly by Hindu and Muslim students, inspiring civic bonds. There are regular Bengali cultural events, involving singing and dancing which Islamists in other parts of the country have equated with 'un-Islamic' behaviour. A teacher at the school explains that there is much enthusiasm for cultural activities amongst his students, but few teachers teach these, concerned it would cause offence to conservatives. During a musical performance that I attended where Chairman Babar was the guest of honour, everything came to a halt when the *azaan* from the mosque sounded. No one, other than the chairman, left to pray. On his return, the female student resumes her singing of the Tagore song.

What is most interesting about the chairman is that although he looks for admiration from the old, secular Project guard, at the same time he attempts to gain social capital from Islamic modernity. For example, he is always shrouded in pristine white *djellabas* and shawls that he acquires while on pilgrimages to Saudi Arabia. His generosity and public spiritedness also extends to the local madrassa, which he funds. This is similar to Magnus Marsden's observations in Pakistan, where he says it is often assumed that the emerging middle classes are attracted to conservative Islam and to reformist parties such as the Jama'at-e-Islami. Yet in Chitral, in Northern Pakistan where he carried out fieldwork, this is complicated by the reality that the emerging elites—some of whom are certainly pious and reform-minded in their approach—seek to convert their wealth into respect by investing in and associating with local cultural groups. These groups are often critical of (and themselves criticised by) puritanical Muslims; however, alliances with them allow the new elites to be presented in a favourable light (2005: 151–3). Gardner and Osella argue that an emulation of orthodox Islamic codes (including Arab styles of dress) is an attempt at consolidating and helping to legitimise recently gained wealth and social status (2003: xvi). Though they write in regards to South Asian migrants to the Middle East, the same argument can be applied to Chairman Babar who is a domestic migrant. Such practices may seem to be backward and anti-modern (it certainly is contradictory to earlier modernisation theory), but religious reform in both instances must be understood within a discourse of multiple modernities. Babar's support for an institution with an ethos of secular, Bengali nationalism (conceived of as embracing Hindus and Muslims) and his own conspicuous religiosity may seem contradictory, but this is simply not the case. In fact, the two coexist and this is what modern Bangladeshi identity consists of, a creative and at times fraught tension between being Muslim and Bengali. What Islamic modernities do firmly come up against though, is the hierarchical split between the cosmopolitan secular self of the Project and that of the working classes in the informal economy outside. During its heyday, pilgrimages to Mecca and other sorts of religious activity carried little social capital, in particular for high-ranking employees. In fact, in keeping with the project of mod-ernisation, this was no less an indicator of an individual/society going 'backwards'.

* * *

The Project practised secularism not merely as an institutional residue from when the Chhatak Cement Factory was under colonial administra-tion (its genesis cannot be ignored), but for other reasons. Firstly, one of the core aims for newly de-colonised states was transforming 'primordial sentiments' of a pre-modern world into progressive 'civil sentiments' of a modern one. This was crucial as they were keen to create a unified national ideology, consisting of new citizens made up of heterogeneous bodies of people, which included new migrants and religious and ethnic minorities. Following developments in Western modernity, the waning of 'primordial' identities, it was believed, would guarantee economic self-reliance and political independence. Secondly, the communal bloodletting at Partition, where religious affiliation became the defining characteristic of community membership, was close in terms of time, within people's living memories (with some even [in]directly involved in them) and also space. The demarcations of the borders which followed were only a few metres away from the Project perimeters in Khonighat. Though much of the hostilities had taken place in urban centres, stories of violence had percolated to the remotest villages, intermingling with local passions and political and economic agendas, creating new rup-tures. Project management would have understood secularism as an attempt to stave off that which religious identities at the time potentially symbolised: discord, anarchy and bloodshed. Uncontrolled, this could be detrimental to the extraction of limestone. Even when the Pakistani state (and later Bangladesh) gave up its own experiments with the doc-trine, attracted instead to ideas of religious modernities, the Project continued to practise it. This is because, the third point, despite count-less numbers choosing to or forced into doing so, not all Bengali Hindus left East Pakistan at the time of Partition.

Five years after Partition, the 1951 Census of East Pakistan shows that 22 per cent of the total population at the time were Hindu.[1] This is despite Pakistan being a Muslim-majority country which for some Hindus meant a loss of status, employment and opportunities. In

Khonighat, Muslim workers made up the bulk of low- and middle-ranking employees, but there was a significant Hindu population too who lived and worked here. They were employed in positions higher up the rungs of the organisation. Throughout the history of East Bengal, what Bengali Hindus lacked in numbers, they made up in influence and power. In pre-Partition Bengal, nearly 75 per cent of the land in East Bengal, including the largest zamindari holdings, belonged to Hindu landlords. They were worked on by Muslim peasants. Muslims were practically non-existent in the civil service and military as well as in the educated, landed, business and entrepreneurial classes. The idea of Pakistan for Bengali Muslims then was an opportunity to rectify this discrepancy: a state where they had greater economic and political autonomy. Van Schendel argues that the Bengali rural majority had imagined Pakistan to be a 'peasant utopia' bringing deliverance from upper-caste Hindu landlords, merchants and moneylenders. Prosperity was far more important to them, he says, than the division of state power along religious lines (2009: 116).[2] Against this backdrop, it was imperative the Project management operated in such a way that it was seen to be even-handed when dealing with Muslim and Hindu employees. It could not afford to let any more of its high-level Hindu officers leave for India with all of their experience and knowledge. Neither could they allow Muslim employees to feel aggrieved and strike. This was a major concern as throughout the first decade of the Pakistan union, there was high labour unrest throughout the industrial sector.

Secular modernism, as exemplified by the Project, involved the conspicuous separation of the communities and the confinement of religious practice to designated spheres. What replaced the role of religion in public life was the new belief in the project of the nation state which had its own concomitant nationalist gospels and prophets, stripped of and devoid of communal sentiments. Secularism indeed took firm root in the everyday practices in Khonighat. Not all social relations adhered to it in the same extent or degree, but this was very much a feature of the formal workings of the organisation. The ideology was not just a top-down affair. Like other features of modernisation, Muslim and Hindu Project employees and their families took up positions at the vanguard of such praxis. An employee's job, status and social reproduction was dictated not by religious or community affiliations, but by qualifications, class and skills: the facets of the new citizenship. It was not just in the workplace but also in the living quarters where people were spatially organised according to grade and not religious identity. Hindu and Muslim families lived next to one another, there were no religious enclaves and friendships were created across communal divides. This was not just amongst the managers but the general workforce too (though Hindus were fewer in number, the lower down the hierarchy one went). Children went to the same school and meals were taken together in the Project canteen. It was very much an example of theories of 'modernity turned into a lived reality' (Strumpell 2008: 314). For many (in particular dependent women) who came to live and work in Khonighat in the 1960s, this would have been the first time they were to live in such 'multicultural' ways, as previously, village life would have been much more homogenous. *'Amra shob shoman'* (we are all the same) is how remaining Project residents continue to describe relations between Hindus and Muslims.

The Project management may have had the desire to be seen to be neutral, but in all issues pertaining to a religious nature, they were actively stage-managing and manipulating. Overt religious symbols such as the mosque and mandir (which still function as intended) were carefully controlled. They were built in architecturally similar ways: squat, square buildings with little aesthetic merit. Roughly the same size (even though Muslims were numerically greater than Hindus), they are constructed out of concrete and metal and painted an institutional dark green colour, discernible from the other buildings within the installation which are all painted yellow. There are no domes, minarets, *murtis* (idols), images, bells or any other idiosyncrasies that may distinguish them apart from one another. The temple was placed near the school, at the foot of the West Khasi Hills and the mosque next to the Project bazaar, besides the *haor*. The uniformity of the structures suggests that difference was thought of as potentially threatening, thus policed against, something that was non-negotiable. Overarching them was a philosophy that attempted to treat Hindu and Muslim staff with equal respect and wished not to be seen to discriminate between them. To avoid accusations of bias or favouritism, the Project merely provided the buildings, but not the upkeep. This was done on *sanda* (donation), collected from worshippers. To prevent embezzlement (and to keep an eye on the goings on), the Project institutionalised the collection. Surviving Project records show that employees had the choice of whether or not they wanted to make contributions to the mosque/mandir from their monthly salaries. Most seemingly did not, suggesting that, by the late 1980s, for many residents religious practice was reduced to a basic ceremonial importance. The *sanda* system is still in operation in Khonighat and the upkeep of the mosque/mandir continues to be footed by remaining residents.

* * *

Parry says the reason why communal tension between different religious and caste groups in the Bhilai Steel Plant (BSP) in Chhattisgarh remains absent is because it is a formal, public sector organisation. The lid to possible aggression is apparently provided by the institutional work culture which finds its origins in the Nehruvian vision of modernity in which divisions of religion, caste and regionalism are to be transcended 'for the greater good of the nation'. He writes 'Nehru's Bhilai was not only about forging steel but about the forging of a new kind of man in a new kind of society. It was to be a catalyst for a rejuvenated civilisation which would blow away the nastier cobwebs of the past' (1999c: 147). In this sense, people who toil together, eat, sleep and drink tea together. It is this that mitigates against communalism, in what locals call a 'mini-India'. Parry describes the demanding, difficult and dangerous jobs workers do, requiring close collaboration and trust. Work groups are made up of the same individuals over a long period with loyalty and friendly rivalry prevalent. The groups are socially heterogeneous and are a mixture of caste and non-caste Hindus, Muslims, Sikhs and Christians. Not all disparities are smoothly negotiated. Parry observes that food brought from home is shovelled on to each other's plates but occasionally he sensed a degree of assertiveness about such generosity between a high-caste and low-caste worker. There is a mixture of housing for high- and low-level employees, work groups are invited to life-cycle rituals and blood is donated for transfusions. A man's identity as a steel-maker is more encompassing at the BSP, eclipsing his ethnic and religious identity. Importantly, it is not only those who come from the bottom of the caste hierarchy who have an investment in such practices but high-caste Brahmins are equally committed.

All of this stands in contrast to the lives of private sector workers in Bhilai where wage levels are lower and fringe benefits poorer than for the public sector workers. Fears of job losses, strikes, closures and lock-outs are common. But it is the contrast in the way labour is organised between the private and public that is most striking (1999c: 136). The private sector shop floor is less of a melting-pot, where 'primordial' loyalties are more of a feature and amongst insecure contract workers a localist 'sons-of-the-soil' politics has taken root (2008: 327). Parry says the difference lies in the institutional cultures: private engineering companies are not set up to engineer a nation. Their priorities are to maximise profits and they have none of the paternalistic social reform agenda that concerns the BSP (1999c: 137). He believes this is not despite capitalism (global or domestic) but precisely because of it. To evade labour laws which provide permanent staff with relative security and other benefits that temporary employees are denied, workers are recruited through contractors, who hire kin, caste-fellows and co-villagers (1999a: 149). The result is that private sector workers are more likely to spend time in social groups that are analogous to those from which they have originated, sticking together within the factory and living with each other outside. The consequence of this is grave, Parry believes, warning that the weakening of formal public sector employment has serious consequences for inter-community relations, making workers insular, inward-looking and setting different segments off one another.

The collapse of formal sector employment and the consequences of the growth of informal labour is the subject of Jan Breman's work. Indeed, he builds on Parry's warning and provides a glimpse of the costs of a growing informal sector and a private sector that provides no social and/or economic stabilisers needed for harmony in heterogeneous and industrialising societies. In the aftermath of the destruction of the Babri Masjid in Ayodhya in 1992, the industrial city of Surat in Gujarat erupted into violence against its minority Muslim population. Paul Brass says such acts are pre-planned and are not due to the 'excessive passion' of followers or 'spontaneous acts of mob fury' (2003: 6/355) as it is often described. It was instigated by Hindu fundamentalists belonging to the BJP and other right-wing groups affiliated to the ideology of Hindutva. The perpetrators were in the main migrant workers to the city. People were beaten, stabbed and set on fire. Men with beards were targeted and some had their trousers pulled down, reminiscent of Partition bloodshed when circumcision determined which religious community one belonged to. The migrant labourers who perpetrated the pogrom were the 'floating mass' of reserve labour who flock to Surat's power-loom and gem-cutting workshops. These 'footloose proletariats' are subject to exceptional repression and exploitation at work. They work in miserable conditions with little or no stability, are outside of the law and beyond the reach of state agencies, hired and fired according to the needs of the bosses. The violence that engulfed Surat is a consequence of the suppressed frustrations of migrant workers, given voice to by Hindu zealots. The city had led the way for the economic liberalisation now sweeping across India. Most of the textile mills date back to the colonial period. In the 1980s they began closing their gates and dismantling, forcing workers out of relatively stable work into the precarious informal sector (2003: 265). Only a small minority of the total working population continue to enjoy the benefits of a permanent job and the laws which protect formal sector labourers. All of this, according to Breman, coalesced into the city becoming fertile ground for a disaster.

Neo-liberal economic policies which saw the closure of public sector mills and factories in Surat also saw the closure of the Khonighat Limestone Mining Project in Bangladesh a decade later, where it became cheaper to import limestone from India than to have an expensive workforce with all of its additional costs. Once the Project shut down, the majority of its workers moved into small-scale private coal enterprises that began to grow. Whilst some have become extremely wealthy from the coal trade, most migrants to the area have not. Men, women and children are at the forefront of an industry that provides them with no safety, little stability and just enough money to live. However, in contrast to Parry and Breman's warnings, in Boropani and Khonighat the growth of a fragmented informal economy has not led to violence. Relations between Hindu and Muslim borderlanders are robust, characterised by friendships, deep-rooted, long-term emotions and connectedness, as well as disagreements and differences that are not necessarily polite: basically the stuff of all human sociality. 'Hindu-Muslim relations' have traditionally, in particular within academic discourse, been characterised as one of profound hostility and polarisation. Such ideas are a world away from the obvious nuances within and between communities and individuals, as well as the commensality and amity that is evident in Khonighat and Boropani where a raucous 'disorganised cosmopolitanism' prevails.

* * *

Shafik is a Muslim and runs a phone credit shop at the Zero Point. He also rents out a tin shed that he owns in Boropani bazaar to Topon Das. Topon belongs to a Hindu caste of silversmiths. He is inundated with orders due to the Eid/Puja festivities. Every day, migrants preparing to go back to their villages bring old silver necklaces that they want melting down and turning into new jewellery. In the afternoons, Shafik buys food from the bazaar and prepares iftar. As Topon complains about a perennial stomach ulcer, he says he is not sure if he will be able to cross the border into Indian Boropani on Eid, only a few days away and an annual ritual for the two friends. 'With this interminable stomach ache and the amount of work I have to do, I doubt that I will survive until the end of today!' he complains. For iftar, there is fruit, puffed rice, lentils, samosas, sweetmeats and orange-flavoured energy drink to wash it down with. Shafik mixes all of the food—sweet, savoury, fruit and processed—in a bowl. This he places on a newspaper in the middle of the floor. Later I learn that the *prasad* (food blessings) given to worshippers at the Khonighat mandir is mixed in the same way and contains comparable foodstuff. It is served in different ways, however: for Muslims it is placed in the middle and shared centrally, for Hindus it is dished out individually.

The sharing of iftar between Shafik and Topon and its apparent absence of any restrictions is not an example of the remnants of the Project's secular past, despite Shafik being of Project stock. Instead, this is an example of what Annu Jalais (2010) says is part of the construction of Bengali notions of relatedness and sociality. In the Sundarbans, the mangrove forests in the south of the Bengal region, the sharing of food and the affective sentiment that this creates is the basis by which disparate Bengali migrants and settled long-term residents bind themselves together in webs of kinship. Jalais convincingly argues that this is crucial in creating relatedness and bonds between people of different religions and castes. The success of it is such that the 'extent to which this "elected kin-making" defies the differences of both jati [caste] and religion is noteworthy', she says. Jalais also suggests that it is around food that tensions between people are resolved and once protagonists partake in shared meals, there is an expectation that they will participate in other annual and life-cycle rituals too (ibid.: 75; 98/99). Whilst Shafik was born in Khonighat (his father was a labourer in the Project), Topon is a long-term settled migrant. It is through sharing food and space, including playing the weekly bazaar lottery, lending each other money and attending social gatherings that they are able to overcome supposed religious divides.

The sun sets, the *azaan* is called and the bazaar comes to a standstill. Shafik (a practising Muslim), Topon (an observant Hindu) and I (a trainee anthropologist) break fast together. Others intermittently join. An old man announces that it pleases God when people share food with each other. On one occasion we are accompanied by a high-caste Hindu NGO worker. Though religious (or in this case, caste) distinction does not prevent participation at these meals, the NGO-wallah is given a stool to sit on and a plate to eat from, thus obvious differences in status are accommodated so that they are not a barrier. Everyone else eats from the same communal pile, sitting on the floor. Arjun Appadurai says food in South Asia carries two diametrically opposed social messages: it can serve to construct social relations characterised by equality, intimacy or solidarity, or it can be used to demarcate rank, distance or segmentation (1981: 507). The example here shows that they may not be exclusive binaries and that rank for example can remain intact at the same time as intimacy or equality. Of all the people who join, often Shafik and Topon (due to the ulcer and his own idea of how to treat it) are the only two who have actually fasted that day.

Once everyone finishes eating, Topon flicks water from a little clay pot over the shack and everyone in it, rubbing it on the framed pictures of the goddesses Kali and Durga that are placed by the door. Incense sticks are lit, purifying the room. Bowing his head in front of the divine, he closes his eyes. All this happens in the same space that moments earlier people had sat down to have iftar. No one is surprised, looks awkward or behaves differently. There is an understanding that while the Muslims present in the room had performed a religious rite by breaking fast at sunset that that too is the time for Hindus to perform the *bikaler prarthona* (evening prayer). The exact time and space is transformed into different ritualistic time and space by members of either religious community.

One evening, I ask Shafik if he has been to see the *murti* (idol) of the Durga that is being constructed in the Project mandir by artisans. The slow formation of the life-like figures which started off as bundles of straw has captured the local attention. The clay has dried to the shade of human flesh. A saree will be wrapped around later, but for the time being it looks like a nude female body. The overt eroticism of the *murti* feels incongruous in Khonighat where Project women (Hindu and Muslim) observe a form of secular purdah. Topon replies on behalf of Shafik. 'He does not like to do such things. He doesn't participate in Hindu festivities'. As a member of the Tabligh-e Jama'at brotherhood, Shafik's understanding of Islam is much more dogmatic than others in Khonighat and Boropani. He believes that whilst the rigours of Ramadan and the festivities of Eid are 'gifts from Allah', the Hindu celebration is performed by non-believers and should be ignored. 'Under Islam, it is not considered right to worship idols', he says. Topon quietly tells me that as a young man Shafik did in fact attend Durga Pujas but stopped once he joined the Tabligh. On the surface, one may expect Shafik and Topon not to have any relations with each other, but for all intents and purposes, they are very close friends. They share resources with each other, but also importantly time, space and companionship. There are obvious differences in how they view the world, dictated by their different understandings of their religion, but these differences do not coalesce into antagonism, hatred, animosity or suspicion. Here, avowedly religious people—not just in the orthodox sense but in that which encompasses all kinds and levels of different commitment—can participate in each other's religious celebrations—or even choose not to—without either entering into a third space of secularism, or needing to band together into oppositional groups and becoming hostile.

I was privy to another experience between the two friends, this time including Habib, the coal depot manager. Talk centred upon a group of Pakistani Tabligh-e Jama'at preachers who had arrived in the area during Ramadan and were staying near Boropani. Outsiders, let alone foreign ones visiting the area, are uncommon and there was much excitement. Shafik says the Pakistanis have been giving electrifying sermons and he would like to attend one. Topon asks if they speak Bangla. 'Everything they say is translated for the audience by their Bengali colleagues', Shafik replies. 'We kicked the Pakistanis out once, what are they doing back again?' Topon jokes, referring to the War of Liberation between East and West Pakistan. 'There is a difference between the army and the people of Pakistan, stupid', Shafik responds. 'These men are here to tell us to do good, to pray and to remember the name of Allah in our lives'. 'But we already know this', Habib interjects mischievously. 'We don't need reminding. Anyway, we have our own pious Bengalis, you for example, to do that for us'. 'They are actually doing it for themselves. They have a calling. They feel they are on a journey to spread Allah's message and is why they are here', Shafik says. 'So if we attend, there is no benefit for us?' Topon asks. 'All the benefit will be theirs? What is the point in us attending then?'

Due to other commitments, the friends don't go, but such interactions where Topon and Habib poke fun at Shafik's show of obvious piety were common. I know another set of friends where the Hindus in the group make jokes about the Muslims amongst them eating beef and then behaving like cattle. Such ritualised banter is acceptable between tight-knit groups of friends, something which outside of the group may lead to real offence. Most interactions between Hindu and Muslim friends that I witness are not so frank. In fact, most heterogeneous friendships avoid broaching the topic of religion and religious conduct altogether. What such interactions suggest is that whilst the aim of secular modernity was to create relative peace, whereby people of different religious backgrounds could cooperate and live alongside one another, what was missing from this meta-narrative was that local and individual forms of interaction that avoided tension, misinterpretation and offence being given/taken, already existed which do not coalesce around religious distinctions. This does not deny or sideline religion to a mythical private sphere. As part of modernist purification, the Project had sought to treat religion as a private matter, exempt from organised, civic life, from employment and governance. However, today a form of disorganised cosmopolitanism reigns, which can be messy and has none of the attempts to neaten human relations as secularism once did. What this means is that despite religious identity being at the forefront of the coal industry in ways that it never was during Project days, the reality is that members of all communities have to work with one another in order to make a living in the industry. It is precisely during religious festivities that members of either community are able to come together to cement their bonds. One crucial reason for all of this is that possible fractures and lines of schisms are not between the communities themselves— united as they are by the need to make a living in this precarious region/industry—but between the general population and the state, of both India and Bangladesh. As a result, it should be no surprise that with the closure of the Project and the collapse of much of what it propagated, violence between communities did not surface. This challenges elite, secular views of lower-class people as prone to communalism as Parry and Breman's work suggest.[3]

On Eid day, *Jamaat* (the main prayer), starts early in the morning. On the side of the quarry lake where the West Khasi Hills are, Indian Muslims come to bathe. Some join the congregation in Khonighat. By now, alongside the border guards, the only people to remain in the borderlands are families of the old Project aristocracy (both Hindu and Muslim), their visiting relatives, coal barons who trace their origins back to the Project and a smattering of long-term resident coal families. Without the labourers to work it, the cross-border coal industry, like the turning off of a piece of large, heavy machinery, gently grinds to a halt. It is most noticeable that few people actually live here permanently. Once the prayer ends, Shafik and I meet Topon (he did not participate in the *Jamaat*) and prepare to walk to the Zero Point in Bangladeshi Boropani from where we hope to cross the border into Indian Boropani. Both friends tell me to go home and change the kurta that I had worn to pray in. 'But it's new', I say, attempting to defend my choice of attire and thinking they thought that I wasn't presentable enough for the visit to the other side. 'The BSF will not allow you inside', they correct me. 'They think all Muslims with beards, hats and kurtas are terrorists. So you must change'. I do as instructed and change into a t-shirt and jeans. On the way, a passer-by tells us that the BSF are apparently not letting people in. He himself though has just returned from Indian Boropani. A student of a madrassa in Sunamgonj, he had accompanied a Bangladeshi imam that morning to lead the *Jamaat* prayer for a group of Indian Muslim coal exporters on the other side. There are no imams there to carry out religious rituals. I ask why the BSF won't let us in. 'Because brother, Bengalis are no good. They go there, get drunk and cause trouble. If I were an Indian, I wouldn't let Bengalis in either. You may have a chance at Puja time'.

At the Zero Point there is a festive feeling, though no apparent signs of anything happening. There are families, couples and male-only groups, all dressed in their Eid best, waiting to go in. They stare at the Indian side, willing the Indian guards to let them in. The BDR are less obstinate, saying it depends upon the BSF. Shafik and Topon, upset that their day has not gone to plan, want to take an unofficial route through the shrubbery, but worry the BSF are stationed in the known areas. 'They will probably beat up anyone they catch trying to cross', Shafik says. 'We will try at Puja time'.

* * *

The fair arrives on boats the day after Eid. They pitch their tents and set their wares in front of the mandir. On the first day of Puja, *Shoshti* (sixth day), the Holy Family is revealed. Alongside Durga, noticeable in her red saree, are her children Lakshmi (Goddess of wealth), Saraswati (Goddess of learning), Kartik (the General of the Army) and Ganesh (God of prosperity). Observed annually throughout East and West Bengal during the lunar month of Aswin, the worship marks the mythical triumph of good over evil. Police officers from the district headquarters are in attendance. Their presence is to ward off incidents of a possible communal nature. Public events and festivals such as this are considered to be flashpoints or even pre-conditions for communal violence. Gyanendra Pandey's (1990) work as part of the subaltern school of thought may explain why, despite communal riots as well as 'village communalism' (Roy 1994: 3) being rare in the district of Sunamgonj, the police are thought to be necessary. Even during Partition, major incidents of violence against Hindus in Sylhet were uncommon (Dasgupta 2001: 345). Pandey says that nineteenth-century British writings on Hindu-Muslim riots characterised them as the 'usual state of Hindu-Muslim co-existence' (1990: 98). The specificities which caused them in the first place were ignored, emptying them of all significance and what applied to one city was thought to apply to the country as a whole. The thinking was that this is, after all, was 'the natural order of things in this kind of society'. Thus the police presence in Khonighat is a remnant of the colonial state that has passed into nationalist understandings of Hindu–Muslim relations. Consequently, the uniformed men sit in a line besides the deities, rifles nonchalantly leaning against them, looking bored.

Present at the mandir are also children and adults, gaping at the brightly lit creations, teachers from the Project school shouting orders and gaggles of Hindu widows from the *haor* in white sarees queuing up for *prasad*. A large number of the people standing around, watching, taking part in the revelries, putting up decorations and even helping to dish out *prasad*, are Muslim by birth. Such pluralistic religious practice is hardly uncommon in the subcontinent and is one of its defining and enduring features. Gardner is right to argue that the term 'syncretism' should be treated with suspicion. It suggests that a 'creole religiosity' is created when two supposedly bounded or pure traditions come together when actually no pure or orthodox form exists in the first place (1993: 213). Islamic puritans reject such localised practices, arguing that they are anti-Islamic, harking back to a pre-Islamic past when Bengalis were in the main Hindu.

The sun sets and the Goddess descends on to earth, taking her position up for the next four days of celebrations. A fire is lit, women ululate and a banana tree, dressed in a saree, is planted next to the mandir. The Brahmin *purohit* (priest) who presides, like the imam of the mosque, is the second generation in his family to lead the congregation in Khonighat. Biplob is a descendant of the Project and also the manager of a successful coal import company. He helps to organise the annual Puja celebrations which he says are still the same as when he was young and haven't changed much since then. 'It's the same *purohit*, the same band members and the same faces'. This year, however, the villagers from the *haor* who usually visit have gone to the Puja ceremony in Boropani instead of coming to the one in the Project, a reason why there are apparently fewer people than usual. The *murtis* that have been staged there, at the home of a Hindu coal baron, are more ostentatious than the modest ones in the Project. 'They have the money to make them big', explains Biplob. 'Whereas we have only one demon that Durga has impaled on her spear, they have the money for two!'

The Hindu population in this part of the Sylhet–Meghalaya borderlands, like that of the Muslim, is made up of a heterogeneous group of people, ostensibly migrants from other parts of Bangladesh. Project descendants are simply one, small group, but there is a more recent and much larger community of Hindu migrants who have moved to Boropani to work in the coal industry. Whilst some work as labourers, they generally hold positions as agents, merchants, clerks and bookkeepers in the cross-border trade. There are an increasing number who are starting their own import businesses. But on the whole, Bangladeshi Hindus are explicitly employed by Bangladeshi Muslim coal barons in order to do business with the Indian side. As the majority of Indian coal export companies are owned by Hindus, it is believed that having a Bangladeshi Hindu to communicate with better facilitates trade with sellers. Some of the largest coal import companies are owned by Muslims but all of their vital managerial roles are performed by Bengali Hindus and is a crucial feature of the workings of the cross-border coal trade. It is not just perceived religious commonality between Bangladeshi and Indian Hindus that is at the root of this phenomenon. The perception is that (similar to Project days), Bangladeshi Hindus are better educated than Bangladeshi Muslims. They are employed to carry out certain roles because they are able to communicate in rudimentary English (spoken by some Garos and Khasis) and Hindi, considered assets in the trade. A Hindu friend explains that Bangladeshi Hindus have to be educated over and above Bangadeshi Muslims because, as he believes, they have fewer opportunities to send their children abroad to work. Hindus do not traditionally have the same family networks in the desired foreign destinations. A shared faith (and position as minorities) does not mean Hindus in Khonighat and Boropani are a united community any more than the Muslim community is. The ideological divisions that the two spaces constitute create enduring fractures and schisms for Muslims and Hindus alike.

Despite Biplob's assertion that things remain the same from his childhood, much has of course fundamentally altered over the years. The large Muslim presence at the Project Durga Puja is a relatively new development and only began after the Project closed down. Ghosh (2006) suggests a lasting feature of Durga Pujas is that they are not static and constantly change throughout history. Chatterjee says the changes to Puja celebrations in Calcutta have not occurred autonomously but are motivated by commercialisation. It is 'spectacle that moves crowds rather than piety' (2008: 338), he says, with some of the more traditional practices being dispensed with, in the Calcutta Pujas. Nonetheless, rites still exist whereby actual religious piety can take place, marking distinctions between the spectacle (or, as Ghosh says, the secular) and the religious, which includes the opportunity to make offerings to the Goddess or watching the *arati* (ecstatic chanting, drumming and dance) (ibid.: 341).

Attik is a descendant of the Project. He now lives in Dhaka where he is a social worker. He is reprimanding a Muslim friend of his who refuses to watch the tree-planting ceremony when I meet them. This friend, a student in Dhaka whose family still live in Khonighat, explains that the reason he does not want to watch the ceremony is because he 'just does not feel like it'. 'But why don't you feel like it? You walked past here yesterday with no problems. The difference today is that there is a Puja', says Attik. 'I don't like big crowds. That's all', comes the reply. 'Your best friend is a Hindu', Attik says.

This is a happy day. You should celebrate it with him as he did when he came to your house on Eid. Instead you stand at a distance. You must understand that

Bengali culture is so rich that Muslims and Hindus have always come together to celebrate. Puja is Eid for everyone. This is what we have to protect.

One has to be wary of understanding all personal, individual actions through sociological factors. There are many reasons why Attik's friend may be refusing to watch the tree-planting ceremony, an important aspect of the Durga Puja celebrations. He may indeed not like large crowds, is avoiding someone, or, as he says, just simply does not feel like it. Attik thinks otherwise and believes it may have a deeper meaning. He explains that during Project days, Muslims were not allowed to watch the ceremony in the Project Puja:

We could see other rituals, but not that one. The Hindu teachers would tell us to go home and study, or that it's late and we should be asleep. What they really thought was that if we were there, we would defile the Goddess. Some Muslims here still believe that they are not allowed to watch. But this is not the case now.

The point here is that the change that has obviously come about in Khonighat which Attik's interaction with his friend refers to could only have occurred with the demise of the Project and the weakening of the management of social and intimate life. Modernisation theory dictated that to create modern and enlightened citizens, religion should be eradicated from the public sphere. Religious difference was considered to be a site of potential discord and, as such, conflict was contained through separation. This meant interlopers, even those with the most benign of intentions such as joining friends to watch a spectacle, were prevented from doing so. The fear of potential violence between the two communities was simply too great to allow any sort of 'deviation' from the master plan. The unintended consequence of this practice was that the secular Project was behaving in similar ways as religious puritans do today, whose own version of modernity attempts to deny that Bengali Hindus and Muslims share a commonality with each other that transcends religious differences. For both the old Project and the new religious puritans, acts such as watching the tree-planting ceremony are considered to be the remnants of a backwards past, something that should and will be done away once their respective master plan is put into place.

* * *

On day two of Puja, *Shoptomi* (seventh day), rumours abound that the guards will open the border, something that failed to happen on Eid. Apparently the day before Eid, a drunken Indian man was seized by the BDR on the Bangladeshi side, hence why the BSF are refusing to let people into the Indian side. I am told that the BDR are holding him because the BSF too have caught Bangladeshis on that side and are not releasing them. That evening Biplob invites me to what is an extant slice of what Hindu–Muslim relations in the Project were once like. In a building in the Khonighat bazaar sits a harmonium, a set of tablas and some worn-out music books. Assembled around them are current Project residents and returnees here for the festivities. They are all males of various ages. I recognise some as teachers from the school, coal managers and students. What they have in common is that they are the three generations of the former Project aristocracy resisting the slipping away of the past. What ensues is an evening of recitals of songs and poetry by Rabindranath Tagore and Kobi Nazrul Islam. Leading them is the school music teacher. He plays the harmonium and chooses the songs. Occasionally, he pronounces that 'in Dhaka they perform this song in such a way … and in Calcutta they execute it like this …', or, 'the popular understanding of this particular Nazrul *geeti* [song] is … however, I like to think it is this …' The youngsters are too reverential to reply, the elders respond accordingly, or in 'mmmmm's' and 'ahhhhhhh's'. Biplob plays the tabla. Various people take it in turns to sing. Mitu, a university student in Sylhet and Shafik's older brother, sings Nazrul *geetis*. In later conversations with him, he explains that the poet is extremely important to his personal philosophy, as 'Nazrul considered people to be human first and foremost. This came before any religious divisions'. Beth Roy argues such cultural forms are associated with upper-caste/class Hindus and newly educated Muslims take them on as symbols of their newly acquired status (1994: 158). Whether this is accurate or not, in Khonighat such forms are utilised by Hindus and Muslims to transgress their supposed differences and to enter into a realm of commonality, of Bengali cultural nationalism.

These people are the remnants of an ideological practice that no longer exists at the border. More than a decade since the Project closed down, this is the lasting memory of secular, urbane *bhadrolok* propriety in amongst what they consider to be a sea of illiteracy and backwardness. It is not that the participants have no religious beliefs; nor are they atheists. Religious life is something that they all, in a variety of ways, participate in. It is that they consider their Bengali culture, tradition and history to be far more salient than their religious identity. Of the Muslims in the group, I do not remember seeing many of them during the Eid *Jamaat* and doubt if they fast. Biplob, though ostensibly a Hindu and who helps to organise the Pujas, does so to support the Project community at large rather than because he is observant. Mitu and his brother Shafik cannot be any more different from one another. Shafik prays five times a day and goes on missionary expeditions around the country with the Tabligh-e Jama'at. For him, his world is shaped by a particular understanding of the Quran. Mitu on the other hand sings and calls himself a humanist. He fasts and observes Eid but these practices coexist with his belief in Bengali humanism. Such evenings, rare as they are, not only continue a link to the past, but by performing it, they actively challenge conservative Islam. At one point in the evening we can hear the drum beats of the *arati* coming from the Boropani puja. Someone sticks their head out of the window and exclaims with regret that the coal baron in Boropani who has staged this year's competing Puja has hired an electronic stereo system. Khonighat on the other hand has had to make do with a traditional, three-man band. Even this is felt with acute distress by those gathered, another illustration of the collapse of something they had profoundly believed in and the rise of the very entity that had caused it.

* * *

The borders remain closed on *Oshtomi* (eighth day). Biplob speaks to a BDR pal who tells him that a Bengali had stolen motorbikes from the Indian side and until the bikes are returned, the BSF will keep the border closed. The BDR on the other hand aren't stopping Indians from coming into Bangladesh. The Brahmin *purohit*, whose restaurant I usually eat in, explains that he crossed legitimately earlier on in the day. Like the madrassa student on Eid, the guards had permitted him to enter because there are no *purohits* in Indian Boropani and he needed to carry out a funeral rite for someone who died there recently. Biplob jokes that it is a good exchange that the two sides have. 'The Indians import our people when the need arises: labourers, imams, *purohits* and in return, they send us their coal'.[4]

The following day, *Nobomi* (ninth day), after goats and ducks are sacrificed at the Project mandir, Khonighat's men and children start walking towards the Zero Point in Boropani. The old are helped by the young, and though most had worn kurtas to the early morning *boli* (sacrifice), by now even the Hindus have changed into shirts and trousers. It is the last day of Puja and there is optimism the border will be opened. People tell each other stories of their adventures on the hills the previous year where there was apparently much merriment. The story of the Indian man found in Bangladesh has developed. Apparently, he was caught attempting to rape a Bangladeshi woman. Apprehended by the BDR, he was sent to the police station in Sunamgonj. The BDR friend of Biplob's says to him 'He raped her. What can we do? We can't just let him off'. The motorbikes too have been found and returned. It is difficult to decipher whether any of this is real, fictitious or nationalist sentiment. At the border, the Indian guards refuse to let the Bangladeshis in. They want the man that has been arrested back. Locals are angry with the BSF but they are frustrated with the BDR too, accusing them of creating trouble for ordinary people simply to scratch at their boredom. It is obvious that those waiting won't be let in and everyone departs. As the cross-border coal trade exemplifies, the ability to negotiate with the state apparatus is a feature of this place, but there are moments such as this when the enormous power disparities, or rather the asymmetry of power between the locals and the state, is brought into sharp focus. What this also confirms is that here both Hindus and Muslims are united, not just in opposition to the Indian state, as represented by the BSF and their actions, but also the Bangladeshi state and the inertia of the BDR. This fits in with the wider perception people have of the state. Where once, during Project days it was considered to be a bountiful provider, today, at best, it is seen as a negative impediment to everyday movements and at worst, greedy and corrupt.

In the evening, hundreds of people clamber into the Khonighat mandir to watch the *arati*. Women and girls sit on one side and men on the other. The Durga is brightly lit and the drums work up a crescendo. Holding a clay pot containing burning coal and incense, one of the *purohit's* assistants swaggers into the centre of the mandir. The young man goes around in circles, moving his legs this way and that, swirling the bowl of smoke as he does so. Another joins him. They go around, avoiding each other, in a trancelike state. Women ululate. Students who live in Sylhet and Dhaka join in. One of them starts talking to Masud, a hijra from Boropani. There are a number of hijras here. They are all wearing make-up, glittery shirts and *lunghis* with heavy pleats at the front like a saree. We are sitting some distance apart, but I can see that the student wants Masud to do something that Masud does not want to comply with. Is he being asked to leave? Is it because he is a hijra? Masud is gruffly dragged up by the arm and so he starts walking towards the entrance of the mandir. Suddenly, the crowd erupts, jeering at the departing hijras. The Project overseer too, sitting in the front row, also tells him to go. '*Ja*', he commands. Slowly, I understand what is happening. The crowd is trying to summon the hijras to dance. It is so aggressive that I initially misinterpret it. It is all a performance, as much as Masud's pretend refusal is. He is simply raising his asking price, so to say. He even makes a show of walking out but returns and stands with his back to the women's section, staring intensely at each and every man in attendance. His moves are slow and tentative. Other hijras join in too. They begin shuffling their feet, lifting their heels and moving their bodies to the music. As it increases in tempo, the crowd becomes boisterous and the hijras and the students fling each other around the mandir. Masud and his sisters dance like Dollywood actresses, writhing around, snaking their hips. Men queue up to dance with them. One grabs Masud in a sexually provocative manner. They fall back on each other and Masud kisses him on the cheek. He replies in kind. The crowd holler, encouraging it further. Finally the *arati* reaches its frenetic end. On the way out, the Project overseer states matter-of-factly that 'this *arati* became Western, didn't it. The culture of it was *onyo rokom* [different]'. I later ask Masud why he thinks the men didn't feel embarrassed being teased in public in such provocative ways by the hijras. 'The people like it. At such a time, anything is possible. Everyone is doing *ananda* [happiness]'.

On *doshomi* (tenth day), Durga leaves earth. Her departure feels apparent. There are no lines of pilgrims coming to the mandir, the flagpoles have been taken down and a snake of chairs is taken back to the school. The physical remains of the Durga and her family are eventually taken out of the mandir. On the way to the *haor* where they will be drowned, Biplob says the Indian man caught by the BDR and the Bangladeshi woman he was found with are actually lovers. He is Hindu, she a Muslim. 'He was caught in her house. He should be released but the BDR won't allow it. They like causing needless problems'. Project residents line the paths that have seen better days. Women, normally not seen in public, are outside of their quarters as the Durga makes her final passage to the *haor* waters. The crowd of people walk through the metal gates: 'Khonighat Limestone Mining Project' inscribed on it. This procession is nothing like the disputed routes that are at the heart of so much communal conflict in India. The Boropani Puja belonging to the Hindu coal baron had already immersed their *murtis* and they, along with their musicians, join the Khonighat group. The students, who danced with the hijras the night before, drive the pushcart, appropriated from a coal heaver, with the Durga on it, into the waters of the *haor*. It is not as dramatic as one expects. Death is quick and without fanfare. I overhear talk that the Project was not going to hold its own separate Puja this year, merging with the Boropani Puja instead because the funds raised from Khonighat residents were simply not sufficient. But opposition to the merger with Boropani was raised by some of the old residents and it did not happen. There is anxiety that in years to come they may be left with no choice.

CONCLUSION

For all over India fences appear to exist rather for the purpose of marking boundaries than for the protection against intruders (Trevelyan 1894).[1]

The village of Shundori Gao is found on the base of the West Khasi Hills, in a particularly lush and beautiful area where the two countries meet. It is only a matter of minutes away from Boropani. The village is one of many to have cropped up over the years at the border. It is essentially a migrant labourer dormitory, where practically all its inhabitants are involved in the coal trade. Towards the end of fieldwork, I was introduced to it by friends from Boropani who wanted to show me how migrant settlers to the village have come up with an innovative way to grow crops. This is a crucial way for such families to get extra nutrition, an activity the old take up, having been spewed out by the industry. In Shundori Gao people have started growing food in poly-bags. It was just the beginning of the experiment and no one was confident of the results. Why bags and not the soil itself? It is not something they want, but are having to do. The soil had been inundated and is now buried under at least 3 feet of sand. The sand runs down with the multitude of tiny streams that connect the hills to the plains. It is particularly bad after the monsoon and has left the entire village looking like a tropical beach, when in the past it was able to grow its own rice. The worst of it is that tube-wells cannot be operated and ponds, used to harvest fish, are drowned in sand. This is a new development here and a massive environmental and social catastrophe, not least because the sand is spreading, colonising more villages. In the last four or five years, a coal mine had started operations on the top of the hill where Shundori Gao is located. This mine has loosened the rocks, and is now sending the sand down. I see women sieving the fine grains for coal: a familiar sight. Elsewhere in Boropani it is soil they sieve. Locals are thinking of building their homes on stilts to avoid the sand. Such everyday catastrophes will not be rare for those involved in the world of coal and limestone extraction along the Sylhet–Meghalaya border. In July 2011, the Supreme Court in Delhi finally allowed the multinational French cement company, Lafarge, to resume supplying limestone to the Chhatak Cement Factory, which it, along with the Spanish cement company, Cementos Morlins, now own. Lafarge had been mining limestone in protected forest land in the East Khasi Hills without official permission. Its seventeen-month stay by the court had turned into a diplomatic tangle between the companies, Delhi and Dhaka, and was finally lifted.

Work continues on the impending fence. In Boropani most people say it is India's prerogative to build what it wants on its own land. Most also agree that it won't last long, pointing to relics on the hillside. One person sums it up by saying:

The Indian state is sixty-two years old. The Bangladeshi state is a mere thirty-eight. The hills themselves are millions of years old. They may stop us from crossing for a few years, but it will never be forever.

Although the fence may bring about significant changes to the livelihoods and the social lives of the inhabitants of Indian and Bangladeshi Boropani, one can be sure that this will not be the last time that utopian master plans of this scale and ambition will be attempted here on the Sylhet–Meghalaya borderlands.

NOTES

INTRODUCTION

1. This is the name I have given it. In order to protect identities, I use pseudonyms for many place and people's names. Unless made explicit, I will in the main be referring to Bangladeshi Boropani throughout this book.

2. Adams (23 Jan. 2011) http://www.guardian.co.uk/commentisfree/libertycentral/2011/jan/23/india-bangladesh-border-shoot-to-kill-policy (accessed 1 Sep. 2011). The India-Pakistan border, also fenced, is arguably even more volatile, a symbol of the relationship between these two states. Exchange of fire between soldiers is common and there is constant fear of border incursions by either side. The Kashmir issue continues to antagonise both sides. The *Economist* magazine considers it to be the 'the world's most dangerous border'. 'The World's Most Dangerous Border' (21–27 May 2001), pp. 11–12.

3. In 2010, the Bangladesh Rifles changed its name to the Border Guards Bangladesh (BGB) following what has been described as a mutiny carried out the year before by the force across the country. I continue to use the name Bangladesh Rifles and BDR as that is what they were called during the period of my fieldwork.

4. Van Schendel believes that by 1948 when the flows of migratory people had reduced, altogether 800,000 people from India had sought refuge in East Pakistan and about a million went in the opposite direction. Depending upon communal strife in either country, this number would steadily go up during the twentieth century (2009: 131–3).

5. In other parts of East Pakistan, in particular in the south-west region of the Chittagong Hill Tracts, these apparatuses were used alongside more far-reaching ways to demarcate territory. The state populated entire frontier zones with supposed 'like-minded' people (i.e. Bengali-speaking Muslims). This was thought to safeguard and buffer the border but in effect it marginalised and undermined the

indigenous people who already lived there, creating long-term tensions that continue to this day.

6. Dasgupta (2001) argues that, during this time, Hindus and Muslims who migrated could easily cross the border to sell their land and properties.

7. Lime burning was an important cottage industry in the Khasi Hills even in pre-colonial days (van Schendel 2001: 409). In the 1700s, Lord Lindsay Robert, then a district official of the British East India Company, describes the hills as an 'open frontier', covered with 'an impenetrable jungle and so infested by elephants, tigers and other wild beasts that … clearing and cultivation [is] attended with great difficulty and expense' (Ludden 2003a: 26). Transportation of the limestone from the hills was difficult. Once it was brought down, the rocks would be burnt into lime besides the banks of the Surma River (Rizvi 1971: 249). The industry employed a 'great number of people'. Importantly, the 'quarriers' were in the main Khasis and the boatmen and the 'limeburners' were 'inhabitants of Sylhet' (ibid.).

8. In some areas customs posts were established to actually prevent cross-border trade, as in the case of jute. East Pakistan tried to block the trade with West Bengal, calling it smuggling, as it attempted to establish its own market in the commodity (ibid. 2001: 408).

9. Jaffrelot writes that between 1950 and 1990 Pakistan and India were very unsuccessful at import substitution, not managing to promote their exports with the 'necessary force' (2004: 173).

10. By 1965, the kilns and boilers in the factory had been converted from coal to gas firing when the fields for the latter were discovered in 1959, obviating the factory's need for coal from Boropani.

11. The 'discovery' of the region and in particular 'civilising' it from impenetrable jungles and the tigers that roamed here remain a leitmotif for the *haor's* current population. They are also, interestingly, a recurring theme in the ethnographies of other factory towns in India (Parry 1999; Sanchez 2009; Jimenez 2005: 338).

12. India too was in love with concrete in the early post-colonial period, Khilnani writes. Millions of tons were required to construct dams and Le Corbusier's Chandigarh, designed as the new capital of Punjab; all were 'spectacular facades, luxurious in their very austerity, upon which the nation watched expectantly as the image of its future was projected' (1997: 61–2).

13. One of the flaws of modernisation theory was that state governments were never exclusively interested in promoting the development goals they were ostensibly committed to and often were not committed to them at all ([Toye 1993] Leys 2005: 114).

14. Across the country too, people were still poor, uneducated, unhealthy and troubled. The Kaptai Hydroelectric Dam in the Kaptai Lake in the Chittagong Hill Tracts was formed by drowning massive amounts of forest land, home to the

indigenous Chakma people. The internal displacements and migrations of 100,000 people that this resulted in was the impetus behind the long, drawn-out conflict between the state and the Chakma. In 1997 a peace accord was drawn up; however, consecutive Bangladeshi governments refuse to enact many of the agreements. Meanwhile, the parliament building, designed by the modernist architect Loius Kahn, also has been largely underused, with opposition parties refusing to sit with those in power and much of the politics being carried out on the streets and universities across the country.

15. I am keenly aware and attempt to avoid James Ferguson's concern that whilst the discourse on multiple modernities deals ostensibly with culture, in the realm of the political-economic, there is much divergence between and within societies. He is right to criticise academics who, in an urge to undo the ethnocentrism so prevalent in the research of non-Western people in an earlier time (in his case Africa), argue that notwithstanding all its problems, African societies are all in fact just as modern as any other place. They just have their own, 'alternative' versions and ways of being modern (2006: 32). He says Africans are puzzled by such claims. In the realm of economics and politics there is definitely no equality. This is something that is palpable in the conditions that surround them: the bad roads, poor healthcare, crumbling buildings and precarious livelihoods. He says the danger of sidestepping such an issue, or rather conflating cultural modernity with economic and political modernity 'deemphasis[es] or overlook[s] the socioeconomic inequalities and questions of global rank that loom so large in African understandings of the modern' (ibid.: 33).

1. THE FUTURE THAT DID NOT HAPPEN

1. James Legge (1861), *Chinese Classics: With a Translation, Critical and Exegetical Notes, Prolegomena, and Corpus Indexes*, vol. 1: *Confucian Analects, the Great Learning, and the Doctrine of the Mean*, Hong Kong: London Missionary Society. Cited in Kipnis 2008.

2. EVERYDAY LIFE AT THE COALFACE

1. Roitman 2005: 155.
2. The entire population of Meghalaya is around 2.2 million people, the majority belonging to the Khasi, Jaintia and the Garo adivasi communities (Karlsson 2009).
3. Bengali Hindus are generally not vegetarian. They eat fish, chicken and goat. I met some who also consumed beef. There are no explicit prohibitions against pork.
4. There are an estimated 70,000 children from Bangladesh, Nepal, Assam, Bihar

and Jharkhand working in these mines (Majumder 3 July 2010) http://www.tehelka.com/story_main45.asp?filename=Ne030710coalchild.asp# (site accessed Oct. 2010).

5. More than half of Grameenphone is owned by the Norwegian telecommunications company Telenor and Banglalink is owned by the Egyptian company Orascom.

6. The Pubali Bank was initially set up to deal with all banking matters relating to the Project, such as salaries, insurance and pensions. It too switched to coal with the closure of the Project. During the period of my fieldwork, the bank closed down and operations were transferred to Sunamgonj.

7. The LC is not too dissimilar to the *hundi* system, the mercantile note of credit that allowed Indian traders and merchants to carry out business with one another across huge swathes of land during the seventeenth, eighteenth and nineteenth centuries (Bayly 1983: 30).

8. Deer have returned to the hills, decades after last being seen in Khonighat. Locals believe this only happened because, with the closure of the Project, the noisy machinery was turned off.

9. It is precisely to avert the stampede of millions of these refugees that India is also building the fence around its neighbour (Gupta 2009).

10. Other unorganised informal work gangs consist mainly of long-term male migrants who surreptitiously work high up in the hills by randomly excavating and digging for coal. Such men do not have access to the larger mines, know-how or literacy to work formally. Other than the (il)licit payment to border guards they have no permits or licences to do what they do. Bangladeshis work with Indian counterparts who notify them of where the seams are. It is important to have mixed work gangs because if a contingent of BSF or BDR guards who have not been paid were to discover them on the hills, having men from both sides of the border helps in the negotiations that may ensue.

3. THE SEXUAL LIVES OF THE BORDERLANDERS

1. Maugham [1943] 2003: 81.

2. I will change the pronouns around inconsistently because this is what the hijras in Boropani do when referring to each other.

3. Cohen says that, in India, the hijras' lack of male genitalia is referred to as 'all India-passes', allowing them to travel on public transportation for free lest the conductor is exposed to the 'hole'. He also heard the 'operative mark' being called a 'passport', allowing hijras to be able to travel to and from Bangladesh without an actual passport (2004: 186).

4. In Boropani hijras speak *ultapalta* with each other when they are in the presence of non-hijras. Over time, hijra friends simply spoke in Bangla when I was around.

Abed explains that it is the same slang that hijras across the border in India also speak. It is taught to new initiates by their guru. Much of the vocabulary does seem similar to that referred to in the literature on Indian hijras.

5. The hijra courts are not something I will be able to discuss in this book, but suffice to say, each community of hijras has the power to arbitrate amongst themselves. Decisions reached during such courts are recognised by the wider hijra society and passed along through the formal hijra networks.

6. A pseudonym for a city in southern India.

7. Reddy argues that this pre-modern construction of sexuality implicitly problematises Foucault's contention regarding the nineteenth-century creation of the 'homosexual' (2005: 239).

8. The president of the All India Hijra Welfare Association stated that 98 per cent of all hijras are castrated men (Talwar 1999: 19). Hermaphrodites are in fact extremely rare. It is beyond the scope of this work to enter into a discussion on whether hijras are on the whole castrated or if it is only a tiny number that are, which has then become an orientalist's fantasy in the same way the Great Indian Rope Trick once was. Nanda says she saw the 'physical results of the operation many times' (1999: xix) and provides references to historical and contemporary examples of it. The heated debate between Carstairs and Opler (1961), termed the 'first anthropological debate on hijras' (Agarwal 1997: 292), questions such assertiveness. It centres on whether hijras are actually castrated men (Opler) or whether they are (intact) male prostitutes and homosexuals who simply wear women's clothes (Carstairs). Shah (1961) also queries whether most hijras are castrated. He says that on the one hand there is a strong belief that they are, but on the other hand 'we do not have a proof [*sic*] that the belief is based on facts. It is likely the belief is a myth'. See Agarwal (1997) and Cohen (2005) for an overview of the debate.

9. The hijra who did express an interest said he has been saving funds in order to do so. Though his plans were opaque at the time, he says he will cross the border into India where, through the hijra network there, he intends to find someone to do it for him.

10. *Kothi* is another contested term and a rather specialised one which I heard only a handful of times. Non-hijras never used it. Cohen argues that in the 1990s before the onslaught of international donors, AIDS funding and national and local NGOs in South Asia, the term *kothi* was used very selectively by a group of male sex workers in Chennai. After this the '"kothi-panthi" framework became important in AIDS prevention research and interventions … as well as an accepted and recognisable feature of "Indian culture" cited by knowledgeable experts' (2005: 284). His argument is that the increased public usage of *kothi* 'is correlated with the increased public visibility of the NGO industry' (ibid.: 285).

11. My point of course differs from that of Cohen's who argues that it is the cas-

tration, or the lack of male genitals, which ensures the 'respectability' of hijras within Indian public life. Hijras who have won political elections assert that because they are unable to reproduce, they are incorruptible, not having to provide for the children they will not have. Cohen writes 'hijra politicians have stressed hijra difference as central to their political integrity. Far from hijras being the weak and corrupt villains of public critique, they emerge in both their own and many popular accounts as having cut away the ties that bind them to others and being, (because of their operations), the only bodies truly able to materialise a democratic polity' (2004: 186). Here, it is precisely because they are able to marry, reproduce and have 'male-only jobs' that make them not as transgressive and beyond the pale as they may otherwise be.

12. They did, on the other hand, take an interest in alcohol smuggling, largely because they make money from it.

13. Both are *ultapalta* terms.

14. See Butler's (1990) argument on gender as performance.

15. Writing about the Pakistani context, Khan says that the 'tolerance' of extramarital homosexual liaisons should not be taken to imply that there is good-humoured indulgence in this regard, which, to the contrary, is derided in public discourse (1997: 277).

16. The hijras all have unprotected sex. In 2007, the rate of HIV/AIDS in India was much higher (0.3 per cent) than it is in Bangladesh (0.1 per cent). This equates to 3,200,000 adults (India) and 19,000 (Bangladesh) (http://www.unicef.org/infobycountry/india_statistics.html and http://www.unicef.org/infobycountry/bangladesh_bangladesh_statistics.html).This is something that neither they nor any of the NGOs based in the area seem to be aware of or concerned about. Equating condom use simply with hygiene, the hijras say it is unnecessary to use them because they have their own systems for purification. This includes washing their genitals and anus with water before and after sex. A hijra friend explained that it is in their advantage that they maintain cleanliness otherwise lovers will not be interested in them (http://www.tehelka.com/story_main49.asp?filename=Ws210411PARAMILITARY.asp; (site accessed 28 May 2011).

4. THE STATE OF RELIEF

1. Bangladesh has an 'unusually large number' of 'indigenous' NGOs. One report puts the figure at 22,000 organisations (DFID 2000). Most are local, small and voluntary. Between 20 and 35 per cent of the country's population is believed to receive some services from an NGO (Lewis 2004: 305).

2. Before 1971, foreign aid to East Pakistan amounted to $4 per person. By the mid-1970s it tripled, continuing to rise during the years of military rule until it reached an all-time high of $20 per Bangladeshi in 1990 (van Schendel 2009:

220). When the first Five Year Plan of the new country was published in 1973, it was projected that 39.44 per cent of the total development investment would be made by foreign aid and by 1978 dependence on foreign aid would decrease to 27 per cent. However the Two Year Plan (1977–9) found that 72 per cent of total developmental investments came from foreign sources. During the Third Five Year Plan (1985–90), the amount increased to 80 per cent. Foreign aid increased to $130 million during fiscal years 1985–6 (Alam 1996: 93).

3. There has been a massive increase in funds going to NGOs, from $120m in 1991 to $188 million in 1994–5 ([World Bank 1996] Lewis 2004: 306–7). It is estimated that NGOs receive about 17 per cent of the total aid flows disbursed to Bangladesh ([DFID 2000] ibid.). The British Department for International Development is the biggest source of foreign aid, providing £170 million a year, aiming to increase to £300 million by 2014 (Wilson: 11 May 2011). Since 1971 aid dependency has remained at a level just under $2billion per year although it is now declining both in real terms and as a proportion of GNP ([Hossain 1990] Lewis 2004: 306–7).

4. I am using a pseudonym for both NGOs to protect the identities of informants.

5. The *haor* region has recently become a site for much development work. The British Department for International Development, amongst other foreign countries, is funding a number of community-based organisations who all work in the *haor*.

6. Bayly suggests this may even be a pre-colonial feature where lower castes were seen as 'unruly' and a danger to hierarchy (1983: 407).

7. In its promotional literature, it states 'in all interactions in the private and in the public sector there is a need for clear rules and the respect of these rules irrespective of power and position. Our procedures are open and fair and we abstain from all forms of corruption and patronage … Our work is based on principles. We are bound to adhere to them even though this may often be difficult in a real life situation'.

5. TEMPLES OF BELIEF

1. Hindus are the largest minority group in Bangladesh. Today their numbers make up just 10 per cent of the population. This number is in marked contrast to the 28 per cent they constituted during the 1941 Census. Richer East Bengali Hindus migrated to West Bengal in the 1930s and 1940s. In the 1950s, 1960s and 1970s, it was poorer Hindus (mainly rural middle-class cultivators and artisans and later the landless) who made the journey westwards (Jalais 2010: 164–5). During the War of Liberation, Pakistani soldiers targeted Hindus for apparently siding with India to break up the Pakistan union. During periods of communal unrest in 1964 and also in the 1965 India–Pakistan war, over 600,000 refugees

left East Pakistan for India (ibid.: 164–5). In the aftermath of the 2001 elections, Hindus again faced brutality for their support of the opposition party when the Bangladesh Nationalist Party in coalition with far-right Islamist parties came to power.

2. Jinnah wanted a state for India's Muslims, not an Islamic theocracy (Alam 1995: xxiv). The 1962 Constitution referred to Pakistan as the Republic of Pakistan. But as the regime politicised itself, Ayub Khan increasingly used religious symbols and religious leaders for political purpose. Later, a constitutional amendment changed the name to the Islamic Republic of Pakistan (Jahan 1972: 65).

3. The issue of scale is crucial here. The arguments which this chapter is based on are from observations of a very specific and relatively small-scale community which is exceptional in many ways. There are no external or local players here who are attempting to foment communal tension for economic, political or electoral gains. If we are to except Brass' (1997; 2003) argument, then this is the source of much of the communal violence that has rocked the subcontinent. In the case of large-scale societies or even nation states, secularism has been the source of tension in the contemporary world, but it is also, nonetheless, an attempt to resolve much of it too. In the case of Bangladeshi society as a whole, the rise of Islamism continues to gain currency and is at the heart of much of its problems, hence I assert that at the national level what is needed is more secularism and not less of it.

4. Marriage partners are also part of this exchange. Exporters are known to marry the daughters of import partners.

CONCLUSION

1. G. Trevelyan (1894), *Cawnpore*, London: Macmillan, quoted in King (1984).

BIBLIOGRAPHY

Abraham, Itty and Willem van Schendel (2005), *Illicit Flows and Criminal Things: States, Borders and the Other Side of Globalization*, Bloomington: Indiana University Press.

Abraham, Leena (2004), 'Redrawing the Lakshman Rekha: Gender Differences and Cultural Constructions in Youth Sexuality in Urban India', in Sanjay Srivastava (ed.), *Sexual Sites, Seminal Attitudes—Sexualities, Masculinities and Culture in South Asia*, New Delhi: Sage Publications.

Agrawal, Anuja (1997), 'Gendered Bodies: The Case of the "Third Gender" in India', *Contributions to Indian Sociology*, 31, pp. 273–97.

Alam, Shamsul, S.M. (1995), *The State, Class Formation and Development in Bangladesh*, Lantham: University Press of America.

Ali, Tariq (1970), *Pakistan: Military Rule or People's Power?* London: Jonathan Cape.

———— (1983), *Can Pakistan Survive? The Death of a State*, London: Penguin.

Altaf, Anjum (Jan. 2010), 'Macaulay's Stepchildren', *Himal South Asia*, 23, 1, pp. 41–3.

Alter, Joseph S. (Feb. 1994a), 'Celibacy, Sexuality, and the Transformation of Gender into Nationalism in North India', *Journal of Asian Studies*, 53, 1, pp. 45–66.

———— (July 1994b), 'Somatic Nationalism: Indian Wrestling and Militant Hinduism', *Modern Asian Studies*, 28, 3, pp. 557–88.

Amin, Ash (1994), 'Models, Fantasies and Phantoms of Transition', in Ash Amin (ed.), *Post-Fordism: A Reader*, Oxford: Blackwell.

Anandhi, S. (2000), 'Reproductive Bodies and Regulated Sexuality: Birth Control Debates in Early Twentieth Century Tamilnadu', in Janaki Nair and Mary E. John (eds), *A Question of Silence: The Sexual Encounters of Modern India*, London: Zed Books.

Appadurai, Arjun (1981), 'Gastro-Politics in Hindu South Asia', *American Ethnologist*, 8, 3, pp. 494–511.

BIBLIOGRAPHY

———— (1996), *Modernity at Large: Cultural Dimensions of Globalization*, Minneapolis: University of Minnesota Press.

Arnold, David (1980), 'Industrial Violence in Colonial India', *Comparative Studies in Society and History*, 22, 2, pp. 234–55.

Arnold, David and Stuart Blackburn (eds) (2004), *Telling Lives in India: Biography, Autobiography and Life History*, Bloomington: Indiana University Press.

Aretxaga, Begona (2003), 'Maddening States', *Annual Review of Anthropology*, 32, pp. 393–410.

Bahl, Vinay (Aug. 1982), 'TISCO Workers' Struggles: 1920–1928', *Social Scientist*, 10, 8, pp. 32–44.

Balachandran, Chandra (2004), 'A Preliminary Report on Emerging Gay Geographies in Bangalore, India', in Sanjay Srivastava (ed.), *Sexual Sites, Seminal Attitudes—Sexualities, Masculinities and Culture in South Asia*, New Delhi: Sage Publications.

Ballard, Chris and Glenn Banks (2003), 'Resource Wars: The Anthropology of Mining', *Annual Review of Anthropology*, 32, pp. 287–313.

Ballard, Roger (Autumn 2006), 'Hawala', *IIAS Newsletter*, 42.

Barth, F (1983), *Sohar: Culture and Society in an Omani Town*, London: Johns Hopkins University Press.

Baruah, Srinath (2000), 'Certain Observations of Informal Border-Trade with Neighbouring Countries and Economic Prospects of the North East Region', in Gurudas Das and R.K. Purkayatha (eds), *Border Trade—North East India and Neighbouring Countries*, Delhi: Akansha Publishing House.

Basu, Amrita (1998), 'Appropriating Gender', in Patricia Jeffery and Amrita Basu (eds), *Appropriating Gender: Women's Activism and Politicised Religion in South Asia*, New York: Routledge.

Bayly, C.A. (1983 [2002]), *Rulers, Townsmen and Bazaars—North Indian Society in the Age of British Expansion 1770–1870*, New Delhi: Oxford University Press.

———— (1985), 'The Pre-History of "Communalism"? Religious Conflict in India 1700–1860', *Modern Asian Studies*, 19, 2, pp. 177–203.

Bayly, Susan (1989), *Saints, Goddesses and Kings: Muslims and Christians in South Indian Society 1700–1900*, Cambridge: Cambridge University Press.

Bear, Laura (2007), *Lines of the Nation: Indian Railway Workers, Bureaucracy, and the Intimate Historical Self*, New York: Columbia University Press.

Berman, Marshall (1982), *All That is Solid Melts into Air—The Experience of Modernity*, London: Verso.

Bloch, Maurice (1998), *How We Think They Think—Anthropological Approaches to Cognition, Memory and Literacy*, Colorado: Westview Press.

Borneman, John (1998), 'Grenzregime (Border Regime): the Wall and its Aftermath', in Thomas Wilson and Hastings Donnan (eds), *Border Identities:*

Nation and State at International Frontiers, Cambridge: Cambridge University Press.

Bowman, Glenn (1989), 'Fucking Tourists: Sexual Relations and Tourism in Jerusalem's Old City', *Critique of Anthropology*, 9, pp. 77–93.

Brass, Paul (1997), *Theft of an Idol—Text and Context in the Representation of Collective Violence*, Princeton: Princeton University Press.

——— (2003), *The Production of Hindu–Muslim Violence in Contemporary India*, Seattle: University of Washington Press.

Brecher, Irvin and S.A. Abbas (1972), *Foreign Aid and Industrial Development in Pakistan*, Cambridge: Cambridge University Press.

Breman, Jan (1999a), 'The Formal Sector—An Introductory Review', in Jonathan Parry, Jan Breman and Karin Kapadia (eds), *The Worlds of Indian Industrial Labour*, Delhi: Sage Publications.

——— (1999b), 'The Informal Sector—A Concluding Review', in Jonathan Parry, Jan Breman and Karin Kapadia (eds), *The Worlds of Indian Industrial Labour*, Delhi: Sage Publications.

——— (2003), *The Labouring Poor in India—Patterns of Exploitation, Subordination and Exclusion*, Delhi: Oxford University Press.

Brown, Wendy (2010), *Walled States, Waning Sovereignties*, New York: Zone Books.

Butalia, Urvashi (2000), *The Other Side of Silence: Voices from the Partition of India*, Durham: Duke University Press.

Butler, Judith (1990), *Gender Trouble*, New York: Routledge.

Caldeira, Teresa and James Holston (2005), 'State and Urban Space in Brazil—From Modernist Planning to Democratic Interventions', in Aihwa Ong and Stephen Collier (eds), *Global Assemblages: Technology, Politics and Ethics*, London: Blackwell.

Cameron, James (1974), *An Indian Summer—A Personal Experience of India*, London: Penguin.

Campbell, Howard (2007), 'Cultural Seduction: American Men, Mexican Women, Cross-border Attraction', *Critique of Anthropology*, 27, pp. 261–84.

Chakrabarty, Bidyut (2002), 'The "Hut" and the "Axe": The 1947 Sylhet Referendum', *Indian Economic and Social History Review*, 4, 39, pp. 317–50.

——— (2004) *The Partition of Bengal and Assam, 1932–1947—Contour of Freedom*, London: Routledge Curzon.

Chakrabarty, Dipesh (1981), 'Communal Riots and Labour: Bengal's Jute Mill-Hands in the 1890s', *Past and Present*, 90, pp. 140–69.

Chandavarkar, Rajnarayan (1994), *The Origins of Industrial Capitalism in India: Business Strategies and the Working Classes in Bombay, 1900–1940*, Cambridge: Cambridge University Press.

BIBLIOGRAPHY

Chatterjee, Partha (1989), 'Colonialism, Nationalism and Colonised Women: The Context in India', *American Ethnologist*, 4, 1–2, pp. 622–33.

——— (1997), *The Present History of West Bengal: Essays in Political Criticism*, Delhi: Oxford University Press, pp. 27–46.

——— (2002), 'Foreword', in K. Sivaramakrishnan and Arjun Agrawal (eds), *Regional Modernities: The Cultural Politics of Development in India*, Stanford: Stanford University Press.

——— (2008), 'Critique of Popular Culture', *Public Culture*, 20, 2, pp. 321–44.

Chatterji, Joya (1994), *Bengal Divided: Hindu Communalism and Partition. 1932–1947*, Cambridge: Cambridge University Press.

——— (1996), 'The Bengali Muslim: a Contradiction in Terms?' *Comparative Studies of South Asia, African and the Middle East*, 16, pp. 16–24.

——— (2001), 'Right or Charity? The Debate Over Relief and Rehabilitation in West Bengal, 1947–1950', in S. Kaul (ed.), *The Partitions of Memory: The Afterlife of the Division of India*, Delhi: Permanent Black, pp. 74–110.

Chauncey, George (1985), 'Christian Brotherhood or Sexual Perversion? Homosexual Identities and the Construction of Sexual Boundaries in the World War One Era', *Journal of Social History*, 19, 2, pp. 189–211.

Cohen, Lawrence (1995a), 'Holi in Banaras and the Mahaland of Modernity', *QLQ A Journal of Lesbian and Gay Studies*, 2, pp. 399–442.

——— (1995b), 'The Pleasures of Castration: The Postoperative Status of Hijras, Jankhas and Academics', in Paul Abramson and Steven Pinkerton (eds), *Sexual Nature, Sexual Culture*, Chicago: University of Chicago Press.

——— (2004), 'Operability: Surgery at the Margins of the State', in Veena Das and Deborah Poole (eds), *Anthropology in the Margins of the State*, Oxford: James Currey.

——— (2005), 'The Kothi Wars: AIDS Cosmopolitanism and the Morality of Classification', in Vincanne Adams and Stacy Leigh Pigg (eds), *Sex in Development: Science, Sexuality and Morality in Global Perspective*, Durham and London: Duke University Press.

Coutin, Susan Bibler (2006), 'Cultural Logics of Belonging and Movement: Transnationalism, Naturalisation and US Immigration Politics', in Aradhana Sharma and Akhil Gupta (eds), *The Anthropology of the State—A Reader*, Oxford: Blackwell.

Crew, Emma (1997), 'The Silent Traditions of Developing Cooks', in R.D. Grillo, and R.L Stirrat (eds), *Discourses of Development: Anthropological Perspectives*, Oxford: Berg.

Das, Gurudas (2000), 'Trade Between the North Eastern Region and Neighbouring Countries. Structures and Implications for Development', in Gurudas Das and R.K. Purkayatha (eds), *Border Trade—North East India and Neighbouring Countries*, Delhi: Akansha Publishing House.

BIBLIOGRAPHY

Das, Gurudas and R.K. Purkayatha (2000) (eds), *Border Trade—North East India and Neighbouring Countries*, Delhi: Akansha Publishing House.

Dasgupta, Anindita (2001), 'Denial and Resistance: Sylheti Partition "Refugees" in Assam', *Contemporary South Asia*, 10, 3, pp. 343–60.

Das, Veena (1990) (ed.), *Mirrors of Violence: Communities, Riots and Survivors in South Asia*, Delhi: Oxford University Press.

———— (2004), 'The Signature of the State: The Paradox of the Illegibility', in Veena Das and Deborah Poole (eds), *Anthropology in the Margins of the State*, Oxford: James Currey.

———— (2010), 'Engaging the Life of the Other: Love and Everyday Life', in Michael Lambeck (ed.), *Ordinary Ethics*, New York: Fordham.

Davidson, James (2001), 'Dover, Foucault and Greek Homosexuality: Penetration and the Truth of Sex', *Past and Present*, 170, pp. 3–51.

De Neve, Geert (2003), 'Expectations and Rewards of Modernity: Commitment and Mobility among Rural Migrants in Tirupur, Tamil Nadu', *Contributions to Indian Sociology*, 37, 1–2, pp. 251–280.

Didier, Brian (2004), 'Conflict Self-Inflicted: Dispute and the Threat of Violence in an Indian Muslim Community', *Journal of Asian Studies*, 63, 1, pp. 61–80.

Donham, Donald L. (2002), 'Freeing South Africa: The "Modernisation" of Male-Male Sexuality in Soweto', in Jonathan Xavier Inda and Renalto Rosaldo (eds), *The Anthropology of Globalisation: A Reader*, Oxford: Blackwell.

Donnan, Hastings and Thomas Wilson (1990), *Borders—Frontiers of Identity, Nation and State*, Oxford: Berg.

Donner, Henrike (2006), 'Committed Mothers and Well-Adjusted Children: Privatisation, Early-Years Education and Motherhood in Calcutta', *Modern Asian Studies*, 40, 2, pp. 371–95.

———— (2008), *Domestic Goddesses: Maternity, Globalisation and Middle Class Identity in Contemporary India*, Aldershot: Ashgate.

Dutta, Rajesh (2000), 'Coal Export from Meghalaya to Bangladesh: A Case Study of the Barsora Trade Route', in Gurudas Das and R.K. Purkayatha (eds), *Border Trade—North East India and Neighbouring Countries*, Delhi: Akansha Publishing House.

Eaton, Richard (1993), *The Rise of Islam and the Bengal Frontier 1204–1760*, Berkley: University of California Press.

Eisenstadt, S.N. (2000), 'Multiple Modernities', *Daedalus*, 129, 1, pp. 1–29.

Engineer, Irfan (1995), 'Religion, State, Secularism', *Economic and Political Weekly*, 30, 43, pp. 2726–8.

Escobar, Arturo (1995), *Encountering Development: The Making and Unmaking of the Third World*, Princeton: Princeton University Press.

Evans-Pritchard, E.E. (1970), 'Sexual Inversion Among the Azande', *American Anthropologist*, 72, 6, pp. 1428–34.

BIBLIOGRAPHY

Featherstone, Mike (1994), 'City Cultures and Post-Modern Lifestyles', in Ash Amin (ed.), *Post-Fordism: A Reader*, Oxford: Blackwell.

Feldman, Shelley (1998), '(Re)presenting Islam: Manipulating Gender, Shifting State Practices, and Class Frustrations in Bangladesh', in Patricia Jeffery and Amrita Basu (eds), *Appropriating Gender: Women's Activism and Politicised Religion in South Asia*, New York: Routledge.

Ferguson, James (1994), *The Anti-Politics Machine—'Development', Depoliticization, and Bureaucratic Power in Lesotho*, Cambridge: Cambridge University Press.

———— (1999), *Expectations of Modernity—Myth and Meanings of Urban Life in the Zambian Copperbelt*, Berkley: University of California Press.

———— (2002), 'Global Disconnect: Abjection and the Aftermath of Modernism', in Jonathan Xavier Inda and Renalto Rosaldo (eds), *The Anthropology of Globalisation: A Reader*, Oxford: Blackwell.

———— (2006), *Global Shadows: Africa in the Neoliberal World Order*, Durham: Duke University Press.

Ferguson, James and Akhil Gupta (2005), 'Spatialising States: Toward an Ethnography of Neo-Liberal Governmentality', in Jonathan Xavier Inda (ed.), *Anthropologies of Modernity: Foucault, Governmentality and Life Politics*, Oxford: Blackwell.

Foucault, Michel (2006), 'Governmentality', in Aradhana Sharma and Akhil Gupta (eds), *The Anthropology of the State—A Reader*, Oxford: Blackwell.

Fox, Kate (2004), *Watching the English: The Hidden Rules of English Behaviour*, London: Hodder & Stoughton.

Freitag, Sandra (1989), *Collective Action and Community—Public Arenas and the Emergence of Communalism in North India*, Berkley: University of California Press.

Gaonkar, Dilip Parameshwar (2001), *Alternative Modernities*, Durham: Duke University Press.

Gardner, Katy (1998), 'Women and Islamic Revivalism in a Bangladeshi Community', in Patricia Jeffery and Amrita Basu (eds), *Appropriating Gender: Women's Activism and Politicised Religion in South Asia*, New York: Routledge.

———— (1997), 'Mixed Messages: Contested "Development" and the Plantation Rehabilitation Project', in R.D. Grillo and R.L. Stirrat (eds), *Discourses of Development: Anthropological Perspectives*, Oxford: Berg.

———— (1993), 'Mullahs, Migrants, Miracles: Travel and Transformation in Sylhet', *Contributions to Indian Sociology*, 27, pp. 213–35.

Gardner, Katy and David Lewis (1996), *Anthropology, Development and the Post-Modern Challenge*, London: Pluto Press.

Gardner, Katy and Filippo Osella (2003), 'Migration, Modernity and Social

Transformation in South Asia: An Overview', Contributions to Indian Sociology, 37, 1–2, pp. v–xxviii.

Geertz, Clifford (ed.) (1963), *Old Societies and New States—The Quest for Modernity in Asia and Africa*, New York: Free Press of Glencoe.

Geeta, V. (Sep. 1994), 'Politics of Population and Development', *Economic and Political Weekly*, 29, 38, pp. 2470–2.

Ghosh, Anjan (2000), 'Spaces of Recognition: Puja and Power in Contemporary Calcutta', *Journal of Southern African Studies*, 26, 2, pp. 289–99.

———— (Mar. 2006), 'Durga Puja: A Consuming Passion', *Seminar*, 559.

Gosh, Sujit (2000), *Politics of Subversion: The Untold Story of Sylhet*, Delhi: BR Publishing Corporation.

Gould, Harold A. (1988 [1963]), 'Lucknow Rickshawallas: The Social Organization of an Occupational Category', in Harold A. Gould (ed.), *Caste Adaptation in Modernizing Indian Society*, New Delhi: Chanakya Publications.

Government of Pakistan (n.d.), *East Bengal Shares Pakistan's Planned Progress—A Review of Seven Years of Economic Development*, Karachi: Government of Pakistan, Department of Advertising, Films and Publications.

Gray, John (2007), *Al-Qaeda and What it Means to be Modern*, London: Faber and Faber.

Grillo, R.D. (1997), 'Discourse of Development: The View from Anthropology', in R.D. Grillo and R.L. Stirrat (eds), *Discourses of Development: Anthropological Perspectives*, Oxford: Berg.

Gupta, Akhil (2006), 'Blurred Boundaries: The Discourse of Corruption, the Culture of Politics and the Imagined State', in Aradhana Sharma and Akhil Gupta (eds), *The Anthropology of the State—A Reader*, Oxford: Blackwell.

Gupta, Divya (14 Nov. 2009), 'Meet a New Community of the Displaced in India: Climate Change', *Tehelka Magazine*, 6, 45.

Gupta, S.D. et al. (2002), 'Coal Mining in Jaintia Hills, Meghalaya: An Ecological Perspective', in P.M. Passah and S. Sarma (eds), *Jaintia Hills—A Meghalaya Tribe: Its Environment, Land and People*, Delhi: Reliance Publishing House.

Hann, Arjan de (2003), 'Calcutta's Labour Migrants: Encounters with Modernity', *Contributions to Indian Sociology*, 37, 1–2, pp. 189–215.

Hansen, Kathryn (2002), 'A Different Desire, a Different Femininity: Theatrical Transvestism in the Parsi, Gujarati and Marathi Theatres 1850–1940', in Ruth Vanita (ed.), *Queering India: Same-Sex Love and Eroticism in Indian Culture and Society*, New York: Routledge.

Hansen, Thomas Blom (1996), 'Recuperating Masculinity: Hindu Nationalism, Violence and the Exorcism of the Muslim "Other"', *Critique of Anthropology*, 16, 2, pp. 137–72.

Hardiman, David (1996), *Feeding the Baniya—Peasants and Usurers in Western India*, Delhi: Oxford University Press.

Harvey, David (1994), 'Flexible Accumulation through Urbanisation: Reflections on "Post Modernism" in the American City', in Ash Amin (ed.), *Post-Fordism: A Reader*, Oxford: Blackwell Publishing.

Haynes, Douglas (1999), 'Just Like a Family—Recalling the Relations of Production in the Textile Industries of Surat and Bhiwandi', in Jonathan Parry, Jan Breman and Karin Kapadia (eds), *The Worlds of Indian Industrial Labour*, Delhi: Sage Publications.

Hefner, Robert W. (1998), Multiple Modernities: Christianity, Islam, and Hinduism in a Globalizing Age', *Annual Review of Anthropology*, 27, pp. 83–104.

Hekma, Gert (1994), 'A Female Soul in a Male Body: Sexual Inversion as Gender Inversion in Nineteenth Century Sexology', in Gilbert Herdt (ed.), *Third Sex, Third Gender*, London: Zone Books.

Herdt, Gilbert (1984), *Ritualised Homosexuality in Melanesia*, London: University of California Press.

———— (ed.) (1994), *Third Sex, Third Gender*, London: Zone Books.

Heuze, Gerard (1996), *Workers of Another Wold: Miners, the Countryside and Coalfields in Dhanbad*, Delhi: Oxford University Press.

Hilhorst, Dorothea (2003), *The Real World of NGOs: Discourses, Diversity and Development*, London: Zed Books.

Hirsch, Jennifer and Holly Wardlow (eds) (2009), *Modern Loves: The Anthropology of Romantic Courtship and Companionate Marriage*, Ann Arbor: The University of Michigan Press.

Hirsch, Jennifer et al. (2009) 'The Social Construction of Sexuality: Companionate Marriage and STD/HIV Risk in a Mexican Migrant Community', in Jennifer Hirsch and Holly Wardlow (eds), *Modern Loves: The Anthropology of Romantic Courtship and Companionate Marriage*, Ann Arbor: The University of Michigan Press.

Holston, James (1999), 'Spaces of Insurgent Citizenship', in James Holston (ed.), *Cities and Citizenship*, Durham: Duke University Press.

———— (2000), 'Alternative Modernities: Statecraft and Religious Imagination in the Valley of the Dawn', *American Ethnologist*, 26, 3, pp. 605–31.

Hulme, David and David Edwards (eds) (1997), *NGOs, States and Donors: Too Close for Comfort?* London: Macmillan Press.

Humphrey, Caroline (2000), 'Rethinking Bribery in Contemporary Russia', in Stephen Lovell, Alena Ledeneva and Andrei Rogachevskii (eds), *Bribery and Blat in Russia—Negotiating Reciprocity from the Middle Ages to the 1990s*, Basingstoke: Macmillan Press.

Hussain, Delwar (2007), 'Globalisation, God and Galloway: The Islamisation of Bangladeshis in London', *Journal of Creative Communications*, 2, 1–2, pp. 189–217.

———— (2009a), 'Hindu–Muslim Bhai Bhai in a Small Town in Bangladesh', *Economic and Political Weekly*, 44, 2, pp. 21–4.

BIBLIOGRAPHY

———— (2009b), 'Life and Death in the Bangladesh–India Margins', in Open Democracy http://www.opendemocracy.net/article/life-and-death-in-the-bangladesh-india-margins (accessed 1 Nov. 2010).

Inda, Jonathan Xavier (2005), 'Analytics of the Modern: An Introduction', in Jonathan Xavier Inda (ed.), *Anthropologies of Modernity: Foucault, Governmentality and Life Politics*, Oxford: Blackwell.

Jaffrelot, Christophe (2004), *A History of Pakistan and its Origins*, London: Anthem Press.

Jaffrey, Zia (1998), *The Invisibles: A Tale of the Eunuchs of India*, London: Phoenix Orion Books.

Jalais, Annu (2010), *Forest of Tigers: People, Politics and Environment in the Sundarbans*, London: Routledge.

Jaguaribe, Beatriz (2001), 'Modernist Ruins: National Narratives and Architectural Forms', in Dilip Parameshwar Gaonkar (ed.), *Alternative Modernities*, Durham: Duke University Press.

Jahan, Rounaq (1972), *Pakistan: Failure in National Integration*, New York: Columbia University Press.

Jalal, Ayesha (1990), *The State of Martial Rule—the Origins of Pakistan's Political Economy of Defence*, Cambridge: Cambridge University Press.

Janeja, Manpreet (2010), *Transactions on Taste: The Collaborative Lives of Everyday Bengali Food*, London: Routledge.

Jeffrey, Craig, Patricia Jeffery and Roger Jeffery (2008), *Degrees Without Freedom? Education, Masculinity and Unemployment in North India*, Stanford: Stanford University Press.

Jimenez, Alberto Corsin (2005), 'Landscaping History: Nitrate Mining in the Atacama Desert in the 20th Century', in Mike Smith and Paul Hesse (eds), *23 South: Archaeology and Environmental History of the Southern Deserts*, National Museum of Australia.

Kabeer, Naila (1991), 'The Quest for National Identity: Bangladesh', in Deniz Kandiyoti (ed.), *Women, Islam and the State*, Philadelphia: Temple University Press.

Karlsson, Bengt G. (2009), 'Nuclear Lives: Uranium Mining, Indigenous Peoples and Development in India', *Economic and Political Weekly*, xliv, 34, pp. 43–9.

Kaviraj, Sudipta (2000), 'Modernity and Politics in India', *Daedalus*, 129, 1, pp. 137–62.

Khan, Bhadruddin (1997), 'Not-So-Gay Life in Pakistan in the 1980s and 1990s', in Stephen O. Murray and Will Roscoe (eds), *Islamic Homosexualities—Culture, History and Literature*, New York and London: New York University Press.

Khan, Mushtaq H. (2000), 'Class, Clientelism and Communal Politics in Con-

BIBLIOGRAPHY

temporary Bangladesh', in K.N. Panikkar, T.J. Byres and U. Patnaik (eds), *The Making of History: Essays Presented to Irfan Habib*, New Delhi: Tulika.

Khan, Sharful Islam, Nancy Hudson Rodd, Sherry Saggers and Abbas Bhuiya (2005), 'Men Who Have Sex with Men's Sexual Relations with Women in Bangladesh', *Culture, Health and Sexuality*, 7, 2, pp. 154–69.

Khan, Zilur Rahman (1985), 'Islam and Bengali Nationalism', *Asian Survey*, 25, 8, pp. 834–51.

Khilnani, Sunil (1999), *The Idea Of India*, London: Penguin.

King, Anthony (1984), *The Bungalow—The Production of a Global Culture*, London: Routledge.

Kipnis, Andrew B. (2007), 'Neoliberalism Reified: Suzhi Discourse and Tropes of Neoliberalism in the People's Republic of China', *JRAI* (N.S.), 13, pp. 383–400.

——— (2008), 'Audit Cultures: Neoliberal Governmentality, Socialist Legacy, or Technologies of Governing?' *American Ethnologist*, 35, 2, pp. 275–89.

Kuhn, Randall (2003), 'Identities in Motion: Social Exchange Networks and Rural-Urban Migration in Bangladesh', *Contributions to Indian Sociology*, 37, 1–2, pp. 312–37.

Kulick, Don (1997), 'A Man in the House: The Boyfriends of Brazilian Travesti Prostitutes', *Social Text*, 52/53, pp. 133–60.

——— (2000), 'Gay and Lesbian Language', *Annual Review of Anthropology*, 29, pp. 243–85.

Kumar, B.B. (2000), 'The Border Trade in North East India: The Historical Perspective', in Gurudas Das and R.K. Purkayatha (eds), *R.K Border Trade— North East India and Neighbouring Countries*, Delhi: Akansha Publishing House.

Lambert, Helen (1996), 'Caste, Gender and Locality in Rural Rajasthan', in Chris Fuller (ed.), *Caste Today*, Delhi: Oxford University Press.

Landell-Mills, Sam (1998), 'The Hardware of Sanctity—Anthropomorphic Objects in Bangladeshi Sufism', in Pnina Werbner and Helene Basu (eds), *Embodying Charisma—Modernity, Locality and the Performance of Emotion in Sufi Cults*, London: Routledge.

Larkin, Brian (1997), 'Indian Films and Nigerian Lovers: Media and the Creation of Parallel Modernities', *Africa: Journal of the International African Institute*, 67, 3, pp. 406–40.

Leach, E.R. (1960), 'The Frontiers of "Burma"', *Comparative Studies in Society and History*, 3, 1, pp. 49–68.

Lewis, David (2003), 'NGOs, Organization Culture, and Institutional Sustainability', *Annals of the American Academy of Political and Social Science*, 590 (Rethinking Sustainable Development), pp. 212–26.

——— (2004), 'On the Difficulty of Studying "Civil Society": Reflections on

BIBLIOGRAPHY

NGOs, State and Democracy in Bangladesh', *Contributions to Indian Sociology*, 38, pp. 299–322.

———— (2010), 'Exchanges of Professionals between the Public and Non-Governmental Sectors: Life-work Histories from Bangladesh', *Modern Asian Studies*, pp. 1–23.

Leys, Colin (2005), 'The Rise and Fall of Development Theory', in Marc Edelman and Angelique Haugerud (eds), *The Anthropology of Globalisation: From Classical Political Economy to Contemporary Neoliberalism*, Oxford: Blackwell.

Lindquist, Johan (Autumn 2006), 'Deep Pockets—Notes on the Indonesian Cockfight in a Globalising World', *IIAS Newsletter*, 42.

Lowenthal, David (1985), *The Past is a Foreign Country*, Cambridge: Cambridge University Press.

Ludden, David (2003a), 'The First Boundary of Bangladesh on Sylhet's Northern Frontiers', *Journal of the Asiatic Society of Bangladesh*, 48, 1, pp. 1–54.

———— (2003b), 'Political Maps and Cultural Territories—The Earliest Boundary Between India and Bangladesh Separated Peoples of the Hills and Plains', in *Himal South Asian* (http://www.himalmag.com/2003/july/perspective.htm).

———— 'Maps in the Mind and the Mobility of Asia', Presidential Address for the Association of Asian Studies, *Journal of Asian Studies*, 62, 3, pp. 1057–78.

———— (2012), 'Spatial Inequity and 1905 in Bengal: Reinterpreting "Partition"', *Modern Asian Studies*, 46, 3, pp. 483–525.

Macdonald, Laura and Arne Ruckert (eds) (2009), *Post Neoliberalism in the Americas*, London: Palgrave Macmillan.

MacGaffey, Janet and Remy Bazenguissa-Ganga (2000), *Congo–Paris: Transnational Traders on the Margins of the Law*, Oxford: James Currey.

Maggi, Wynne (2009), '"Heart Struck": Love Marriage as a Marker of Ethnic Identity among the Kalash of North West Pakistan', in Jennifer Hirsch and Holly Wardlow (eds), *Modern Loves: The Anthropology of Romantic Courtship and Companionate Marriage*, Ann Arbor: The University of Michigan Press.

Mamdani, Mahmood (2002), 'Good Muslims, Bad Muslims: A Political Perspective on Culture and Terrorism', *American Anthropologist*, 104, 3, pp. 766–75.

Marmon, Shaun (1995), *Eunuchs and Sacred Boundaries in Islamic Society*, New York: Oxford University Press.

Marsden, Magnus (2005), *Living Islam: Muslim Religious Experience in Pakistan's North-West Frontier*, Cambridge: Cambridge University Press.

Mathur, Nayanika (2010), 'Paper Tiger? The Everyday Life of the State in the Indian Himalaya', Unpublished PhD Thesis: University of Cambridge.

Maugham, W. Somerset (2003 [1943]), *The Razor's Edge*, New York: Vintage International.

BIBLIOGRAPHY

Mbembé, Achille (2000), 'At the Edge of the World: Boundaries, Territoriality and Sovereignty in Africa', *Public Culture*, 12, 1, pp. 259–84.

McMichael, Philip (ed.) (2009), *Contesting Development—Critical Struggles for Social Change*, London: Routledge.

———— (2009), 'Global Citizenship and Multiple Sovereignties: Reconstituting Modernity', in Atasoy Yildiz (ed.), *Hegemonic Transitions, the State and Crisis in Neoliberal Capitalism*, London: Routledge.

Mehta, Sukehtu (2004), *Maximum City: Bombay Lost and Found*, London: Penguin.

Menon, Ritu (1998), 'Reproducing the Legitimate Community: Secularity, Sexuality and the State in Post-Partition India', in Patricia Jeffery and Amrita Basu (eds), *Appropriating Gender: Women's Activism and Politicised Religion in South Asia*, New York: Routledge.

Metcalf, Thomas (1989), *An Imperial Vision: Indian Architecture and Britain's Raj*, Delhi: Oxford University Press.

Metcalf, Barbara (1998), 'Women and Men in a Contemporary Pietist Movement: The Case of the Tablighi Jama'at', in Patricia Jeffery and Amrita Basu (eds), *Appropriating Gender: Women's Activism and Politicised Religion in South Asia*, New York: Routledge.

———— (2004), 'The Past in the Present: Instruction, Pleasure and Blessing in Maulana Muhammad Zakarriyya's Aap Biitii', in David Arnold and Stuart Blackburn (eds), *Telling Lives in India: Biography, Autobiography and Life History*, Bloomington: Indiana University Press.

Mills, Mary Beth (1999), 'Migrant Labour Takes a Holiday: Reworking Modernity and Marginality in Contemporary Thailand', *Critique of Anthropology*, 19, 1, pp. 31–51.

Minwalla, Omar, Simon Rosser, Jamie Feldman and Christine Varga (2005), 'Identity Experience among Progressive Gay Muslims in North America: A Qualitative Study within Al-Fatiha', *Culture, Health and Sexuality*, 7, 2, pp. 113–28.

Mody, Perveez (2008), *The Intimate State—Love, Marriage and the Law in Delhi*, London: Routledge.

Moodie, T. Dunbar and Vivienne Ndatshe (1994), *Going for Gold—Men, Mines, and Migration*, Berkley: University of California Press.

Moody, Roger (2007), *Rocks and Hard Places—The Globalisation of Mining*, London: Zed Books.

Mujtaba, Hasan (1997), 'The Other Side of Midnight: Pakistani Male Prostitutes', in Stephen O. Murray and Will Roscoe (eds), *Islamic Homosexualities—Culture, History and Literature*, New York and London: New York University Press.

Mukhtar, Ahmad (195–) [Precise date unknown], *The Industrial Development of Pakistan*, n.p.

BIBLIOGRAPHY

Murray, Stephen O. (1997), 'The Will to Know: Islamic Accommodations of Male Homosexuality', in Stephen O. Murray and Will Roscoe (eds), *Islamic Homosexualities—Culture, History and Literature*, New York and London: New York University Press.

———— (2000), *Homosexualities*, Chicago: The University of Chicago Press.

Nair, Janaki and Mary E. John (2000), *A Question of Silence: The Sexual Encounters of Modern India*, London: Zed Books.

Nanda, Serena (1999), *Neither Man, Nor Woman*, Belmont: Wadsworth Publishing Company.

Nandy, Ashis (1983), *The Intimate Enemy: Loss and Recovery of Self under Colonialism*, Delhi: Oxford University Press.

———— (1990), 'The Politics of Secularism and the Recovery of Religious Tolerance', in Veena Das (ed.), *Mirrors of Violence: Communities, Riots and Survivors in South Asia*, Delhi: Oxford University Press.

Naqvi, Nauman and Hasan Mujtaba (1997), 'Two Baluchis, a Sindhi Zenana and the Status of Hijras in Contemporary Pakistan', in Stephen O. Murray and Will Roscoe (eds), *Islamic Homosexualities—Culture, History and Literature*, New York and London: New York University Press.

Nash, June (1979), *We Eat the Mines and the Mines Eat Us—Dependency and Exploitation in the Bolivian Tin Mines*, New York: Columbia University Press.

———— (1992), *I Spent My Life in the Mines—The Story of Juan Rojas, Bolivian Tin Miner*, New York: Columbia University Press.

Navaro-Yashin, Yael (2003), '"Life is Dead Here" Sensing the Political in "No-Man's-Land"', *Anthropological Theory*, 3, 1, pp. 107–25.

Ong, Aihwa (1999), *Flexible Citizenship: The Cultural Logics of Transnationality*, Durham, NC and London: Duke University Press.

———— (2005), 'Graduated Sovereignty in South East Asia', in Jonathan Xavier Inda (ed.), *Anthropologies of Modernity: Foucault, Governmentality and Life Politics*, Oxford: Blackwell.

———— (2006), *Neoliberalism as Exception: Mutations in Citizenship and Sovereignty*, Durham: Duke University Press.

Opler, Morris E. (1961), 'Further Comparative Notes on the Hijarā of India', *American Anthropologist*, 63, 6, pp. 1331–2.

Ornati, O.A. (1955), *Jobs and Workers in India*. Institute of Industrial and Labour Relations, Ithaca: Cornell University Press.

Pandey, Gyanendra (1990), 'The Colonial Construction of "Communalism": British Writings on Banaras in the Nineteenth Century', in Veena Das (ed.), *Mirrors of Violence: Communities, Riots and Survivors in South Asia*, Delhi: Oxford University Press.

Parker, Andrew et al. (eds) (1992), *Nationalisms and Sexualities*, London: Routledge.

BIBLIOGRAPHY

Parry, Jonathan (1999a), 'Two Cheers for Reservation: The Satnamis and the Steel Plant', in Ramachandra Guha and Jonathan Parry (eds), *Institutions and Inequalities: Essays in Honour of Andre Beteille*, Oxford: Oxford University Press.

———— (1999b), 'Introduction', in Jonathan Parry, Jan Breman and Karin Kapadia (eds), *The Worlds of Indian Industrial Labour*, Delhi: Sage Publications.

———— (1999c) 'Lords of Labour: Working and Shirking in Bhilai', in Jonathan Parry, Jan Breman and Karin Kapadia (eds), *The Worlds of Indian Industrial Labour*, Delhi: Sage Publications.

———— (2000), 'The Crisis of Corruption and "the Idea of India": The Worm's Eye View', in Italo Pardo (ed.), *Morals of Legitimacy: Between Agency and System*, New York: Berghahn Books.

———— (2001), 'Ankalu's Errant Wife: Sex, Marriage and Industry in Contemporary Chhattisgarh', *Modern Asian Studies*, 35, 4, pp. 783–820.

———— (2003), 'Nehru's Dream and the Village "Waiting Room": Long-Distance Labour Migrants to a Central Indian Steel Town', *Contributions to Indian Sociology*, 37, 1–2, pp. 217–49.

———— (2004), 'The Marital History of a "Thumb-Impression Man"', in David Arnold and Stuart Blackburn (eds), *Telling Lives in India: Biography, Autobiography and Life History*, Bloomington: Indiana University Press.

———— (2008), 'Cosmopolitan Values in a Central Indian Steel Town', in Pnina Werbner (ed.), *Anthropology and the New Cosmopolitanism: Rooted, Feminist and Vernacular Perspectives*, Oxford: Berg.

Phillips, Sarah, D. (2005), 'Will the Market Set Them Free? Women, NGOs and Social Enterprise in Ukraine', *Human Organisation*, 64, 3, pp. 251–64.

Piot, Charles (1999), *Remotely Global—Village Modernity in West Africa*, Chicago: The University of Chicago Press.

Preston, Laurence (1987), 'A Right to Exist: Eunuchs and the State in Nineteenth-Century India', *Modern Asian Studies*, 21, 2, pp. 371–87.

Preston, P.W. (1994), *Discourses of Development: State, Market and Polity in the Analysis of Complex Change*, Aldershot: Avebury.

Rahman, Aminur (1999), *Women and Microcredit in Rural Bangladesh. Anthropological Study of the Rhetoric and Realities of Grameen Bank Lending*, Colorado: Westview Press.

Rai, R.K. (2002), 'Implication of Coal Mining on Environment in Jaintia Hills, Meghalaya', in P.M. Passah and S. Sarma (eds), *Jaintia Hills—A Meghalaya Tribe: Its Environment, Land and People*, Delhi: Reliance Publishing House.

Rao, Mohan (Jan. 1994), 'An Imagined Reality: Malthusianism, Neo-Malthusianism and Population Myth', *Economic and Political Weekly*, 29, 5, pp. 40–52.

Reddy, Gayatri (2005), *With Respect to Sex—Negotiating Hijra Identity in South India*, London: University of Chicago Press.

BIBLIOGRAPHY

———— (2009), 'The Bonds of Love: Companionate Marriage and the Desire for Intimacy among Hijras in Hyderabad, India', in Jennifer Hirsch and Holly Wardlow (eds), *Modern Loves: The Anthropology of Romantic Courtship and Companionate Marriage*, Ann Arbor: The University of Michigan Press.

Riaz, Ali (2003), 'God Willing: The Politics and Ideology of Islamism in Bangladesh', *Comparative Studies of South Asia and the Middle East*, 23, 1–2, pp. 301–20.

Ringrose, Kathryn (1994), 'Living in the Shadows: Eunuchs and Gender in Byzantium', in Gilbert Herdt (ed.), *Third Sex, Third Gender*, London: Zone Books.

Rizvi, S.H.M. and Shibani Roy (2006), *Khasi Tribe of Meghalaya*, Delhi: B.R. Publishing Corporation.

Rizvi, S.N.H (1971), *Bangladesh*, District Gazetteer: Sylhet.

Roberts, Michael (1990), 'Noise as Cultural Struggle: Tom-Tom Beating, the British and Communal Disturbances in Sri Lanka, 1880–1930s', in Veena Das (ed.), *Mirrors of Violence: Communities, Riots and Survivors in South Asia*, Delhi: Oxford University Press.

Robinson, Kathryn (1986), *Stepchildren of Progress—The Political Economy of Development in an Indonesian Mining Town*, New York: State University of New York Press.

Rofel, Lisa (1999), *Other Modernities—Gendered Yearnings in China after Socialism*, Berkeley: University of California Press.

Roitman, Janet (2004), 'Productivity in the Margins: Reconstituting State Power in the Chad Basin', in Veena Das and Deborah Poole (eds), *Anthropology in the Margins of the State*, Oxford: James Currey.

———— (2005), *Fiscal Disobedience: An Anthropology of Economic Regulation in Central Africa*, Oxford: Princeton University Press.

Roy, Asim (1982), 'The Pir—Tradition: A Case Study in Islamic Syncretism in Traditional Bengal', in Fred. W. Clothey (ed.), *Images of Man: Religion and Historical Process in South Asia*, Madras: New Era Publication.

Roy, Beth (1994), *Some Trouble with Cows—Making Sense of Social Conflict*, Berkeley: University of California Press.

Rozario, Santi (2006), 'The New Burqa in Bangladesh: Empowerment or Violation of Women's Rights?' *Women's Studies International Forum*, 29, 4, pp. 368–80.

Saha, Antu (2007), *Ethnic Identities and the Role of Religion on the India–Bangladesh Borderland*, Lewiston: The Edwin Mellon Press.

Sanchez, Andrew (2009a), *Deadwood and paternalism: Rationalising casual Labour in an Indian Company Town*, unpublished manuscript.

———— (2009b), 'Workers, Netas and Goondas: The Casualisation of Labour in an Indian Company Town', unpublished PhD thesis: London School of Economics.

BIBLIOGRAPHY

Santos-Granero, Fernando (1998), 'Writing History into the Landscape: Space, Myth, and Ritual in Contemporary Amazonia', *American Ethnologist*, 25, 2, pp. 128–48.

Sarkar, Tanika (1998), 'Woman, Community, and Nation—A Historical Trajectory for Hindu Identity Politics', in Patricia Jeffery and Amrita Basu (eds), *Appropriating Gender: Women's Activism and Politicised Religion in South Asia*, New York: Routledge.

Schendel, Willem van (2001), 'Working Through Partition—Making a Living in the Bengal Borderlands', *International Review of Social History*, 46, 3, pp. 393–421.

——— (2005), 'Introduction: The Making of Illicitness', in Willem van Schendel and Itty Abraham (eds), *Illicit Flows and Criminal Things: States, Borders, and the Other Side of Globalization*, Bloomington: Indiana University Press.

——— (2005), 'Illegal but Licit: Transnational Flows and Permissive Polities in Asia', *IIAS Newsletter*, 38 (Sep. 2005), 32.

——— (2005), *The Bengal Borderland: Beyond State and Nation in South Asia*, London: Anthem Press.

——— (2005), 'Spaces of Engagement: How Borderlands, Illegal Flows, and Territorial States Interlock', in Willem van Schendel and Itty Abraham (eds), *Illicit Flows and Criminal Things: States, Borders, and the Other Side of Globalization*, Bloomington: Indiana University Press.

——— (Autumn 2006), 'The Borderlands of Legality', *IIAS Newsletter*, 42.

——— (2006), 'Underworlds & Borderlands', *IIAS Newsletter* (Special Issue, Sep. 2006), 1–21; Guest Editor and Introduction, 'The Boundaries of Legality'.

——— (2006) 'Quit India! Explaining Mass Deportations of Bangladeshi Immigrants', in *At the Crossroads: South Asian Research, Policy and Development in a Globalized World*, Karachi: Sama Editorial and Publishing Services.

——— (Aug. 2006), 'Guns and Gas in Southeast Asia: Transnational Flows in the Burma–Bangladesh Borderland', *Kyoto Review of Southeast Asia*.

——— (2006), 'Stretching Labour Historiography: Pointers from South Asia', *International Review of Social History*, 51, pp. 229–61.

——— (2009), *A History of Bangladesh*, Cambridge: Cambridge University Press.

Scheper-Hughes, Nancy (2002), 'The Global Traffic in Human Organs', in Jonathan Xavier Inda and Renalto Rosaldo (eds), *The Anthropology of Globalisation: A Reader*, Oxford: Blackwell.

Schielke, Samuli (2009), 'Being good in Ramadan: Ambivalence, Fragmentation and the Moral Self in the Lives of Young Egyptians', *Journal of the Royal Anthropological Institute*, pp. 24–40.

BIBLIOGRAPHY

Scott, James (1985), *Weapons of the Weak: Everyday Forms of Peasant Resistance*, New Haven: Yale University Press.

———— (1990), *Domination and the Arts of Resistance: Hidden Transcripts*, New Haven: Yale University Press.

———— (1998), *Seeing Like a State: How Certain Schemes to Improve the Human Condition have Failed*, New Haven: Yale University Press.

Seabrook, Jeremy (2001), *Freedom Unfinished—Fundamentalism and Popular Resistance in Bangladesh Today*, London: Zed Books.

Sen, Samita (1999), 'At the Margins—Women Workers in the Bengal Jute Industry', in Jonathan Parry, Jan Breman and Karin Kapadia (eds), *The Worlds of Indian Industrial Labour*, Delhi: Sage Publications.

———— (2000), 'Offences Against Marriage: Negotiating Custom in Colonial Bengal', in Janaki Nair and Mary E. John (eds), *A Question of Silence: The Sexual Encounters of Modern India*, London: Zed Books.

Shah, Alpa (2006), 'The Labour of Love: Seasonal Migration from Jharkhand to the Brick Kilns of Other States in India', *Contributions to Indian Sociology*, 40, 91, pp. 92–118.

Shah, A.M. (1961), 'A Note on the Hijadas of Gujarat', *American Anthropologist*, 63, 6, pp. 1325–30.

Sharma, Aradhana and Akhil Gupta (eds) (2006), *The Anthropology of the State—A Reader*, Oxford: Blackwell.

Sharma, B.R. (1970), *The Indian Industrial Worker: Issues in Perspective*, Delhi: Vikas Publishing.

Sharma, Satish Kumar (1989), *Hijras: The Labelled Deviants*, New Delhi: Gyan Publishing House.

Shifflett, Crandall (1991), *Coal Towns—Life, Work and Culture in Company Towns of Southern Appalachia 1880–1960*, Knoxville: The University of Tennessee Press.

Simeon, Dilip (1999), 'Work and Resistance in the Jharia Coalfields', in Jonathan Parry, Jan Breman and Karin Kapadia (eds), *The Worlds of Indian Industrial Labour*, Delhi: Sage Publications.

Singer, Milton (1971), 'Beyond Tradition and Modernity in Madras', *Comparative Studies in Society and History*, 13, pp. 160–95.

———— (1972), 'Industrial Leadership, the Hindu Ethic and the Spirit of Socialism', in Milton Singer (ed.), *When a Great Tradition Modernizes: An Anthropological Approach to Indian Civilization*, Delhi: Vikas Publishing House.

Sisson, Richard and Leo Rose (1990), *War and Secession—Pakistan, India and the Creation of Bangladesh*, Berkley: University of California Press.

Sivaramakrishnan, K. and Arjun Agrawal (2002) 'Regional Modernities in Stories and Practices of Development', in K. Sivaramakrishnan and Arjun

BIBLIOGRAPHY

Agrawal (eds), *Regional Modernities: The Cultural Politics of Development in India*, Stanford: Stanford University Press.

Smillie, Ian (2005), 'Criminality and the Global Diamond Trade: A Methodological Case Study', in Willem van Schendel and Itty Abraham (eds), *Illicit Flows and Criminal Things: States, Borders, and the Other Side of Globalization*, Bloomington: Indiana University Press.

Sobhan, Rehman (1982), *The Crisis of External Dependence: the Political Economy of Foreign Aid to Bangladesh*, London: Zed Press.

——— (1997), 'The Political Economy of Micro Credit', in Geoffrey Wood and Iffath Sharif (eds), *Who Needs Credit? Poverty and Finance in Bangladesh*, London: Zed Books.

Srivastava, Sanjay (2004), *Sexual Site, Seminal Attitudes—Sexualities, Masculinities and Culture in South Asia*, New Delhi: Sage Publications.

——— (2007), *Passionate Modernity—Sexuality, Class and Consumption in India*, New Delhi: Routledge.

Stoler, Ann L. (1989), 'Making Empire Respectable: The Politics of Race and Sexual Morality in 20th-Century Colonial Cultures', *American Ethnologist*, 16, 4, pp. 634–60.

Strumpell, C. (2008), '"We work together, we eat together": Conviviality and Modernity in a Company Settlement in South Orissa', *Contributions to Indian Sociology*, 42, 3, pp. 351–81.

Sweet, Michael and Leonard Zwilling (1996), '"Like a City Ablaze": The Third Sex and the Creation of Sexuality in Jain Religious Literature', *Journal of the History of Sexuality*, 6, 3, pp. 359–84.

Talwar, Rajesh (1999), *The Third Sex and Human Rights*, New Delhi: Gyan Publishing House.

Tarlo, Emma (2001), 'Paper Truths: The Emergency and Slum Clearance Through Forgotten Files', in Chris Fuller and Veronique Benei (eds), *The Everyday State and Society in Modern India*, London: Hurst.

Taussig, Michael (1980), *The Devil and Commodity Fetishism in South America*, Chapel Hill: The University of North Carolina Press.

Taylor, Marcus (2009), 'Contradiction and Transformation of Neoliberalism in Latin America: From Structural Adjustment to "Empowering the Poor"', in Laura Macdonald and Arne Ruckert (eds), *Post Neoliberalism in the Americas*, London: Palgrave Macmillan.

Tsing, Anna Lowenhaupt (1995), *In the Realm of the Diamond Queen: Marginality in an Out-of-the-Way Place*, Princeton: Princeton University Press.

——— (2000), 'Inside the Economy of Appearances', *Public Culture*, 12, 1, pp. 115–44.

Unnithan-Kumar, Maya (2003), 'Spirits of the Womb: Migration, Reproductive Choice and Healing in Rajasthan', in F. Osella and K. Gardner (eds),

BIBLIOGRAPHY

Migration, Modernity and Social Transformation in South Asia, Special Issue of *Contributions to Indian Sociology*, Delhi: Institute of Economic Growth.

Vanita, Ruth (2002), 'Introduction', in Ruth Vanita (ed.), *Queering India: Same-Sex Love and Eroticism in Indian Culture and Society*, New York: Routledge.

Vanita, Ruth and Saleem Kidwai (eds) (2000), *Same Sex Love in India: Readings from Literature and History*, New York: St. Martin's Press.

Vatuk, Sylvia (2004), 'Hamara Daur-i-Hayat: An Indian Muslim Woman Writes Her Life', in David Arnold and Stuart Blackburn (eds), *Telling Lives in India: Biography, Autobiography and Life History*, Bloomington: Indiana University Press.

Werbner, Pnina (2010), 'The Place(s) of Transgressive Sexuality in South Asia: from Ritual to Popular Culture', in Karen Isaksen Leonard, Gayatri Reddy and Ann Grodzins Gold (eds), *Histories of Intimacies and Situated Ethnography. Special Issue in Honour of Sylvia Vatuk*, New Delhi: Manohar, pp. 185–208.

Werbner, Pnina and Helene Basu (eds) (1998), *Embodying Charisma—Modernity, Locality and the Performance of Emotion in Sufi Cults*, London: Routledge.

White, Sarah (1992), *Arguing with the Crocodile: Gender and Class in Bangladesh*, London: Zed Books.

Wikan, Unni (1977), 'Man Becomes Woman: Transsexualism in Oman as a Key to Gender Roles', *Man*, 12, 2, pp. 304–19.

——— (1978), 'The Omani Xanith: A Third Gender Role', *Man*, 13, 3, pp. 473–5.

Wood, Geoff (1997), 'States Without Citizens: The Problem of the Franchise State', in David Hulme and David Edwards (eds), *NGOs, States and Donors: Too Close for Comfort?* London: Macmillan Press.

Wood, Geoff and Iffath Sharif (eds) (1997), *Who Needs Credit? Poverty and Finance in Bangladesh*, London: Zed Books.

Woost, Michael (1997), 'Alternative Vocabularies of Development? "Community" and "Participation" in Development Discourse in Sri Lanka', in R.D. Grillo and R.L. Stirrat (eds), *Discourses of Development: Anthropological Perspectives*, Oxford: Berg.

Yildiz, Atasoy (ed.) (2009) *Hegemonic Transitions, the State and Crisis in Neoliberal Capitalism*, London: Routledge.

Internet

Adams, Brad (23 Jan. 2011), 'India's Shoot-to-Kill Policy on the Bangladesh Border' (http://www.guardian.co.uk/commentisfree/libertycentral/2011/jan/23/india-bangladesh-border-shoot-to-kill-policy; accessed 1 Sep. 2011).

BIBLIOGRAPHY

Anderson, Benedict (24 Aug. 1995), 'Dojo on the Corner' (www.lrb.co.uk/v17/n16/benedict-anderson/dojo-on-the-corner; accessed 20 Jan. 2010).

Azad, Kalam Abdul (2 Oct. 2011), 'Sylhet Tension May Boil Over into Major Conflict' (http://www.thedailystar.net/story.php?nid=129068; accessed 1 Nov. 2010).

Bangladesh Bureau of Statistics (http://www.bbs.gov.bd/dataindex/census/bang_atg.pdf; accessed 1 Apr. 2009).

CNN (13 May 2008), 'Serial Bomb Blasts Leave 60 Dead in India' (http://articles.cnn.com/2008-05-13/world/india.bombs_1_hanuman-temple-jaipur-new-delhi?_s=PM:WORLD; accessed 23 Sep. 2010).

The Daily Star (13 Mar. 2010), 'BSF Retreated from Sylhet Border: BDR' (http://www.thedailystar.net/newDesign/latest_news.php?nid=22672; accessed 1 Nov. 2010).

Economist (21–7 May 2011), 'A Rivalry that Threatens the World' (http://www.economist.com/node/18712274; accessed May 2011).

——— (21–7 May 2011), 'The World's Most Dangerous Border' (http://www.economist.com/node/18712525; accessed May 2011).

Gilani, Iftikhar and Samarth Saran (21 Apr. 2011), 'Home ministry running away from talking sex to forces: But, it fears that skepticism may lead to spread of AIDS and other diseases' (http://www.tehelka.com/story_main49.asp?filename=Ws210411PARAMILITARY.asp; accessed 28 May 2011).

Guardian (30 Oct. 2008), 'Deadly Bomb Blasts Rock North-East India' (http://www.guardian.co.uk/world/2008/oct/30/india-terrorism; accessed 23 Sep. 2010).

The Hindu (9 Mar. 2010), 'Ease Barriers to Unlock South Asian Potential' (http://beta.thehindu.com/business/article223446.ece; accessed Apr. 2010).

——— (17 Mar. 2010), 'India, Bangladesh to Discuss Teesta Water-Sharing' (http://beta.thehindu.com/news/national/article253918.ece; accessed Apr. 2010).

Majumder, Kunal (3 July 2010), 'Half-life of the Coal Child' (http://www.tehelka.com/story_main45.asp?filename=Ne030710coalchild.asp#; accessed Oct. 2010).

Pegu, Manoranjan (28 Dec. 2010), 'Peripheral Economy, Global Capital and Movements in Bangladesh: An Interview with Anu Muhammad' (http://radicalnotes.com/index2.php?option=com_content&task=view&id=151&pop=1&page=0&Itemid=39; accessed 30 Dec. 2010).

Ruram, Tapon (19 June 2007), 'Sancred' (http://www.normisjon.no/index.php?kat_id=351&art_id=10902; accessed 1 May 2011).

The Shillong Times (10 Apr. 2010), 'Tiwari Moots Action Plan for Export Promotion' (http://www.theshillongtimes.com/c-10-aprl.htm; accessed Apr. 2010).

BIBLIOGRAPHY

Singh, Sanjay, K. (7 July 2011), 'Lafarge Gets SC Nod for Meghalaya Mining' (http://articles.economictimes.indiatimes.com/2011–07–07/news/2974 7697_1_government-of-meghalaya-rs-lafarge-surma-cement-project-chhatak; accessed 28 Sep. 2011).

South Asian Media, 'Haats Near India–BD Border to Open Soon' (http://www.southasianmedia.net/index_story.cfm?id=616675&category=Frontend&Country=MAIN; accessed Apr. 2010).

The Times (31 Oct. 2008), 'Multiple Bomb Blasts Rock India's Assam State (http://www.timesonline.co.uk/tol/news/world/asia/article5045940.ece; accessed 23 Sep. 2010).

Wilson, Elliot (11 May 2011), 'Breaking the Bank: The Vendetta Against Bangladesh's Nobel Peace Prize Winner' (www.spectator.co.uk/essays/all/6937648/breaking-the-bank.thtml; accessed 25 May 2011).

INDEX

INDEX